American Casebook Series
Hornbook Series and Basic Legal Texts
Black Letter Series and Nutshell Series

of

WEST PUBLISHING COMPANY
P.O. Box 64526
St. Paul, Minnesota 55164–0526

Accounting

FARIS' ACCOUNTING AND LAW IN A NUTSHELL, 377 pages, 1984. Softcover. (Text)

FIFLIS, KRIPKE AND FOSTER'S TEACHING MATERIALS ON ACCOUNTING FOR BUSINESS LAWYERS, Third Edition, 838 pages, 1984. (Casebook)

SIEGEL AND SIEGEL'S ACCOUNTING AND FINANCIAL DISCLOSURE: A GUIDE TO BASIC CONCEPTS, 259 pages, 1983. Softcover. (Text)

Administrative Law

BONFIELD AND ASIMOW'S STATE AND FEDERAL ADMINISTRATIVE LAW, 826 pages, 1989. (Casebook)

GELLHORN AND BOYER'S ADMINISTRATIVE LAW AND PROCESS IN A NUTSHELL, Second Edition, 445 pages, 1981. Softcover. (Text)

MASHAW AND MERRILL'S CASES AND MATERIALS ON ADMINISTRATIVE LAW—THE AMERICAN PUBLIC LAW SYSTEM, Second Edition, 976 pages, 1985. (Casebook) 1989 Supplement.

ROBINSON, GELLHORN AND BRUFF'S THE ADMINISTRATIVE PROCESS, Third Edition, 978 pages, 1986. (Casebook)

Admiralty

HEALY AND SHARPE'S CASES AND MATERIALS ON ADMIRALTY, Second Edition, 876 pages, 1986. (Casebook)

MARAIST'S ADMIRALTY IN A NUTSHELL, Second Edition, 379 pages, 1988. Softcover. (Text)

SCHOENBAUM'S HORNBOOK ON ADMIRALTY AND MARITIME LAW, Student Edition, 692 pages, 1987 with 1989 pocket part. (Text)

Agency—Partnership

FESSLER'S ALTERNATIVES TO INCORPORATION FOR PERSONS IN QUEST OF PROFIT, Second Edition, 326 pages, 1986. Softcover. Teacher's Manual available. (Casebook)

HENN'S CASES AND MATERIALS ON AGENCY, PARTNERSHIP AND OTHER UNINCORPORATED BUSINESS ENTERPRISES, Second Edition, 733 pages, 1985. Teacher's Manual available. (Casebook)

REUSCHLEIN AND GREGORY'S HORNBOOK ON THE LAW OF AGENCY AND PARTNERSHIP, Second Edition, Approximately 750 pages, October, 1989 Pub. (Text)

SELECTED CORPORATION AND PARTNERSHIP STATUTES, RULES AND FORMS. Softcover. Approximately 700 pages, 1989.

STEFFEN AND KERR'S CASES ON AGENCY-PARTNERSHIP, Fourth Edition, 859 pages, 1980. (Casebook)

STEFFEN'S AGENCY-PARTNERSHIP IN A NUTSHELL, 364 pages, 1977. Softcover. (Text)

Agricultural Law

MEYER, PEDERSEN, THORSON AND DAVIDSON'S AGRICULTURAL LAW: CASES AND MATERIALS, 931 pages, 1985. Teacher's Manual available. (Casebook)

Alternative Dispute Resolution

KANOWITZ' CASES AND MATERIALS ON ALTER-

Alternative Dispute Resolution—Cont'd

NATIVE DISPUTE RESOLUTION, 1024 pages, 1986. Teacher's Manual available. (Casebook)

RISKIN AND WESTBROOK'S DISPUTE RESOLUTION AND LAWYERS, 468 pages, 1987. Teacher's Manual available. (Casebook)

RISKIN AND WESTBROOK'S DISPUTE RESOLUTION AND LAWYERS, Abridged Edition, 223 pages, 1987. Softcover. Teacher's Manual available. (Casebook)

TEPLE AND MOBERLY'S ARBITRATION AND CONFLICT RESOLUTION, (The Labor Law Group). 614 pages, 1979. (Casebook)

American Indian Law

CANBY'S AMERICAN INDIAN LAW IN A NUTSHELL, Second Edition, 336 pages, 1988. Softcover. (Text)

GETCHES AND WILKINSON'S CASES AND MATERIALS ON FEDERAL INDIAN LAW, Second Edition, 880 pages, 1986. (Casebook)

Antitrust—see also Regulated Industries, Trade Regulation

FOX AND SULLIVAN'S CASES AND MATERIALS ON ANTITRUST, Approximately 1100 pages, 1989. (Casebook)

GELLHORN'S ANTITRUST LAW AND ECONOMICS IN A NUTSHELL, Third Edition, 472 pages, 1986. Softcover. (Text)

HOVENKAMP'S BLACK LETTER ON ANTITRUST, 323 pages, 1986. Softcover. (Review)

HOVENKAMP'S HORNBOOK ON ECONOMICS AND FEDERAL ANTITRUST LAW, Student Edition, 414 pages, 1985. (Text)

OPPENHEIM, WESTON AND MCCARTHY'S CASES AND COMMENTS ON FEDERAL ANTITRUST LAWS, Fourth Edition, 1168 pages, 1981. (Casebook) 1985 Supplement.

POSNER AND EASTERBROOK'S CASES AND ECONOMIC NOTES ON ANTITRUST, Second Edition, 1077 pages, 1981. (Casebook) 1984–85 Supplement.

SULLIVAN'S HORNBOOK OF THE LAW OF ANTITRUST, 886 pages, 1977. (Text)

Appellate Advocacy—see Trial and Appellate Advocacy

Architecture and Engineering Law

SWEET'S LEGAL ASPECTS OF ARCHITECTURE, ENGINEERING AND THE CONSTRUCTION PROCESS, Fourth Edition, 889 pages, 1989. Teacher's Manual available. (Casebook)

Art Law

DUBOFF'S ART LAW IN A NUTSHELL, 335 pages, 1984. Softcover. (Text)

Banking Law

LOVETT'S BANKING AND FINANCIAL INSTITUTIONS LAW IN A NUTSHELL, Second Edition, 464 pages, 1988. Softcover. (Text)

SYMONS AND WHITE'S TEACHING MATERIALS ON BANKING LAW, Second Edition, 993 pages, 1984. Teacher's Manual available. (Casebook) 1987 Supplement.

Business Planning—see also Corporate Finance

PAINTER'S PROBLEMS AND MATERIALS IN BUSINESS PLANNING, Second Edition, 1008 pages, 1984. (Casebook) 1987 Supplement.

See also Selected Corporation and Partnership Statutes, Rules and Forms

SELECTED CORPORATION AND PARTNERSHIP STATUTES, RULES AND FORMS. Approximately 700 pages, 1989. Softcover.

Civil Procedure—see also Federal Jurisdiction and Procedure

AMERICAN BAR ASSOCIATION SECTION OF LITIGATION—READINGS ON ADVERSARIAL JUSTICE: THE AMERICAN APPROACH TO ADJUDICATION, 217 pages, 1988. Softcover. (Coursebook)

CLERMONT'S BLACK LETTER ON CIVIL PROCEDURE, Second Edition, 332 pages, 1988. Softcover. (Review)

COUND, FRIEDENTHAL, MILLER AND SEXTON'S CASES AND MATERIALS ON CIVIL PROCEDURE, Fifth Edition, Approximately 1280 pages, 1989. Teacher's Manual available. (Casebook)

COUND, FRIEDENTHAL, MILLER AND SEXTON'S CIVIL PROCEDURE SUPPLEMENT. Approximately 450 pages, 1989. Softcover. (Casebook Supplement)

FEDERAL RULES OF CIVIL PROCEDURE—EDUCATIONAL EDITION. Softcover. Approximately 600 pages, 1989.

Civil Procedure—Cont'd

FRIEDENTHAL, KANE AND MILLER'S HORN-BOOK ON CIVIL PROCEDURE, 876 pages, 1985. (Text)

KANE AND LEVINE'S CIVIL PROCEDURE IN CALIFORNIA: STATE AND FEDERAL Approximately 500 pages, 1989. Softcover. Casebook Supplement.

KANE'S CIVIL PROCEDURE IN A NUTSHELL, Second Edition, 306 pages, 1986. Softcover. (Text)

KOFFLER AND REPPY'S HORNBOOK ON COMMON LAW PLEADING, 663 pages, 1969. (Text)

MARCUS, REDISH AND SHERMAN'S CIVIL PROCEDURE: A MODERN APPROACH, 1027 pages, 1989. Teacher's Manual available. (Casebook)

MARCUS AND SHERMAN'S COMPLEX LITIGATION—CASES AND MATERIALS ON ADVANCED CIVIL PROCEDURE, 846 pages, 1985. Teacher's Manual available. (Casebook) 1989 Supplement.

PARK'S COMPUTER-AIDED EXERCISES ON CIVIL PROCEDURE, Second Edition, 167 pages, 1983. Softcover. (Coursebook)

SIEGEL'S HORNBOOK ON NEW YORK PRACTICE, 1011 pages, 1978, with 1987 pocket part. (Text)

Commercial Law

BAILEY AND HAGEDORN'S SECURED TRANSACTIONS IN A NUTSHELL, Third Edition, 390 pages, 1988. Softcover. (Text)

EPSTEIN, MARTIN, HENNING AND NICKLES' BASIC UNIFORM COMMERCIAL CODE TEACHING MATERIALS, Third Edition, 704 pages, 1988. Teacher's Manual available. (Casebook)

HENSON'S HORNBOOK ON SECURED TRANSACTIONS UNDER THE U.C.C., Second Edition, 504 pages, 1979, with 1979 pocket part. (Text)

MURRAY'S COMMERCIAL LAW, PROBLEMS AND MATERIALS, 366 pages, 1975. Teacher's Manual available. Softcover. (Coursebook)

NICKLES' BLACK LETTER ON COMMERCIAL PAPER, 450 pages, 1988. Softcover. (Review)

NICKLES, MATHESON AND DOLAN'S MATERI-ALS FOR UNDERSTANDING CREDIT AND PAYMENT SYSTEMS, 923 pages, 1987. Teacher's Manual available. (Casebook)

NORDSTROM, MURRAY AND CLOVIS' PROBLEMS AND MATERIALS ON SALES, 515 pages, 1982. (Casebook)

NORDSTROM, MURRAY AND CLOVIS' PROBLEMS AND MATERIALS ON SECURED TRANSACTIONS, 594 pages, 1987. (Casebook)

RUBIN AND COOTER'S THE PAYMENT SYSTEM: CASES, MATERIALS AND ISSUES, Approximately 885 pages, 1989. (Casebook)

SELECTED COMMERCIAL STATUTES. Softcover. Approximately 1600 pages, 1989.

SPEIDEL'S BLACK LETTER ON SALES AND SALES FINANCING, 363 pages, 1984. Softcover. (Review)

SPEIDEL, SUMMERS AND WHITE'S COMMERCIAL LAW: TEACHING MATERIALS, Fourth Edition, 1448 pages, 1987. Teacher's Manual available. (Casebook)

SPEIDEL, SUMMERS AND WHITE'S COMMERCIAL PAPER: TEACHING MATERIALS, Fourth Edition, 578 pages, 1987. Reprint from Speidel et al., Commercial Law, Fourth Edition. Teacher's Manual available. (Casebook)

SPEIDEL, SUMMERS AND WHITE'S SALES: TEACHING MATERIALS, Fourth Edition, 804 pages, 1987. Reprint from Speidel et al., Commercial Law, Fourth Edition. Teacher's Manual available (Casebook)

SPEIDEL, SUMMERS AND WHITE'S SECURED TRANSACTIONS: TEACHING MATERIALS, Fourth Edition, 485 pages, 1987. Reprint from Speidel et al., Commercial Law, Fourth Edition. Teacher's Manual available. (Casebook)

STOCKTON'S SALES IN A NUTSHELL, Second Edition, 370 pages, 1981. Softcover. (Text)

STONE'S UNIFORM COMMERCIAL CODE IN A NUTSHELL, Third Edition, Approximately 540 pages, 1989. Softcover. (Text)

UNIFORM COMMERCIAL CODE, OFFICIAL TEXT WITH COMMENTS. Softcover. 1155 pages, 1987.

WEBER AND SPEIDEL'S COMMERCIAL PAPER IN A NUTSHELL, Third Edition, 404 pages,

Commercial Law—Cont'd

1982. Softcover. (Text)

WHITE AND SUMMERS' HORNBOOK ON THE UNIFORM COMMERCIAL CODE, Third Edition, Student Edition, 1386 pages, 1988. (Text)

Community Property

MENNELL AND BOYKOFF'S COMMUNITY PROPERTY IN A NUTSHELL, Second Edition, 432 pages, 1988. Softcover. (Text)

VERRALL AND BIRD'S CASES AND MATERIALS ON CALIFORNIA COMMUNITY PROPERTY, Fifth Edition, 604 pages, 1988. (Casebook)

Comparative Law

BARTON, GIBBS, LI AND MERRYMAN'S LAW IN RADICALLY DIFFERENT CULTURES, 960 pages, 1983. (Casebook)

GLENDON, GORDON AND OSAKWE'S COMPARATIVE LEGAL TRADITIONS: TEXT, MATERIALS AND CASES ON THE CIVIL LAW, COMMON LAW AND SOCIALIST LAW TRADITIONS, 1091 pages, 1985. (Casebook)

GLENDON, GORDON AND OSAKWE'S COMPARATIVE LEGAL TRADITIONS IN A NUTSHELL. 402 pages, 1982. Softcover. (Text)

LANGBEIN'S COMPARATIVE CRIMINAL PROCEDURE: GERMANY, 172 pages, 1977. Softcover. (Casebook)

Computers and Law

MAGGS AND SPROWL'S COMPUTER APPLICATIONS IN THE LAW, 316 pages, 1987. (Coursebook)

MASON'S USING COMPUTERS IN THE LAW: AN INTRODUCTION AND PRACTICAL GUIDE, Second Edition, 288 pages, 1988. Softcover. (Coursebook)

Conflict of Laws

CRAMTON, CURRIE AND KAY'S CASES—COMMENTS—QUESTIONS ON CONFLICT OF LAWS, Fourth Edition, 876 pages, 1987. (Casebook)

HAY'S BLACK LETTER ON CONFLICT OF LAWS, Approximately 325 pages, 1989. Softcover. (Review)

SCOLES AND HAY'S HORNBOOK ON CONFLICT OF LAWS, Student Edition, 1085 pages, 1982, with 1989 pocket part. (Text)

SEIGEL'S CONFLICTS IN A NUTSHELL, 470

pages, 1982. Softcover. (Text)

Constitutional Law—Civil Rights—see also Foreign Relations and National Security Law

ABERNATHY'S CASES AND MATERIALS ON CIVIL RIGHTS, 660 pages, 1980. (Casebook)

BARRON AND DIENES' BLACK LETTER ON CONSTITUTIONAL LAW, Second Edition, 310 pages, 1987. Softcover. (Review)

BARRON AND DIENES' CONSTITUTIONAL LAW IN A NUTSHELL, 389 pages, 1986. Softcover. (Text)

ENGDAHL'S CONSTITUTIONAL FEDERALISM IN A NUTSHELL, Second Edition, 411 pages, 1987. Softcover. (Text)

FARBER AND SHERRY'S HISTORY OF THE AMERICAN CONSTITUTION, Approximately 476 pages, August, 1989 Pub. Softcover. (Text)

GARVEY AND ALEINIKOFF'S MODERN CONSTITUTIONAL THEORY: A READER, Approximately 494 pages, 1989. Softcover. (Reader)

LOCKHART, KAMISAR, CHOPER AND SHIFFRIN'S CONSTITUTIONAL LAW: CASES—COMMENTS—QUESTIONS, Sixth Edition, 1601 pages, 1986. (Casebook) 1989 Supplement.

LOCKHART, KAMISAR, CHOPER AND SHIFFRIN'S THE AMERICAN CONSTITUTION: CASES AND MATERIALS, Sixth Edition, 1260 pages, 1986. Abridged version of Lockhart, et al., Constitutional Law: Cases—Comments—Questions, Sixth Edition. (Casebook) 1989 Supplement.

LOCKHART, KAMISAR, CHOPER AND SHIFFRIN'S CONSTITUTIONAL RIGHTS AND LIBERTIES: CASES AND MATERIALS, Sixth Edition, 1266 pages, 1986. Reprint from Lockhart, et al., Constitutional Law: Cases—Comments—Questions, Sixth Edition. (Casebook) 1989 Supplement.

MARKS AND COOPER'S STATE CONSTITUTIONAL LAW IN A NUTSHELL, 329 pages, 1988. Softcover. (Text)

NOWAK, ROTUNDA AND YOUNG'S HORNBOOK ON CONSTITUTIONAL LAW, Third Edition, 1191 pages, 1986 with 1988 pocket part. (Text)

ROTUNDA'S MODERN CONSTITUTIONAL LAW:

Constitutional Law—Civil Rights—Cont'd

CASES AND NOTES, Third Edition, 1085 pages, 1989. (Casebook) 1989 Supplement.

VIEIRA'S CIVIL RIGHTS IN A NUTSHELL, 279 pages, 1978. Softcover. (Text)

WILLIAMS' CONSTITUTIONAL ANALYSIS IN A NUTSHELL, 388 pages, 1979. Softcover. (Text)

Consumer Law—see also Commercial Law

EPSTEIN AND NICKLES' CONSUMER LAW IN A NUTSHELL, Second Edition, 418 pages, 1981. Softcover. (Text)

SELECTED COMMERCIAL STATUTES. Softcover. Approximately 1600 pages, 1989.

SPANOGLE AND ROHNER'S CASES AND MATERIALS ON CONSUMER LAW, 693 pages, 1979. Teacher's Manual available. (Casebook) 1982 Supplement.

Contracts

CALAMARI, AND PERILLO'S BLACK LETTER ON CONTRACTS, 397 pages, 1983. Softcover. (Review)

CALAMARI AND PERILLO'S HORNBOOK ON CONTRACTS, Third Edition, 1049 pages, 1987. (Text)

CALAMARI, PERILLO AND BENDER'S CASES AND PROBLEMS ON CONTRACTS, Second Edition, approximately 846 pages, 1989. Teacher's Manual Available. (Casebook)

CORBIN'S TEXT ON CONTRACTS, One Volume Student Edition, 1224 pages, 1952. (Text)

FESSLER AND LOISEAUX'S CASES AND MATERIALS ON CONTRACTS—MORALITY, ECONOMICS AND THE MARKET PLACE, 837 pages, 1982. Teacher's Manual available. (Casebook)

FRIEDMAN'S CONTRACT REMEDIES IN A NUTSHELL, 323 pages, 1981. Softcover. (Text)

FULLER AND EISENBERG'S CASES ON BASIC CONTRACT LAW, Fourth Edition, 1203 pages, 1981 (Casebook)

HAMILTON, RAU AND WEINTRAUB'S CASES AND MATERIALS ON CONTRACTS, 830 pages, 1984. (Casebook)

JACKSON AND BOLLINGER'S CASES ON CONTRACT LAW IN MODERN SOCIETY, Second Edition, 1329 pages, 1980. Teacher's Manual available. (Casebook)

KEYES' GOVERNMENT CONTRACTS IN A NUTSHELL, 423 pages, 1979. Softcover. (Text)

SCHABER AND ROHWER'S CONTRACTS IN A NUTSHELL, Second Edition, 425 pages, 1984. Softcover. (Text)

SUMMERS AND HILLMAN'S CONTRACT AND RELATED OBLIGATION: THEORY, DOCTRINE AND PRACTICE, 1074 pages, 1987. Teacher's Manual available. (Casebook)

Copyright—see Patent and Copyright Law

Corporate Finance

HAMILTON'S CASES AND MATERIALS ON CORPORATION FINANCE, Second Edition, approximately 1177 pages, 1989. (Casebook)

Corporations

HAMILTON'S BLACK LETTER ON CORPORATIONS, Second Edition, 513 pages, 1986. Softcover. (Review)

HAMILTON'S CASES ON CORPORATIONS—INCLUDING PARTNERSHIPS AND LIMITED PARTNERSHIPS, Third Edition, 1213 pages, 1986. Teacher's Manual available. (Casebook) 1986 Statutory Supplement.

HAMILTON'S THE LAW OF CORPORATIONS IN A NUTSHELL, Second Edition, 515 pages, 1987. Softcover. (Text)

HENN'S TEACHING MATERIALS ON THE LAW OF CORPORATIONS, Second Edition, 1204 pages, 1986. Teacher's Manual available. (Casebook)

See Selected Corporation and Partnership Statutes

HENN AND ALEXANDER'S HORNBOOK ON LAWS OF CORPORATIONS, Third Edition, Student Edition, 1371 pages, 1983, with 1986 pocket part. (Text)

SELECTED CORPORATION AND PARTNERSHIP STATUTES, RULES AND FORMS. Softcover. Approximately 650 pages, 1989.

SOLOMON, SCHWARTZ AND BAUMAN'S MATERIALS AND PROBLEMS ON CORPORATIONS: LAW AND POLICY, Second Edition, 1391 pages, 1988. Teacher's Manual available. (Casebook)

See also Selected Corporation and Partnership Statutes

Corrections

KRANTZ' CASES AND MATERIALS ON THE LAW OF CORRECTIONS AND PRISONERS' RIGHTS, Third Edition, 855 pages, 1986. (Casebook) 1988 Supplement.

KRANTZ' THE LAW OF CORRECTIONS AND PRISONERS' RIGHTS IN A NUTSHELL, Third Edition, 407 pages, 1988. Softcover. (Text)

POPPER'S POST-CONVICTION REMEDIES IN A NUTSHELL, 360 pages, 1978. Softcover. (Text)

ROBBINS' CASES AND MATERIALS ON POST-CONVICTION REMEDIES, 506 pages, 1982. (Casebook)

Creditors' Rights

BANKRUPTCY CODE, RULES AND FORMS, LAW SCHOOL EDITION. Approximately 820 pages, 1989. Softcover.

EPSTEIN'S DEBTOR-CREDITOR RELATIONS IN A NUTSHELL, Third Edition, 383 pages, 1986. Softcover. (Text)

EPSTEIN, LANDERS AND NICKLES' CASES AND MATERIALS ON DEBTORS AND CREDITORS, Third Edition, 1059 pages, 1987. Teacher's Manual available. (Casebook)

LOPUCKI'S PLAYER'S MANUAL FOR THE DEBTOR-CREDITOR GAME, 123 pages, 1985. Softcover. (Coursebook)

NICKLES AND EPSTEIN'S BLACK LETTER ON CREDITORS' RIGHTS AND BANKRUPTCY, 576 pages, 1989. (Review)

RIESENFELD'S CASES AND MATERIALS ON CREDITORS' REMEDIES AND DEBTORS' PROTECTION, Fourth Edition, 914 pages, 1987. (Casebook)

WHITE'S CASES AND MATERIALS ON BANKRUPTCY AND CREDITORS' RIGHTS, 812 pages, 1985. Teacher's Manual available. (Casebook) 1987 Supplement.

Criminal Law and Criminal Procedure—see also Corrections, Juvenile Justice

ABRAMS' FEDERAL CRIMINAL LAW AND ITS ENFORCEMENT, 866 pages, 1986. (Casebook) 1988 Supplement.

AMERICAN CRIMINAL JUSTICE PROCESS: SELECTED RULES, STATUTES AND GUIDELINES. Approximately 700 pages, 1989. Softcover.

CARLSON'S ADJUDICATION OF CRIMINAL JUSTICE: PROBLEMS AND REFERENCES, 130 pages, 1986. Softcover. (Casebook)

DIX AND SHARLOT'S CASES AND MATERIALS ON CRIMINAL LAW, Third Edition, 846 pages, 1987. (Casebook)

GRANO'S PROBLEMS IN CRIMINAL PROCEDURE, Second Edition, 176 pages, 1981. Teacher's Manual available. Softcover. (Coursebook)

HEYMANN AND KENETY'S THE MURDER TRIAL OF WILBUR JACKSON: A HOMICIDE IN THE FAMILY, Second Edition, 347 pages, 1985. (Coursebook)

ISRAEL, KAMISAR AND LAFAVE'S CRIMINAL PROCEDURE AND THE CONSTITUTION: LEADING SUPREME COURT CASES AND INTRODUCTORY TEXT, Approximately 735 pages, Revised 1989 Edition. Softcover. (Casebook)

ISRAEL AND LAFAVE'S CRIMINAL PROCEDURE—CONSTITUTIONAL LIMITATIONS IN A NUTSHELL, Fourth Edition, 461 pages, 1988. Softcover. (Text)

JOHNSON'S CASES, MATERIALS AND TEXT ON CRIMINAL LAW, Third Edition, 783 pages, 1985. Teacher's Manual available. (Casebook)

JOHNSON'S CASES AND MATERIALS ON CRIMINAL PROCEDURE, 859 pages, 1988. (Casebook) 1989 Supplement.

KAMISAR, LAFAVE AND ISRAEL'S MODERN CRIMINAL PROCEDURE: CASES, COMMENTS AND QUESTIONS, Sixth Edition, 1558 pages, 1986. (Casebook) 1989 Supplement.

KAMISAR, LAFAVE AND ISRAEL'S BASIC CRIMINAL PROCEDURE: CASES, COMMENTS AND QUESTIONS, Sixth Edition, 860 pages, 1986. Softcover reprint from Kamisar, et al., Modern Criminal Procedure: Cases, Comments and Questions, Sixth Edition. (Casebook) 1989 Supplement.

LAFAVE'S MODERN CRIMINAL LAW: CASES, COMMENTS AND QUESTIONS, Second Edition, 903 pages, 1988. (Casebook)

LAFAVE AND ISRAEL'S HORNBOOK ON CRIMINAL PROCEDURE, Student Edition, 1142 pages, 1985, with 1988 pocket part. (Text)

LAFAVE AND SCOTT'S HORNBOOK ON CRIMINAL LAW, Second Edition, 918 pages, 1986.

Criminal Law and Criminal Procedure— Cont'd

(Text)

LANGBEIN'S COMPARATIVE CRIMINAL PROCE-DURE: GERMANY, 172 pages, 1977. Softcover. (Casebook)

LOEWY'S CRIMINAL LAW IN A NUTSHELL, Second Edition, 321 pages, 1987. Softcover. (Text)

LOW'S BLACK LETTER ON CRIMINAL LAW, 433 pages, 1984. Softcover. (Review)

SALTZBURG'S CASES AND COMMENTARY ON AMERICAN CRIMINAL PROCEDURE, Third Edition, 1302 pages, 1988. Teacher's Manual available. (Casebook) 1989 Supplement.

UVILLER'S THE PROCESSES OF CRIMINAL JUSTICE: INVESTIGATION AND ADJUDICATION, Second Edition, 1384 pages, 1979. (Casebook) 1979 Statutory Supplement. 1986 Update.

VORENBERG'S CASES ON CRIMINAL LAW AND PROCEDURE, Second Edition, 1088 pages, 1981. Teacher's Manual available. (Casebook) 1987 Supplement.

Decedents' Estates—see Trusts and Estates

Domestic Relations

CLARK'S CASES AND PROBLEMS ON DOMESTIC RELATIONS, Third Edition, 1153 pages, 1980. Teacher's Manual available. (Casebook)

CLARK'S HORNBOOK ON DOMESTIC RELATIONS, Second Edition, Student Edition, 1050 pages, 1988. (Text)

KRAUSE'S BLACK LETTER ON FAMILY LAW, 314 pages, 1988. Softcover. (Review)

KRAUSE'S CASES, COMMENTS AND QUESTIONS ON FAMILY LAW, Third Edition, approximately 1200 pages, October, 1989 Pub. (Casebook)

KRAUSE'S FAMILY LAW IN A NUTSHELL, Second Edition, 444 pages, 1986. Softcover. (Text)

KRAUSKOPF'S CASES ON PROPERTY DIVISION AT MARRIAGE DISSOLUTION, 250 pages, 1984. Softcover. (Casebook)

Economics, Law and—see also Antitrust, Regulated Industries

GOETZ' CASES AND MATERIALS ON LAW AND ECONOMICS, 547 pages, 1984. (Casebook)

Education Law

ALEXANDER AND ALEXANDER'S THE LAW OF SCHOOLS, STUDENTS AND TEACHERS IN A NUTSHELL, 409 pages, 1984. Softcover. (Text)

Employment Discrimination—see also Women and the Law

JONES, MURPHY AND BELTON'S CASES AND MATERIALS ON DISCRIMINATION IN EMPLOYMENT, (The Labor Law Group). Fifth Edition, 1116 pages, 1987. (Casebook)

PLAYER'S CASES AND MATERIALS ON EMPLOYMENT DISCRIMINATION LAW, Second Edition, 782 pages, 1984. Teacher's Manual available. (Casebook)

PLAYER'S FEDERAL LAW OF EMPLOYMENT DISCRIMINATION IN A NUTSHELL, Second Edition, 402 pages, 1981. Softcover. (Text)

PLAYER'S HORNBOOK ON EMPLOYMENT DISCRIMINATION LAW, Student Edition, 708 pages, 1988. (Text)

Energy and Natural Resources Law—see also Oil and Gas

LAITOS' CASES AND MATERIALS ON NATURAL RESOURCES LAW, 938 pages, 1985. Teacher's Manual available. (Casebook)

SELECTED ENVIRONMENTAL LAW STATUTES—EDUCATIONAL EDITION. Softcover. Approximately 850 pages, 1989.

Environmental Law—see also Energy and Natural Resources Law; Sea, Law of

BONINE AND MCGARITY'S THE LAW OF ENVIRONMENTAL PROTECTION: CASES—LEGISLATION—POLICIES, 1076 pages, 1984. Teacher's Manual available. (Casebook)

FINDLEY AND FARBER'S CASES AND MATERIALS ON ENVIRONMENTAL LAW, Second Edition, 813 pages, 1985. (Casebook) 1988 Supplement.

FINDLEY AND FARBER'S ENVIRONMENTAL LAW IN A NUTSHELL, Second Edition, 367 pages, 1988. Softcover. (Text)

RODGERS' HORNBOOK ON ENVIRONMENTAL LAW, 956 pages, 1977, with 1984 pocket

Environmental Law—Cont'd

part. (Text)

SELECTED ENVIRONMENTAL LAW STATUTES—
EDUCATIONAL EDITION. Softcover. Approximately 850 pages, 1989.

Equity—see Remedies

Estate Planning—see also Trusts and Estates; Taxation—Estate and Gift

LYNN'S AN INTRODUCTION TO ESTATE PLANNING IN A NUTSHELL, Third Edition, 370 pages, 1983. Softcover. (Text)

Evidence

BROUN AND BLAKEY'S BLACK LETTER ON EVIDENCE, 269 pages, 1984. Softcover. (Review)

BROUN, MEISENHOLDER, STRONG AND MOSTELLER'S PROBLEMS IN EVIDENCE, Third Edition, 238 pages, 1988. Teacher's Manual available. Softcover. (Coursebook)

CLEARY, STRONG, BROUN AND MOSTELLER'S CASES AND MATERIALS ON EVIDENCE, Fourth Edition, 1060 pages, 1988. (Casebook)

FEDERAL RULES OF EVIDENCE FOR UNITED STATES COURTS AND MAGISTRATES. Softcover. 378 pages, 1989.

GRAHAM'S FEDERAL RULES OF EVIDENCE IN A NUTSHELL, Second Edition, 473 pages, 1987. Softcover. (Text)

KIMBALL'S PROGRAMMED MATERIALS ON PROBLEMS IN EVIDENCE, 380 pages, 1978. Softcover. (Coursebook)

LEMPERT AND SALTZBURG'S A MODERN APPROACH TO EVIDENCE: TEXT, PROBLEMS, TRANSCRIPTS AND CASES, Second Edition, 1232 pages, 1983. Teacher's Manual available. (Casebook)

LILLY'S AN INTRODUCTION TO THE LAW OF EVIDENCE, Second Edition, 585 pages, 1987. (Text)

MCCORMICK, SUTTON AND WELLBORN'S CASES AND MATERIALS ON EVIDENCE, Sixth Edition, 1067 pages, 1987. (Casebook)

MCCORMICK'S HORNBOOK ON EVIDENCE, Third Edition, Student Edition, 1156 pages, 1984, with 1987 pocket part. (Text)

ROTHSTEIN'S EVIDENCE IN A NUTSHELL: STATE AND FEDERAL RULES, Second Edition,

514 pages, 1981. Softcover. (Text)

Federal Jurisdiction and Procedure

CURRIE'S CASES AND MATERIALS ON FEDERAL COURTS, Third Edition, 1042 pages, 1982. (Casebook) 1985 Supplement.

CURRIE'S FEDERAL JURISDICTION IN A NUTSHELL, Second Edition, 258 pages, 1981. Softcover. (Text)

FEDERAL RULES OF CIVIL PROCEDURE—EDUCATIONAL EDITION. Softcover. Approximately 600 pages, 1989.

REDISH'S BLACK LETTER ON FEDERAL JURISDICTION, 219 pages, 1985. Softcover. (Review)

REDISH'S CASES, COMMENTS AND QUESTIONS ON FEDERAL COURTS, Second Edition, 1122 pages, 1989. (Casebook)

VETRI AND MERRILL'S FEDERAL COURTS PROBLEMS AND MATERIALS, Second Edition, 232 pages, 1984. Softcover. (Coursebook)

WRIGHT'S HORNBOOK ON FEDERAL COURTS, Fourth Edition, Student Edition, 870 pages, 1983. (Text)

Foreign Relations and National Security Law

FRANCK AND GLENNON'S FOREIGN RELATIONS AND NATIONAL SECURITY LAW, 941 pages, 1987. (Casebook)

Future Interests—see Trusts and Estates

Health Law—see Medicine, Law and

Human Rights—see International Law

Immigration Law

ALEINIKOFF AND MARTIN'S IMMIGRATION PROCESS AND POLICY, 1042 pages, 1985. (Casebook) 1987 Supplement.

WEISSBRODT'S IMMIGRATION LAW AND PROCEDURE IN A NUTSHELL, 345 pages, 1984, Softcover. (Text)

Indian Law—see American Indian Law

Insurance Law

DEVINE AND TERRY'S PROBLEMS IN INSURANCE LAW, Approximately 230 pages, 1989. Softcover. Teacher's Manual available. (Course book)

Insurance Law—Cont'd

DOBBYN'S INSURANCE LAW IN A NUTSHELL, Second Edition, approximately 285 pages, 1989. Softcover. (Text)

KEETON'S CASES ON BASIC INSURANCE LAW, Second Edition, 1086 pages, 1977. Teacher's Manual available. (Casebook)

KEETON AND WIDISS' INSURANCE LAW, Student Edition, 1359 pages, 1988. (Text)

WIDISS AND KEETON'S COURSE SUPPLEMENT TO KEETON AND WIDISS' INSURANCE LAW, 502 pages, 1988. Softcover. (Casebook)

YORK AND WHELAN'S CASES, MATERIALS AND PROBLEMS ON GENERAL PRACTICE INSURANCE LAW, Second Edition, 787 pages, 1988. Teacher's Manual available. (Casebook)

International Law—see also Sea, Law of

BUERGENTHAL'S INTERNATIONAL HUMAN RIGHTS IN A NUTSHELL, 283 pages, 1988. Softcover. (Text)

BUERGENTHAL AND MAIER'S PUBLIC INTERNATIONAL LAW IN A NUTSHELL, 262 pages, 1985. Softcover. (Text)

FOLSOM, GORDON AND SPANOGLE'S INTERNATIONAL BUSINESS TRANSACTIONS—A PROBLEM-ORIENTED COURSEBOOK, 1160 pages, 1986. Teacher's Manual available. (Casebook) 1989 Documents Supplement.

FOLSOM, GORDON AND SPANOGLE'S INTERNATIONAL BUSINESS TRANSACTIONS IN A NUTSHELL, Third Edition, 509 pages, 1988. Softcover. (Text)

HENKIN, PUGH, SCHACHTER AND SMIT'S CASES AND MATERIALS ON INTERNATIONAL LAW, Second Edition, 1517 pages, 1987. (Casebook) Documents Supplement.

JACKSON AND DAVEY'S CASES, MATERIALS AND TEXT ON LEGAL PROBLEMS OF INTERNATIONAL ECONOMIC RELATIONS, Second Edition, 1269 pages, 1986. (Casebook) 1989 Documents Supplement.

KIRGIS' INTERNATIONAL ORGANIZATIONS IN THEIR LEGAL SETTING, 1016 pages, 1977. Teacher's Manual available. (Casebook) 1981 Supplement.

WESTON, FALK AND D'AMATO'S INTERNATIONAL LAW AND WORLD ORDER—A PROBLEM-ORIENTED COURSEBOOK, 1195 pages, 1980. Teacher's Manual available. (Casebook)

Documents Supplement.

Interviewing and Counseling

BINDER AND PRICE'S LEGAL INTERVIEWING AND COUNSELING, 232 pages, 1977. Teacher's Manual available. Softcover. (Coursebook)

SHAFFER AND ELKINS' LEGAL INTERVIEWING AND COUNSELING IN A NUTSHELL, Second Edition, 487 pages, 1987. Softcover. (Text)

Introduction to Law—see Legal Method and Legal System

Introduction to Law Study

DOBBYN'S SO YOU WANT TO GO TO LAW SCHOOL, Revised First Edition, 206 pages, 1976. Softcover. (Text)

HEGLAND'S INTRODUCTION TO THE STUDY AND PRACTICE OF LAW IN A NUTSHELL, 418 pages, 1983. Softcover (Text)

KINYON'S INTRODUCTION TO LAW STUDY AND LAW EXAMINATIONS IN A NUTSHELL, 389 pages, 1971. Softcover. (Text)

Jurisprudence

CHRISTIE'S JURISPRUDENCE—TEXT AND READINGS ON THE PHILOSOPHY OF LAW, 1056 pages, 1973. (Casebook)

Juvenile Justice

FOX'S CASES AND MATERIALS ON MODERN JUVENILE JUSTICE, Second Edition, 960 pages, 1981. (Casebook)

FOX'S JUVENILE COURTS IN A NUTSHELL, Third Edition, 291 pages, 1984. Softcover. (Text)

Labor Law—see also Employment Discrimination, Social Legislation

FINKIN, GOLDMAN AND SUMMERS' LEGAL PROTECTION OF INDIVIDUAL EMPLOYEES, (The Labor Law Group). Approximately 1000 pages, December, 1989 Pub. (Casebook)

GORMAN'S BASIC TEXT ON LABOR LAW— UNIONIZATION AND COLLECTIVE BARGAINING, 914 pages, 1976. (Text)

GRODIN, WOLLETT AND ALLEYNE'S COLLECTIVE BARGAINING IN PUBLIC EMPLOYMENT, (The Labor Law Group). Third Edition, 430 pages, 1979. (Casebook)

Labor Law—Cont'd

LESLIE'S LABOR LAW IN A NUTSHELL, Second Edition, 397 pages, 1986. Softcover. (Text)

NOLAN'S LABOR ARBITRATION LAW AND PRACTICE IN A NUTSHELL, 358 pages, 1979. Softcover. (Text)

OBERER, HANSLOWE, ANDERSEN AND HEINSZ' CASES AND MATERIALS ON LABOR LAW—COLLECTIVE BARGAINING IN A FREE SOCIETY, Third Edition, 1163 pages, 1986. (Casebook) Statutory Supplement.

RABIN, SILVERSTEIN AND SCHATZKI'S LABOR AND EMPLOYMENT LAW: PROBLEMS, CASES AND MATERIALS IN THE LAW OF WORK, (The Labor Law Group). 1014 pages, 1988. Teacher's Manual available. (Casebook) 1988 Statutory Supplement.

Land Finance—Property Security—see Real Estate Transactions

Land Use

CALLIES AND FREILICH'S CASES AND MATERIALS ON LAND USE, 1233 pages, 1986. (Casebook) 1988 Supplement.

HAGMAN AND JUERGENSMEYER'S HORNBOOK ON URBAN PLANNING AND LAND DEVELOPMENT CONTROL LAW, Second Edition, Student Edition, 680 pages, 1986. (Text)

WRIGHT AND GITELMAN'S CASES AND MATERIALS ON LAND USE, Third Edition, 1300 pages, 1982. Teacher's Manual available. (Casebook) 1987 Supplement.

WRIGHT AND WRIGHT'S LAND USE IN A NUTSHELL, Second Edition, 356 pages, 1985. Softcover. (Text)

Legal History—see also Legal Method and Legal System

PRESSER AND ZAINALDIN'S CASES AND MATERIALS ON LAW AND JURISPRUDENCE IN AMERICAN HISTORY, Second Edition, approximately 1092 pages, 1989. Teacher's Manual available. (Casebook)

Legal Method and Legal System—see also Legal Research, Legal Writing

ALDISERT'S READINGS, MATERIALS AND CASES IN THE JUDICIAL PROCESS, 948 pages, 1976. (Casebook)

BERCH AND BERCH'S INTRODUCTION TO LEGAL

METHOD AND PROCESS, 550 pages, 1985. Teacher's Manual available. (Casebook)

BODENHEIMER, OAKLEY AND LOVE'S READINGS AND CASES ON AN INTRODUCTION TO THE ANGLO-AMERICAN LEGAL SYSTEM, Second Edition, 166 pages, 1988. Softcover. (Casebook)

DAVIES AND LAWRY'S INSTITUTIONS AND METHODS OF THE LAW—INTRODUCTORY TEACHING MATERIALS, 547 pages, 1982. Teacher's Manual available. (Casebook)

DVORKIN, HIMMELSTEIN AND LESNICK'S BECOMING A LAWYER: A HUMANISTIC PERSPECTIVE ON LEGAL EDUCATION AND PROFESSIONALISM, 211 pages, 1981. Softcover. (Text)

KELSO AND KELSO'S STUDYING LAW: AN INTRODUCTION, 587 pages, 1984. (Coursebook)

KEMPIN'S HISTORICAL INTRODUCTION TO ANGLO-AMERICAN LAW IN A NUTSHELL, Second Edition, 280 pages, 1973. Softcover. (Text)

REYNOLDS' JUDICIAL PROCESS IN A NUTSHELL, 292 pages, 1980. Softcover. (Text)

Legal Research

COHEN'S LEGAL RESEARCH IN A NUTSHELL, Fourth Edition, 452 pages, 1985. Softcover. (Text)

COHEN, BERRING AND OLSON'S HOW TO FIND THE LAW, Ninth Edition, approximately 800 pages, October, 1989 Pub. (Coursebook)

Legal Research Exercises, 3rd Ed., for use with Cohen, Berring and Olson, 229 pages, 1989. Teacher's Manual available.

COHEN, BERRING AND OLSON'S FINDING THE LAW, approximately 565 pages, 1989. Softcover reprint from Cohen, Berring and Olson's How to Find the Law, Ninth Edition. (Coursebook)

ROMBAUER'S LEGAL PROBLEM SOLVING—ANALYSIS, RESEARCH AND WRITING, Fourth Edition, 424 pages, 1983. Teacher's Manual with problems available. (Coursebook)

STATSKY'S LEGAL RESEARCH AND WRITING, Third Edition, 252 pages, 1986. Softcover. (Coursebook)

TEPLY'S PROGRAMMED MATERIALS ON LEGAL RESEARCH AND CITATION, Third Edition, ap-

Legal Research—Cont'd

proximately 450 pages, 1989. Softcover. (Coursebook)

Student Library Exercises, 3rd ed., 391 pages, 1989. Answer Key available.

Legal Writing

CHILD'S DRAFTING LEGAL DOCUMENTS: MATERIALS AND PROBLEMS, 286 pages, 1988. Softcover. Teacher's Manual available. (Coursebook)

DICKERSON'S MATERIALS ON LEGAL DRAFTING, 425 pages, 1981. Teacher's Manual available. (Coursebook)

FELSENFELD AND SIEGEL'S WRITING CONTRACTS IN PLAIN ENGLISH, 290 pages, 1981. Softcover. (Text)

GOPEN'S WRITING FROM A LEGAL PERSPECTIVE, 225 pages, 1981. (Text)

MELLINKOFF'S LEGAL WRITING—SENSE AND NONSENSE, 242 pages, 1982. Softcover. Teacher's Manual available. (Text)

PRATT'S LEGAL WRITING: A SYSTEMATIC APPROACH, Approximately 412 pages, 1989. Teacher's Manual available. (Coursebook)

RAY AND RAMSFIELD'S LEGAL WRITING: GETTING IT RIGHT AND GETTING IT WRITTEN, 250 pages, 1987. Softcover. (Text)

SQUIRES AND ROMBAUER'S LEGAL WRITING IN A NUTSHELL, 294 pages, 1982. Softcover. (Text)

STATSKY AND WERNET'S CASE ANALYSIS AND FUNDAMENTALS OF LEGAL WRITING, Third Edition, 424 pages, 1989. (Text)

WEIHOFEN'S LEGAL WRITING STYLE, Second Edition, 332 pages, 1980. (Text)

Legislation

DAVIES' LEGISLATIVE LAW AND PROCESS IN A NUTSHELL, Second Edition, 346 pages, 1986. Softcover. (Text)

ESKRIDGE AND FRICKEY'S CASES AND MATERIALS ON LEGISLATION: STATUTES AND THE CREATION OF PUBLIC POLICY, 937 pages, 1988. Teacher's Manual available. (Casebook)

NUTTING AND DICKERSON'S CASES AND MATERIALS ON LEGISLATION, Fifth Edition, 744 pages, 1978. (Casebook)

STATSKY'S LEGISLATIVE ANALYSIS AND

DRAFTING, Second Edition, 217 pages, 1984. Teacher's Manual available. (Text)

Local Government

FRUG'S CASES AND MATERIALS ON LOCAL GOVERNMENT LAW, 1005 pages, 1988. (Casebook)

MCCARTHY'S LOCAL GOVERNMENT LAW IN A NUTSHELL, Second Edition, 404 pages, 1983. Softcover. (Text)

REYNOLDS' HORNBOOK ON LOCAL GOVERNMENT LAW, 860 pages, 1982, with 1987 pocket part. (Text)

VALENTE'S CASES AND MATERIALS ON LOCAL GOVERNMENT LAW, Third Edition, 1010 pages, 1987. Teacher's Manual available. (Casebook) 1989 Supplement.

Mass Communication Law

GILLMOR AND BARRON'S CASES AND COMMENT ON MASS COMMUNICATION LAW, Fifth Edition, approximately 1068 pages, September 1989 Pub. Teacher's Manual available. (Casebook)

GINSBURG'S REGULATION OF BROADCASTING: LAW AND POLICY TOWARDS RADIO, TELEVISION AND CABLE COMMUNICATIONS, 741 pages, 1979 (Casebook) 1983 Supplement.

ZUCKMAN, GAYNES, CARTER AND DEE'S MASS COMMUNICATIONS LAW IN A NUTSHELL, Third Edition, 538 pages, 1988. Softcover. (Text)

Medicine, Law and

FURROW, JOHNSON, JOST AND SCHWARTZ' HEALTH LAW: CASES, MATERIALS AND PROBLEMS, 1005 pages, 1987. Teacher's Manual available. (Casebook)

KING'S THE LAW OF MEDICAL MALPRACTICE IN A NUTSHELL, Second Edition, 342 pages, 1986. Softcover. (Text)

SHAPIRO AND SPECE'S CASES, MATERIALS AND PROBLEMS ON BIOETHICS AND LAW, 892 pages, 1981. (Casebook)

SHARPE, FISCINA AND HEAD'S CASES ON LAW AND MEDICINE, 882 pages, 1978. (Casebook)

Military Law

SHANOR AND TERRELL'S MILITARY LAW IN A NUTSHELL, 378 pages, 1980. Softcover.

Military Law—Cont'd

(Text)

Mortgages—see Real Estate Transactions

Natural Resources Law—see Energy and Natural Resources Law, Environmental Law

Negotiation

GIFFORD'S LEGAL NEGOTIATION: THEORY AND APPLICATIONS, 225 pages, 1989. Softcover. (Text)

PECK'S CASES AND MATERIALS ON NEGOTIATION, (The Labor Law Group). Second Edition, 280 pages, 1980. (Casebook)

WILLIAMS' LEGAL NEGOTIATION AND SETTLEMENT, 207 pages, 1983. Softcover. Teacher's Manual available. (Coursebook)

Office Practice—see also Computers and Law, Interviewing and Counseling, Negotiation

HEGLAND'S TRIAL AND PRACTICE SKILLS IN A NUTSHELL, 346 pages, 1978. Softcover (Text)

STRONG AND CLARK'S LAW OFFICE MANAGEMENT, 424 pages, 1974. (Casebook)

Oil and Gas—see also Energy and Natural Resources Law

HEMINGWAY'S HORNBOOK ON OIL AND GAS, Second Edition, Student Edition, 543 pages, 1983, with 1989 pocket part. (Text)

KUNTZ, LOWE, ANDERSON AND SMITH'S CASES AND MATERIALS ON OIL AND GAS LAW, 857 pages, 1986. Teacher's Manual available. (Casebook) Forms Manual. Revised.

LOWE'S OIL AND GAS LAW IN A NUTSHELL, Second Edition, 465 pages, 1988. Softcover. (Text)

Partnership—see Agency—Partnership

Patent and Copyright Law

CHOATE, FRANCIS, AND COLLINS' CASES AND MATERIALS ON PATENT LAW, INCLUDING TRADE SECRETS, COPYRIGHTS, TRADEMARKS, Third Edition, 1009 pages, 1987. (Casebook)

MILLER AND DAVIS' INTELLECTUAL PROPERTY—PATENTS, TRADEMARKS AND COPYRIGHT IN A NUTSHELL, 428 pages, 1983. Softcover.

(Text)

NIMMER'S CASES AND MATERIALS ON COPYRIGHT AND OTHER ASPECTS OF ENTERTAINMENT LITIGATION ILLUSTRATED—INCLUDING UNFAIR COMPETITION, DEFAMATION AND PRIVACY, Third Edition, 1025 pages, 1985. (Casebook) 1989 Supplement.

Products Liability

FISCHER AND POWERS' CASES AND MATERIALS ON PRODUCTS LIABILITY, 685 pages, 1988. Teacher's Manual available. (Casebook)

NOEL AND PHILLIPS' CASES ON PRODUCTS LIABILITY, Second Edition, 821 pages, 1982. (Casebook)

PHILLIPS' PRODUCTS LIABILITY IN A NUTSHELL, Third Edition, 307 pages, 1988. Softcover. (Text)

Professional Responsibility

ARONSON, DEVINE AND FISCH'S PROBLEMS, CASES AND MATERIALS IN PROFESSIONAL RESPONSIBILITY, 745 pages, 1985. Teacher's Manual available. (Casebook)

ARONSON AND WECKSTEIN'S PROFESSIONAL RESPONSIBILITY IN A NUTSHELL, 399 pages, 1980. Softcover. (Text)

MELLINKOFF'S THE CONSCIENCE OF A LAWYER, 304 pages, 1973. (Text)

PIRSIG AND KIRWIN'S CASES AND MATERIALS ON PROFESSIONAL RESPONSIBILITY, Fourth Edition, 603 pages, 1984. Teacher's Manual available. (Casebook)

ROTUNDA'S BLACK LETTER ON PROFESSIONAL RESPONSIBILITY, Second Edition, 414 pages, 1988. Softcover. (Review)

SCHWARTZ AND WYDICK'S PROBLEMS IN LEGAL ETHICS, Second Edition, 341 pages, 1988. (Coursebook)

SELECTED STATUTES, RULES AND STANDARDS ON THE LEGAL PROFESSION. Softcover. Approximately 450 pages, 1989.

SUTTON AND DZIENKOWSKI'S CASES AND MATERIALS ON PROFESSIONAL RESPONSIBILITY FOR LAWYERS, Approximately 800 pages, 1989. Teacher's Manual available. (Casebook)

WOLFRAM'S HORNBOOK ON MODERN LEGAL ETHICS, Student Edition, 1120 pages, 1986. (Text)

Property—see also Real Estate Transactions, Land Use, Trusts and Estates

BERNHARDT'S BLACK LETTER ON PROPERTY, 318 pages, 1983. Softcover. (Review)

BERNHARDT'S REAL PROPERTY IN A NUTSHELL, Second Edition, 448 pages, 1981. Softcover. (Text)

BOYER'S SURVEY OF THE LAW OF PROPERTY, Third Edition, 766 pages, 1981. (Text)

BROWDER, CUNNINGHAM, NELSON, STOEBUCK AND WHITMAN'S CASES ON BASIC PROPERTY LAW, Fifth Edition, approximately 1200 pages, 1989. (Casebook)

BRUCE, ELY AND BOSTICK'S CASES AND MATERIALS ON MODERN PROPERTY LAW, Second Edition, 953 pages, 1989. Teacher's Manual available. (Casebook)

BURKE'S PERSONAL PROPERTY IN A NUTSHELL, 322 pages, 1983. Softcover. (Text)

CUNNINGHAM, STOEBUCK AND WHITMAN'S HORNBOOK ON THE LAW OF PROPERTY, Student Edition, 916 pages, 1984, with 1987 pocket part. (Text)

DONAHUE, KAUPER AND MARTIN'S CASES ON PROPERTY, Second Edition, 1362 pages, 1983. Teacher's Manual available. (Casebook)

HILL'S LANDLORD AND TENANT LAW IN A NUTSHELL, Second Edition, 311 pages, 1986. Softcover. (Text)

KURTZ AND HOVENKAMP'S CASES AND MATERIALS ON AMERICAN PROPERTY LAW, 1296 pages, 1987. Teacher's Manual available. (Casebook) 1988 Supplement.

MOYNIHAN'S INTRODUCTION TO REAL PROPERTY, Second Edition, 239 pages, 1988. (Text)

UNIFORM LAND TRANSACTIONS ACT, UNIFORM SIMPLIFICATION OF LAND TRANSFERS ACT, UNIFORM CONDOMINIUM ACT, 1977 OFFICIAL TEXT WITH COMMENTS. Softcover. 462 pages, 1978.

Psychiatry, Law and

REISNER'S LAW AND THE MENTAL HEALTH SYSTEM, CIVIL AND CRIMINAL ASPECTS, 696 pages, 1985. (Casebook) 1987 Supplement.

Real Estate Transactions

BRUCE'S REAL ESTATE FINANCE IN A NUTSHELL, Second Edition, 262 pages, 1985. Softcover. (Text)

MAXWELL, RIESENFELD, HETLAND AND WARREN'S CASES ON CALIFORNIA SECURITY TRANSACTIONS IN LAND, Third Edition, 728 pages, 1984. (Casebook)

NELSON AND WHITMAN'S BLACK LETTER ON LAND TRANSACTIONS AND FINANCE, Second Edition, 466 pages, 1988. Softcover. (Review)

NELSON AND WHITMAN'S CASES ON REAL ESTATE TRANSFER, FINANCE AND DEVELOPMENT, Third Edition, 1184 pages, 1987. (Casebook)

NELSON AND WHITMAN'S HORNBOOK ON REAL ESTATE FINANCE LAW, Second Edition, 941 pages, 1985 with 1989 pocket part. (Text)

OSBORNE'S CASES AND MATERIALS ON SECURED TRANSACTIONS, 559 pages, 1967. (Casebook)

Regulated Industries—see also Mass Communication Law, Banking Law

GELLHORN AND PIERCE'S REGULATED INDUSTRIES IN A NUTSHELL, Second Edition, 389 pages, 1987. Softcover. (Text)

MORGAN, HARRISON AND VERKUIL'S CASES AND MATERIALS ON ECONOMIC REGULATION OF BUSINESS, Second Edition, 666 pages, 1985. (Casebook)

Remedies

DOBBS' HORNBOOK ON REMEDIES, 1067 pages, 1973. (Text)

DOBBS' PROBLEMS IN REMEDIES. 137 pages, 1974. Teacher's Manual available. Softcover. (Coursebook)

DOBBYN'S INJUNCTIONS IN A NUTSHELL, 264 pages, 1974. Softcover. (Text)

FRIEDMAN'S CONTRACT REMEDIES IN A NUTSHELL, 323 pages, 1981. Softcover. (Text)

LEAVELL, LOVE AND NELSON'S CASES AND MATERIALS ON EQUITABLE REMEDIES, RESTITUTION AND DAMAGES, Fourth Edition, 1111 pages, 1986. Teacher's Manual available. (Casebook)

MCCORMICK'S HORNBOOK ON DAMAGES, 811 pages, 1935. (Text)

Remedies—Cont'd

O'CONNELL'S REMEDIES IN A NUTSHELL, Second Edition, 320 pages, 1985. Softcover. (Text)

YORK, BAUMAN AND RENDLEMAN'S CASES AND MATERIALS ON REMEDIES, Fourth Edition, 1029 pages, 1985. Teacher's Manual available. (Casebook)

Sea, Law of

SOHN AND GUSTAFSON'S THE LAW OF THE SEA IN A NUTSHELL, 264 pages, 1984. Softcover. (Text)

Securities Regulation

HAZEN'S HORNBOOK ON THE LAW OF SECURITIES REGULATION, Student Edition, 739 pages, 1985, with 1988 pocket part. (Text)

RATNER'S MATERIALS ON SECURITIES REGULATION, Third Edition, 1000 pages, 1986. Teacher's Manual available. (Casebook) 1989 Supplement.

See Selected Securities and Business Planning Statutes

RATNER'S SECURITIES REGULATION IN A NUTSHELL, Third Edition, 316 pages, 1988. Softcover. (Text)

SELECTED SECURITIES AND BUSINESS PLANNING STATUTES, RULES AND FORMS. Softcover. 493 pages, 1987.

Social Legislation

HOOD AND HARDY'S WORKERS' COMPENSATION AND EMPLOYEE PROTECTION IN A NUTSHELL, 274 pages, 1984. Softcover. (Text)

LaFRANCE'S WELFARE LAW: STRUCTURE AND ENTITLEMENT IN A NUTSHELL, 455 pages, 1979. Softcover. (Text)

MALONE, PLANT AND LITTLE'S CASES ON WORKERS' COMPENSATION AND EMPLOYMENT RIGHTS, Second Edition, 951 pages, 1980. Teacher's Manual available. (Casebook)

Sports Law

SCHUBERT, SMITH AND TRENTADUE'S SPORTS LAW, 395 pages, 1986. (Text)

Tax Practice and Procedure

GARBIS, STRUNTZ AND RUBIN'S CASES AND MATERIALS ON TAX PROCEDURE AND TAX FRAUD, Second Edition, 687 pages, 1987. (Casebook)

Taxation—Corporate

KAHN AND GANN'S CORPORATE TAXATION, Third Edition, approximately 978 pages, 1989. Teacher's Manual available. (Casebook)

WEIDENBRUCH AND BURKE'S FEDERAL INCOME TAXATION OF CORPORATIONS AND STOCKHOLDERS IN A NUTSHELL, Third Edition, 309 pages, 1989. Softcover. (Text)

Taxation—Estate & Gift—see also Estate Planning, Trusts and Estates

McNULTY'S FEDERAL ESTATE AND GIFT TAXATION IN A NUTSHELL, Fourth Edition, 496 pages, 1989. Softcover. (Text)

PENNELL'S CASES AND MATERIALS ON INCOME TAXATION OF TRUSTS, ESTATES, GRANTORS AND BENEFICIARIES, 460 pages, 1987. Teacher's Manual available. (Casebook)

Taxation—Individual

DODGE'S THE LOGIC OF TAX, Approximately 330 pages, September, 1989 Pub. Softcover. (Text)

GUNN AND WARD'S CASES, TEXT AND PROBLEMS ON FEDERAL INCOME TAXATION, Second Edition, 835 pages, 1988. Teacher's Manual available. (Casebook)

HUDSON AND LIND'S BLACK LETTER ON FEDERAL INCOME TAXATION, Second Edition, 396 pages, 1987. Softcover. (Review)

KRAGEN AND McNULTY'S CASES AND MATERIALS ON FEDERAL INCOME TAXATION—INDIVIDUALS, CORPORATIONS, PARTNERSHIPS, Fourth Edition, 1287 pages, 1985. (Casebook)

McNULTY'S FEDERAL INCOME TAXATION OF INDIVIDUALS IN A NUTSHELL, Fourth Edition, 503 pages, 1988. Softcover. (Text)

POSIN'S HORNBOOK ON FEDERAL INCOME TAXATION, Student Edition, 491 pages, 1983, with 1989 pocket part. (Text)

ROSE AND CHOMMIE'S HORNBOOK ON FEDERAL INCOME TAXATION, Third Edition, 923 pages, 1988, with 1989 pocket part. (Text)

SELECTED FEDERAL TAXATION STATUTES AND REGULATIONS. Softcover. Approximately 1550 pages, 1990.

SOLOMON AND HESCH'S PROBLEMS, CASES AND MATERIALS ON FEDERAL INCOME TAXATION OF INDIVIDUALS, 1068 pages, 1987.

Taxation—Individual—Cont'd

Teacher's Manual available. (Casebook)

Taxation—International

DOERNBERG'S INTERNATIONAL TAXATION IN A NUTSHELL, 325 pages, 1989. Softcover. (Text)

KAPLAN'S FEDERAL TAXATION OF INTERNATIONAL TRANSACTIONS: PRINCIPLES, PLANNING AND POLICY, 635 pages, 1988. (Casebook)

Taxation—Partnership

BERGER AND WIEDENBECK'S CASES AND MATERIALS ON PARTNERSHIP TAXATION, 788 pages, 1989. Teacher's Manual available. (Casebook)

Taxation—State & Local

GELFAND AND SALSICH'S STATE AND LOCAL TAXATION AND FINANCE IN A NUTSHELL, 309 pages, 1986. Softcover. (Text)

HELLERSTEIN AND HELLERSTEIN'S CASES AND MATERIALS ON STATE AND LOCAL TAXATION, Fifth Edition, 1071 pages, 1988. (Casebook)

Torts—see also Products Liability

CHRISTIE'S CASES AND MATERIALS ON THE LAW OF TORTS, 1264 pages, 1983. (Casebook)

DOBBS' TORTS AND COMPENSATION—PERSONAL ACCOUNTABILITY AND SOCIAL RESPONSIBILITY FOR INJURY, 955 pages, 1985. Teacher's Manual available. (Casebook)

KEETON, KEETON, SARGENTICH AND STEINER'S CASES AND MATERIALS ON TORT AND ACCIDENT LAW, Second Edition, approximately 1307 pages, 1989. (Casebook)

KIONKA'S BLACK LETTER ON TORTS, 339 pages, 1988. Softcover. (Review)

KIONKA'S TORTS IN A NUTSHELL: INJURIES TO PERSONS AND PROPERTY, 434 pages, 1977. Softcover. (Text)

MALONE'S TORTS IN A NUTSHELL: INJURIES TO FAMILY, SOCIAL AND TRADE RELATIONS, 358 pages, 1979. Softcover. (Text)

PROSSER AND KEETON'S HORNBOOK ON TORTS, Fifth Edition, Student Edition, 1286 pages, 1984 with 1988 pocket part. (Text)

ROBERTSON, POWERS AND ANDERSON'S CASES AND MATERIALS ON TORTS, 932 pages, 1989. Teacher's Manual available. (Casebook)

Trade Regulation—see also Antitrust, Regulated Industries

McMANIS' UNFAIR TRADE PRACTICES IN A NUTSHELL, Second Edition, 464 pages, 1988. Softcover. (Text)

OPPENHEIM, WESTON, MAGGS AND SCHECHTER'S CASES AND MATERIALS ON UNFAIR TRADE PRACTICES AND CONSUMER PROTECTION, Fourth Edition, 1038 pages, 1983. Teacher's Manual available. (Casebook) 1986 Supplement.

SCHECHTER'S BLACK LETTER ON UNFAIR TRADE PRACTICES, 272 pages, 1986. Softcover. (Review)

Trial and Appellate Advocacy—see also Civil Procedure

APPELLATE ADVOCACY, HANDBOOK OF, Second Edition, 182 pages, 1986. Softcover. (Text)

BERGMAN'S TRIAL ADVOCACY IN A NUTSHELL, 402 pages, 1979. Softcover. (Text)

BINDER AND BERGMAN'S FACT INVESTIGATION: FROM HYPOTHESIS TO PROOF, 354 pages, 1984. Teacher's Manual available. (Coursebook)

CARLSON AND IMWINKELRIED'S DYNAMICS OF TRIAL PRACTICE: PROBLEMS AND MATERIALS, 414 pages, 1989. Teacher's Manual available. (Coursebook)

GOLDBERG'S THE FIRST TRIAL (WHERE DO I SIT? WHAT DO I SAY?) IN A NUTSHELL, 396 pages, 1982. Softcover. (Text)

HAYDOCK, HERR, AND STEMPEL'S FUNDAMENTALS OF PRE-TRIAL LITIGATION, 768 pages, 1985. Softcover. Teacher's Manual available. (Coursebook)

HEGLAND'S TRIAL AND PRACTICE SKILLS IN A NUTSHELL, 346 pages, 1978. Softcover. (Text)

HORNSTEIN'S APPELLATE ADVOCACY IN A NUTSHELL, 325 pages, 1984. Softcover. (Text)

JEANS' HANDBOOK ON TRIAL ADVOCACY, Student Edition, 473 pages, 1975. Softcover. (Text)

MARTINEAU'S CASES AND MATERIALS ON AP-

Trial and Appellate Advocacy—Cont'd

PELLATE PRACTICE AND PROCEDURE, 565 pages, 1987. (Casebook)

NOLAN'S CASES AND MATERIALS ON TRIAL PRACTICE, 518 pages, 1981. (Casebook)

SONSTENG, HAYDOCK AND BOYD'S THE TRIALBOOK: A TOTAL SYSTEM FOR PREPARATION AND PRESENTATION OF A CASE, 404 pages, 1984. Softcover. (Coursebook)

Trusts and Estates

ATKINSON'S HORNBOOK ON WILLS, Second Edition, 975 pages, 1953. (Text)

AVERILL'S UNIFORM PROBATE CODE IN A NUTSHELL, Second Edition, 454 pages, 1987. Softcover. (Text)

BOGERT'S HORNBOOK ON TRUSTS, Sixth Edition, Student Edition, 794 pages, 1987. (Text)

CLARK, LUSKY AND MURPHY'S CASES AND MATERIALS ON GRATUITOUS TRANSFERS, Third Edition, 970 pages, 1985. (Casebook)

DODGE'S WILLS, TRUSTS AND ESTATE PLANNING–LAW AND TAXATION, CASES AND MATERIALS, 665 pages, 1988. (Casebook)

KURTZ' PROBLEMS, CASES AND OTHER MATERIALS ON FAMILY ESTATE PLANNING, 853 pages, 1983. Teacher's Manual available. (Casebook)

MCGOVERN'S CASES AND MATERIALS ON WILLS, TRUSTS AND FUTURE INTERESTS: AN INTRODUCTION TO ESTATE PLANNING, 750 pages, 1983. (Casebook)

MCGOVERN, KURTZ AND REIN'S HORNBOOK ON WILLS, TRUSTS AND ESTATES–INCLUDING TAXATION AND FUTURE INTERESTS, 996 pages, 1988. (Text)

MENNELL'S WILLS AND TRUSTS IN A NUTSHELL, 392 pages, 1979. Softcover. (Text)

SIMES' HORNBOOK ON FUTURE INTERESTS, Second Edition, 355 pages, 1966. (Text)

TURANO AND RADIGAN'S HORNBOOK ON NEW YORK ESTATE ADMINISTRATION, 676 pages, 1986. (Text)

UNIFORM PROBATE CODE, OFFICIAL TEXT WITH COMMENTS. 578 pages, 1987. Softcover.

WAGGONER'S FUTURE INTERESTS IN A NUTSHELL, 361 pages, 1981. Softcover. (Text)

WATERBURY'S MATERIALS ON TRUSTS AND ESTATES, 1039 pages, 1986. Teacher's Manual available. (Casebook)

Water Law—see also Energy and Natural Resources Law, Environmental Law

GETCHES' WATER LAW IN A NUTSHELL, 439 pages, 1984. Softcover. (Text)

SAX AND ABRAMS' LEGAL CONTROL OF WATER RESOURCES: CASES AND MATERIALS, 941 pages, 1986. (Casebook)

TRELEASE AND GOULD'S CASES AND MATERIALS ON WATER LAW, Fourth Edition, 816 pages, 1986. (Casebook)

Wills—see Trusts and Estates

Women and the Law—see also Employment Discrimination

KAY'S TEXT, CASES AND MATERIALS ON SEX–BASED DISCRIMINATION, Third Edition, 1001 pages, 1988. (Casebook)

THOMAS' SEX DISCRIMINATION IN A NUTSHELL, 399 pages, 1982. Softcover. (Text)

Workers' Compensation—see Social Legislation

AN INTRODUCTION TO THE
ANGLO-AMERICAN LEGAL SYSTEM
READINGS AND CASES
Second Edition

By

Edgar Bodenheimer
Professor of Law Emeritus
University of California, Davis

John Bilyeu Oakley
Professor of Law
University of California, Davis

Jean C. Love
Professor of Law
University of California, Davis

AMERICAN CASEBOOK SERIES

WEST PUBLISHING CO.
ST. PAUL, MINN., 1988

COPYRIGHT © 1980 By WEST PUBLISHING CO.
COPYRIGHT © 1988 By WEST PUBLISHING CO.
                      50 West Kellogg Boulevard
                      P.O. Box 64526
                      St. Paul, Minnesota 55164–0526

Library of Congress Cataloging in Publication Data

An Introduction to the Anglo-American legal system: readings and cases / by Edgar Bodenheimer,
    John Bilyeu Oakley, Jean C. Love.
    p. cm.—(American casebook series)
    Includes index.
    ISBN 0-314-36662-8
    1. Law—United States—Cases. 2. Common law—United States—Cases. 3. Common law—
Great Britain—Cases. I. Bodenheimer, Edgar, 1908–   II. Oakley, John Bilyeu. III. Love, Jean C.
IV. Series.

KF379.B63   1988   340.5'7—dc19

ISBN 0-314-36662-8   88–5661 CIP

        (B., O., & L.) Anglo–Amer.Legal Sys.ACB
        1st Reprint—1989

Preface to the First Edition

This volume has grown out of earlier unpublished materials which the senior author has tested in the classroom with several variations. The work originated with materials assembled by Professor Bodenheimer in 1967 for a year-long course in the legal process and its historical foundations. In 1976 and 1977 Professors Bodenheimer and Love edited and substantially revised these materials to fit the needs of the intensive, 15 hour course called introduction to the Anglo-American Legal System that is offered to beginning students at the University of California at Davis. In 1979 and 1980, Professors Bodenheimer and Oakley made further extensive revisions, casting the materials into the form in which they are now published. While our intent has been primarily to provide teaching materials for Introduction to Law courses such as that at Davis, we have also attempted to put these materials into a form that will be useful as a reference work for potential and beginning law students, as well as a primer for educated lay persons who seek to increase their understanding of the role and structure of law in modern Anglo-American society.

The preparation of the materials was guided by the conviction that students entering law school need to become acquainted with some basic distinctions and classifications which form part of the conceptual apparatus of the law. Furthermore, a legal system like Anglo-American law, which has historical roots in many important areas, cannot be understood without some knowledge of English legal history, including the rudiments of the forms of action at common law and the reasons for the rise of the rival system of equity. Of equal significance is the need to expose the beginning student to the methodological tools used by American courts in dealing with judicial precedents and statutory enactments. This work follows the customary method of using illustrative cases as well as theoretical discussions in describing the operation of *stare decisis,* the difficult art of determining the *ratio decidendi* of a case, the relative roles of logic and policy in the legal process, and the intricacies of statutory interpretation.

We wish to thank the authors and publishers who have graciously consented to our use of their copyrighted works. We are deeply indebted to Chancellor James Meyer, Vice-Chancellor Leon Mayhew, and Dean of Law Richard C. Wydick of the University of California at Davis for the Financial support which made the production of the manuscript possible. We also wish to express our gratitude to Carole

Hinkle for the painstaking manner in which she prepared the final copy of the manuscript.

EDGAR BODENHEIMER
JOHN B. OAKLEY
JEAN C. LOVE

Davis, California
July, 1980

Preface to the Second Edition

A comment on the first edition of this book contained the observation that students, although receiving a great deal of information, were asked to do little in the way of active problem-solving.[1] The authors have taken up this challenge in the new edition by substantially increasing the amount of cases and other problems designed to test the reasoning powers of the students.

Other changes from the first edition include an expansion of the materials on separation of powers, against the background of the United States Supreme Court decision in *Immigration and Naturalization Service v. Chadha*, as well as a new section on Treaties and Executive Agreements. The description of the American court system has been brought up to date and new developments on retroactivity of overruling decisions have been reported. Additions of some textual materials, notes by the editors, and a few cases are found in the chapters on *ratio decidendi*, logic and policy, and statutory interpretation. The selected references to literature at the end of each chapter have been updated.

EDGAR BODENHEIMER
JOHN B. OAKLEY
JEAN C. LOVE

Davis, California
April 5, 1988

*

1. Gerwin and Shupack, "Karl Llewellyn's Legal Method Course: Elements of Law and Its Teaching Materials," 33 *J.Leg. Ed.* 64, 77–78 (1983).

Summary of Contents

Table of Contents

Table of Cases

The principal cases are in bold type. Cases cited or discussed in the text are roman type. References are to pages. Cases cited in principal cases and within other quoted materials are not included.

Introduction

THE NATURE AND FUNCTIONS
OF LAW

A. PREFATORY COMMENTS

It is not possible to gain an insight into the nature of any institution of human life without an inquiry into the purposes or functions which the particular institution is designed to accomplish. Nobody can intelligently discuss problems of government and arrive at a considered judgment with respect to the policies which should be promoted by public officials or agencies without first forming an opinion as to the general aims and ends for which governments are established. This is equally true for the institution of law, at least in the secular, political sense with which we are concerned. We treat law as a particular kind of governmental institution. From this perspective, we assert that no official within the institution of law—no judge, attorney or other person with official duties in the administration of law—can adequately discharge his or her duties unless familiar with the general purposes which the law is supposed to perform for society.

There exists in the law a separate discipline designed to investigate the nature of law, its guiding ideas and social goals, and the general character of the methods and techniques employed for the effectuation of its ends. This discipline is known as "Jurisprudence." This subject, in most of its ramifications, is dealt with in a separate course in many law schools. The subject cannot in its full scope be taught to students who have not as yet acquired a background in the positive rules, sources, and methodology of the law. And yet beginning students who have decided to launch upon a legal career ought to engage at least in some initial and preliminary reflection upon the meaning of the institution to the service of which they intend to devote their lives and best energies.

B. DEFINITIONS OF LAW

Such reflection, unfortunately, is rendered difficult by the fact that there is no general agreement among jurists and other legal thinkers as to what the goals and purposes of legal regulation are or ought to be. There does exist a large measure of consensus as to the minimum objectives which the institution of law is designed to serve. But when we turn from the minimum and most elementary goals of legal control to the broader ends and ideals for the attainment of which the law can be used by men, we shall encounter a perplexing multitude and variety of viewpoints. Let us set out a number of definitions of law which may be considered representative and which have influenced the course of legal development:

> Cicero—"Law is the highest reason, implanted in nature, which commands what ought to be done and forbids the opposite." (*De Legibus,* Bk. I.)

> St. Thomas Aquinas—"Law is an ordinance of reason for the common good, made by him who has care of the community, and promulgated." (*Summa Theologica,* Part II, First Part, Qu. 90, Art. 4.)

> Hobbes—"Civil Law is to every Subject, those Rules, which the Commonwealth hath commanded him, by Word, Writing, or other sufficient Sign of the Will, to make use of for the Distinction of Right and Wrong; that is to say, of what is contrary, and what is not contrary to the Rule." (*Leviathan,* Ch. XXVI.)

> Austin—"Every positive law . . . is set by a sovereign person, or a sovereign body of persons, to a member or members of the independent political society wherein that person or body is sovereign or supreme. Or (changing the expression) it is set by a monarch or sovereign member to a person or persons in a state of subjection to its author." (*The Province of Jurisprudence Determined,* Lecture VI.)

> Locke—"The end of law is not to abolish or restrain, but to preserve and enlarge freedom." (*Two Treatises on Civil Government,* Bk. II, Ch. VI.)

> Jhering—"Law is the sum of the conditions of social life in the widest sense of the term, as secured by the power of the State through the means of external compulsion." (*Law as a Means to an End,* Ch. VIII.)

> Carter—"Law is not a command or body of commands, but consists of rules springing from the social standard of justice or from the habits and customs from which that standard has itself been derived." ("The Ideal and the Actual," 24 Am.L.Rev. 752.)

> Recaséns–Siches—"Law was not born into human life by reason of the desire to render tribute or homage to the idea of justice, but to fulfill an inescapable urgency for security and certainty in social life. The question of why and wherefore men make law is not answered in the structure of the idea of justice, nor in the suite of outstanding values which accompany it as presupposed by it, but in a subordinate value—security—corresponding to a human need." ("Human Life, Society and Law, Ch. VI, in *Latin–American Legal Philosophy.*)

The definitions of law set forth above are heterogeneous but not necessarily contradictory. Each of them accentuates an element or ingredient in social control through law which may be considered indispensable or at least desirable for the effective operation of a sound legal system. As you re-read the above definitions, ask yourself what each author perceives to be the role of law in human affairs.

Chapter I

LAW AND THE PROCESS OF CLASSIFICATION

A. THE MEANING AND IMPORTANCE OF CLASSIFICATION

One of the main objectives of the law is to bring a measure of order into the chaotic world of reality, to regulate the relations between people, and to adjust their conflicting interests. Such ordering of human affairs cannot, as a matter of basic social policy, be done on an individual basis, i.e., by determining for each citizen what his individual rights and duties should be. It must be done on a *generalized* basis, by dividing the citizens into certain legally significant groups or categories and fixing the rights, duties, and privileges of each of these groups. A major function of a legal system is thus to *classify* things and phenomena found in the external world, i.e., to group and segregate them into classes, and to explain the distinctions and relationships between the classes.

Classification means, figuratively speaking, that one takes objects which are equal or quite similar in their appearance, characteristics, and qualities, puts them into a bottle, and marks the bottle with a label. For instance, we put stones consisting of a compound called beryl and being of a yellowish-green color into a bottle and label it "emerald." We fill a bottle with stones consisting of corundum and characterized by a transparent blue color and give it the tag "sapphire." We then compare the two types of stone *as a class* (not individually) and note their characteristics and distinctions.

The law constantly combines individual persons in generalized abstractions, such as creditor and debtor, vendor and purchaser, citizen and alien, landlord and tenant, owner and possessor, bailor and bailee, employer and employee. Sometimes it is very hard to determine in an individual case whether or not a certain person does or does not fall within some classification which carries with it specific legal rights or duties, or to which some other legal consequence attaches. There are cases, for example, in which it is difficult to decide whether a certain

4

person who pays for the services of others has hired "employees" or entered into contracts for personal services by "independent contractors." A host of legal consequences from tax law to tort law turn on this classification.

The law is filled with such problems of debatable classification. Precise and orderly thought is an essential virtue for a lawyer, because such thought assists in unraveling the complexities of a given set of circumstances and evaluating their legal consequences in light of the applicable legal classifications. Rigorous thought about the terms and justifications of legal classifications cannot eliminate ambiguity from the law, but it can do much to reduce it.

Besides its importance as a basic element of legal reasoning, classification is an aspect of law of special significance for two related reasons. First, American law is derived from governments subject to written constitutions, which impose upon the law itself classifications of permissible and impermissible legal rules. Second, one of the most important constitutional criteria for the validity of a rule of law is that it apply to people equally. This raises a paradox of sorts—how can classifications whose whole purpose it is to treat people and things differently, be reconciled with the constitutional mandate of human equality under the law?

In the United States, judges have the ultimate power to determine whether legal rules are valid under the constitutions of the federal government and the various states. At its most basic level, constitutional law prescribes the existence and limitations of the power of particular institutions of government to impose legal consequences on particular classifications of things and phenomena. Thus all constitutional law may be seen as a problem of the classification of governmental power. For example, does the Constitution classify the licensing of automobile drivers as a function of state governments, or of the federal government? This will determine which government has the power to license drivers. But even the appropriate government's power is not absolute. For instance, an automobile driver licensing law which requires licensees to execute loyalty oaths might be classified as an unreasonable infringement of free speech, and unconstitutional for that reason alone, even though the law was enacted by the government with the general authority to regulate driver licensing.

A special problem of American constitutional law is the right to "the equal protection of the laws." The American legal system is in large part premised upon a profound (though not yet wholly fulfilled) commitment to treating all people as equal in the eyes of the law. How can American law both classify people for purposes of treating them differently, as landlords are treated differently than tenants, while still purporting to afford them "equal protection"? The answer is that equality does not preclude classification; the legal equality of people under the law does not mean that all classifications of people into groups accorded different legal treatment are unconstitutional, nor does it mean that only identically situated identical twins (if there were any) would have any claim to equal legal treatment. Concern for equality under law is basically concern for the justification of legal classifications in terms of the purpose which those classifications are intended to accomplish.

All people have certain similarities and certain differences, all are members of the human race and yet all are unique individuals. The law treats people differently to a greater or lesser extent according to how classifications of their similarities and differences are manipulated. The constitutional norm of equality under the law does not prohibit classifications which treat people differently, but it does demand that such classifications be justified by some goal other than the unequal treatment itself, and that the classifications serve that goal in some direct or even essential way. This problem of the "nexus" between legal classifications and the purposes they serve is one of the most intractable of American constitutional law. The basic principle is that classifications serving a reasonable purpose are permitted, while unreasonable discrimination is outlawed.

Suppose, for example, that the legislature wants to promote traffic safety. It decides to accomplish this by limiting the number of vehicles on public highways. Can the legislature accordingly prohibit anyone from operating a vehicle on the public highways except adult males? except adults with perfect vision uncorrected by lenses? except adults who have never been convicted of a serious crime? except adults who have never been cited for a traffic violation? Each of these statutory classifications of who may drive on the public highways would reduce the number of cars being driven, and to that extent would probably promote traffic safety. Yet you will probably want to object that some or all of these classifications are somehow "unfair"; your perceptions of unfairness will reflect your individual reaction to the importance of the goal of traffic safety and the degree to which each classification serves that goal, as weighed against the value of treating people as equals despite such differing characteristics as gender, acuity of vision, or arrest and conviction records—characteristics which vary in the degree to which they are within the control of an individual, and which also vary in their relevance to whether a given individual is or is not likely to be a safe driver. Much of American constitutional law confronts courts and lawyers with similar problems of whether a particular legal classification is in some fundamental sense unfair, and of the extent to which considerations of fairness ought to play a role in determining whether a legal classification is valid under the "equal protection clause" or any other clause of the Constitution.

B. SOME BASIC DISTINCTIONS AND CLASSIFICATIONS OF THE LAW

Among the myriad classifications of a highly developed legal system most are of a highly technical character, just as distinctions between particular species of beetles or pine trees turn upon the technical minutiae of biological classification. At this point in your study of legal classification you will be introduced solely to some very broad and basic terms and classifications which do not pertain to specific legal topics but to law, legal science, or legal systems in general.

1. INTERNATIONAL LAW AND MUNICIPAL LAW

The chief difference between these two branches of the law is that international law deals with the external (foreign) affairs of nations, while municipal law regulates their internal affairs. International law is concerned with usages, customs, rules, and contractual arrangements which nation states have consented to observe in their dealings with each other. The law contained in treaties and other agreements between nations, the law found in the decisions of international courts, and the law developed by the United Nations are examples of legal source materials pertaining to the field of international law.

One of the problems of the study of international law is that nations consider themselves "sovereign," that is, subject to no higher authority. How can sovereign nations be bound by rules of international law, then, if there is no way to enforce those rules except by one sovereign nation declaring war on another? Some theorists contend for this reason that "international law" is not law at all, because it is for the most part observed by consent rather than enforced by higher authority. (Some enforcement powers are lodged in the U.N. Security Council, but weakened by the veto prerogative vested in five nations.) Other theorists point out that certain rules of international law are so universally observed even by unwilling nations that it is the concept of sovereignty, rather than the concept of international law, which needs reexamination.

In any event, international law is clearly distinguishable from municipal law, which is the domestic law of a state or nation. Municipal law regulates primarily the relations between individuals, as well as the relations between individuals and their government. International law regulates primarily the relations between states, although international agreements may establish rights and responsibilities on the part of individuals. The federal law of the United States, the law of the state of California, the law of Mexico and of France are examples of systems of municipal law. In countries with a federal structure, municipal law is of a multiple character. In the United States, for example, there are the laws made by Congress, the laws of the fifty states, and the laws of cities and counties, among others.

One problem you should be aware of is that the states of the American union are sometimes referred to as "sovereign" states. The sovereignty of these states is, however, of considerably smaller scope than the sovereignty of nations. The United States Constitution carves out large areas of regulation in which federal power is paramount over state power. Constitutionally authorized federal laws and treaties take precedence over inconsistent state laws. It is doubtful, under these circumstances, whether the term "state sovereignty" conveys any clearly discernible meaning.

2. CIVIL LAW AND COMMON LAW

Most of the municipal legal systems of the world may be said to belong to one of two large groups of legal orders which are distinguished from each other by their historical origins and also by certain structural characteristics. These two groups are the Civil Law and the Common Law.[1]

The civil law system grew out of ancient Roman law, which reached its highest development in the Roman Empire during the first two centuries A.D. The civil law may be described as a modern adaptation of Roman law, but it is important to note that many changes were made in the course of time in all of the modern civil law systems which set them to a substantial extent apart from ancient Roman law.

The civil law system is today in effect in Continental Europe (although the Roman law influence has always been weaker in the Scandinavian countries than in the rest of Continental Europe), in Latin America, in Japan, and (with some admixture of common law) in the Union of South Africa.

Civil law ingredients of varying degrees of strength can be found in the laws of the Islamic world. The law of the Soviet Union and the countries within its orbit may also be said to fall within the sphere of the civil law, although some writers have favored a separate classification. A study of recent codes in the Soviet Union and East European countries reveals many similarities in structure, interpretative techniques, and conceptual apparatus with the typical civil law approach.

The law of the People's Republic of China, after the Chinese Revolution of 1949, followed the Soviet model in many important respects. After the Sino–Soviet split and the Cultural Revolution, the influence of Soviet law diminished. Furthermore, during the 1960's and 1970's the role of law as such was downgraded. Law was believed to be a reactionary institution that could ultimately be dispensed with in a socialist society.

A change in the attitude towards law has occurred in the 1980's. China has enacted codes of civil law, criminal law, and criminal procedure. Respect for law is encouraged by the government, although mediation—pursuant to a tradition going back to Confucius—is preferred to litigation as a mode of conflict resolution. One reason for the new approach to law has been the recent increase in trade with foreign

---

1. When we speak of the Common Law as distinguished from the Civil Law, we are using the term Common Law in a broad sense, which includes Equity (see infra Ch. II.C).

nations, including the United States. Such trade requires rules and orderly procedures for resolving contractual and other disagreements.

The state of Louisiana, which was acquired in 1803 from the French, is in part a civil law jurisdiction. Its comprehensive civil code, which covers the fields of contracts, torts, property, family law and inheritance, may be traced back to the Napoleonic code of 1804. But Louisiana has also had a strong influx of the common law, especially in the areas of procedure and evidence. Other New World jurisdictions which form a blend of the civil law and common law are Puerto Rico and the Canadian province of Quebec.

The common law is a system which had its roots in medieval England. It was shaped in the courts of the English king and applied on a nationwide basis, on the assumption that it represented the common customs and convictions of all Englishmen. Its counterpart in medieval times was the custom of the manor (feudal estate), as distinguished from the custom of the realm.

The common law was adopted by the American states during and after the War of Independence, and after the attainment of independence it became the foundation of the laws of the several states. Other common law jurisdictions are England, Scotland (with a strong civil law admixture), Ireland, Canada (with the partial exception of Quebec), Australia, and New Zealand. India may be called a common law jurisdiction in a limited sense, inasmuch as the influence of Hindu customary law is also substantial.

Few generalizations can be made with respect to the legal systems of the black African countries. Elements of the civil law, common law, and tribal customary law can be found in varying proportions, and modern codifications are in progress in many of these states.

Although substantial differences exist between legal systems within the civil law group and also (to a lesser extent) between legal systems in the common law group, there are some characteristics which civil law systems share when compared with their common law counterparts. The starting point of legal reasoning in civil law countries is almost always a statute or code provision. Judicial precedents, at least in theory, play a secondary role; their authority is considered to be no greater than that of legal writers. However, in actual practice prior decisions are widely followed by the courts. In the common law orbit, legal arguments often center around the interpretation and applicability of earlier judicial decisions, especially those rendered by the highest court of the jurisdiction in question; but statutes and administrative regulations are gaining an ever-increasing importance.

Certain differences also exist in the structure of legal procedure in the two rival systems. The judges in civil law jurisdictions take a very active part in the interrogation of witnesses and conduct of the proceedings, and the role of counsel is correspondingly diminished. Under the system of the common law, the initiative in a court trial is exercised primarily by the attorneys for the parties, while the judge plays a less active role. Civil law systems, because of the dominant position of the judge, are often referred to as "inquisitorial," in juxtaposition to the "adversarial" model of the common law, in which the attorneys for the parties bear primary responsibility for shaping the content and course of litigation. As with differences in legal reasoning, these differences in the role of the judge between civil law and common law systems are tending to narrow over time. In constitutional and administrative litigation especially, modern American judges play an increasingly active role in the definition of issues and the development of facts at trial.

3. PUBLIC LAW AND PRIVATE LAW

The municipal law of a state or country is frequently subdivided into public and private law, although there is some disagreement as to where the dividing line should be drawn. Private law, generally speaking, is concerned with disputes among private citizens or private organizations. These disputes may arise out of a contract, or out of a wrongful act (tort), or out of a business transaction, or they may involve family relations or ownership of property. The basic private law subjects are Contracts, Torts and Property. After taking courses in the fundamentals of these subjects, you will be ready to study some of the other important private law subjects which are special applications of contract, tort and property law principles, such as Commercial Law, Trusts and Estates, Corporations, Securities Law and Labor Law.

Public law, in its most general sense, involves relations between private citizens or organizations and the government. The protection of civil liberties, the protection of the citizen against arbitrary acts of executive or administrative organs, the validity of legislation, and governmental regulation of trade and commerce are subjects which belong to the field of public law. Important public law courses are Constitutional Law, Administrative Law, Taxation, and Trade Regulation.

The field of procedure should also be classified as a public law subject, because it deals with the rules followed by public organs—the courts—in conducting their business. The course in Civil Procedure introduces you to the operation of courts and court systems; related courses are Evidence, Conflict of Laws, and Federal Jurisdiction. Criminal Law is also a public law subject, because it is concerned with public sanctions—sanctions imposed by the state in the form of imprisonment, fines, etc.—upon offenders against the public order. Criminal Procedure covers the operation of courts in the enforcement of the criminal law.

4. SUBSTANTIVE LAW AND ADJECTIVE LAW

A classification which cuts across the division of the law into public law and private law is that which differentiates between substantive and adjective law. Substantive law creates, defines, and delimits rights, duties, and obligations. Adjective law prescribes the forms of procedure by which substantive rights or obligations are enforced by the courts or other public agencies. Adjective law is simply another term for procedural law.

Substantive law tells me *what* rights I have if X violates his contract with me (Can I get damages? Do I have the right to cancel the contract?), or if Y negligently drives his car into mine (May I recover for mental shock? May I recover if I, too, have been negligent?).

The adjective law informs me as to *how* I have to go about enforcing my rights. Where should I file my complaint? What should be the content of the complaint? Do I have the right to a jury trial? What kind of evidence offered in support of my claim will be accepted by the court? If the decision goes against me, do I have a right to a new trial, or may I file an appeal? How can I enforce a judgment or decree in my favor?

5. LEGISLATION, CASE LAW, CUSTOMARY LAW

The term "legislation" is today applied for the most part to the deliberate creation of legal norms or precepts by an organ of government which is set up for this purpose and which gives articulate, authoritative expression to such legal precepts in a formalized legal document.[2] This formalized legal document is often a statute or code. The legislative acts of Congress and of the several state legislatures are known as "statutes." A code, as distinguished from a statute, contains a systematic compilation of related enactments (as, for example, the Penal Code of the State of California which specifies most crimes under California law and the procedure for prosecuting them).

There also exists today a large body of law promulgated by the executive and administrative agencies of government in the exercise of a limited legislative authority. This type of law is usually published in the form of executive orders or administrative regulations. Such law is similar in character to statutory law.

Case law originates in the decisions of courts or other tribunals having power to decide particular controversies. In the course of determining such controversies, the tribunal will often find that no legislative law dispositive of the dispute in question is in existence, or that the available legislative law is ambiguous in its application to the problem at hand. In such a case the court must articulate and apply a legal norm or principle which will decide the dispute between the parties. Many of the rules and principles of the Common Law and of Equity originated in this fashion. One of the most difficult problems for legal historians, political scientists and philosophers of law is to determine what has been, and what ought to be the source for judicially created rules of decision. When no legislative law clearly applies, are

2. Some legislation, as for example in California, is created by the popular "initiative" process.

judges bound in any way in their fashioning of case law? Must the judge reach the decision which best accords with custom, or precedent (that is, case law formulated by prior judges in more or less analogous cases), or justice (and if so, what if the judge's view of justice is different from that of society as a whole)?

While clear answers to these questions are hard to find, and even harder to defend, there does exist in the American legal system a substantial degree of consensus on the important differences between legislation and case law. A rule of legislative law is cast in an authoritative textual form and, unless the statute is unconstitutional, judges are bound by the statute as interpreted by them. A judge is not considered free to revise a statute, ignore it or supplant it with a rule which seems to the judge to be better reasoned. Much greater flexibility falls to the judge under the various views of the judicial role in dealing with case law. While subordinate courts must adhere to case law promulgated by courts of higher jurisdiction, courts of parallel jurisdiction are generally free to follow separate paths in the formulation of case law. Moreover, a court is not bound to follow its own precedents, and may elect to refuse to follow a case law rule which it promulgated earlier (generally when the court was composed of a different set of judges). Thus courts take much greater liberties with case law than they are permitted to take with legislative law.

In one sense, legislation and case law come together when vague or ambiguous legislation must be interpreted by a court. Various courts of parallel jurisdiction may confront the same statutory language in different cases, and come to inconsistent results. This frequently happens in cases involving vague clauses of the Constitution. The Supreme Court of Oregon, for example, might decide that capital punishment is unconstitutional under the Eighth Amendment to the Constitution; this would not be binding on the Supreme Court of Arizona's consideration of the same question. The United States Supreme Court is the court of supreme jurisdiction in the construction of the federal Constitution, however, so once the United States Supreme Court decides the status of capital punishment under the federal Constitution, that result is binding on all other courts in the country. (But nothing is simple in our federal system—all the states have their own constitutions, whose construction is the ultimate responsibility of each of their highest courts. Thus even after the United States Supreme Court has upheld the death penalty under the federal Constitution, the supreme court of a state with a cruel-and-unusual-punishment clause in its own constitution might still rule that the death penalty is forbidden in that state by the state constitution, even though it is permitted by the federal Constitution. On all questions of state law—whether involving state statutes, the case law of state courts, or the state constitution—the highest court of the relevant state has the last word, just as the Supreme Court of the United States has the last word on all matters of federal law.)

Another type of law, in the opinion of some, is customary law. Unlike legislation and case law, customary law is not set by an organ of government but develops through actual and continuous practice in the community, accompanied by the conviction that the mode of behavior evinced by the practice is legally obligatory. To some extent international law may be said to be the most important modern form of customary law. Other examples of customary law are generally found in primitive legal systems, including the feudal antecedents of the Anglo–American legal system: unwritten rules of inheritance and testamentary disposition (i.e., by will) of property; rules concerning the tenure and cultivation of land; impediments to marriage recognized in a tribal community but not formalized in a legal enactment; commercial usages of traders and shippers.

In modern American society the principal importance of customary practice is not as a body of law which is obligatory of its own force, but rather as a source of case law. American courts have shown a marked propensity for converting vocational or business customs, such as accustomed ways of behavior in the medical profession, the commercial usages of bankers or conventional methods of operating a mine, into legally obligatory standards of behavior by incorporating custom into case law when no other standard of behavior has been set by statute. It is important to note, however, that courts have not abandoned the traditional flexibility of case law even when incorporating customary standards of behavior into case law; many courts have refused to give legal effect to a custom found to be "unreasonable" from the perspective of public policy, social justice, or the interests of outsiders not fairly charged with knowledge of the custom.

6. LEGISLATIVE, EXECUTIVE, JUDICIAL POWER

Art. III, Sec. 1 of the Constitution of California provides: "The powers of the Government of the State of California shall be divided into three separate departments—the Legislative, Executive, and Judicial; and no person charged with the exercise of powers properly belonging to one of these departments shall exercise any functions appertaining to either of the others, except as in this Constitution expressly directed or permitted." Most state constitutions have similar provisions, and the separation of powers principle also underlies the fabric of the federal Constitution.

Such constitutional divisions of governmental powers into legislative, executive, and judicial powers make it necessary to define or at least circumscribe the meaning of these basic concepts of our public law. This task is not an easy one, because there exist borderline or twilight zones in which these concepts overlap or shade into one another. It is possible, however, to define at least the hard core of these notions.

The most characteristic feature of legislative activity in the American legal system was well explained by Oliver Wendell Holmes, Jr., writing for the United States Supreme Court in Prentis v. Atlantic Coast Line Co., 211 U.S. 210, 226, 29 S.Ct. 67, 69, 53 L.Ed. 150 (1908). Legislation, said Mr. Justice Holmes, "looks to the future and changes existing conditions by making a new rule to be applied thereafter to all or some part of those subject to its power." Legislation is, essentially, the making of new law by means of a formalized pronouncement of a law-making body. The law enacted by a legislative organ consists typically of general rules, principles, or other normative pronouncements which permit, command, or disallow a certain course of conduct. Legislation normally deals with classes of persons and an indefinite number of situations. A disposition or command that is addressed to one or a few named persons or a single concrete situation is not a legislative act in the genuine sense of the term.

Congress does, however, have power to enact Private Laws, which are published in the official collection of federal statutes known as Statutes at Large. Typical examples of private laws are the following: (1) enactments excepting named individuals from immigration or naturalization requirements established by general laws; (2) enactments granting certain individuals compensation not authorized by the Federal Tort Claims Act; (3) waivers of claims that the Federal Government has against particular persons under a general law. Private acts are of an essentially executive character, since they deal with one individual situation. When a bill for such a law is introduced by a senator or congressperson, there is rarely any discussion on the floor of Congress; there may be a limited discussion in a subcommittee. Such legislation is sanctioned by long usage which can be traced back to the powers of the English Parliament. Most state constitutions prohibit such granting of privileges or immunities to specific persons.[3]

An executive or administrative act may be defined as an exercise of governmental power in a concrete situation to accomplish some public purpose. If the President of the United States sends a note to a foreign government protesting against an inimical act directed against the United States, he acts in an executive capacity. If the Department of the Interior authorizes the construction of a new six-lane highway, it proceeds in an administrative fashion.

Executive or administrative power is in its essence the power to act according to discretion for the public advantage. Under a purely executive type of government, the public officials of the state would have unlimited discretion to act for the sake of what they conceive to be the public good. Under a "government of laws," such as ours, executive and administrative discretion is limited by a large and intricate network of legal rules and regulations. Under our system of government, executive and administrative power must be exercised according to law.

---

3. See, for example, California Constitution, Art. I, Sec. 7(b): "A citizen or class of citizens may not be granted privileges or immunities not granted on the same terms to all citizens." For a discussion of private bills see Note, 79 Harvard Law Review 1684 (1966).

Judicial power is employed for the purpose of settling controversies between private individuals or groups, or between private persons and the government, or between different units of government. In the words of Justice Holmes, "judicial inquiry investigates, declares, and enforces liabilities as they stand on present or past facts and under laws supposed already to exist." [4]

A judicial act is distinguished from a legislative act by the fact that the latter determines the rights of individuals generally and in the abstract, while adjudication is in most cases the concrete application of a legal rule to a dispute between the parties before a court. Judicial action is, on the other hand, distinguished from executive action in that the latter is not, or at least not necessarily or typically, undertaken for the purpose of settling a dispute.

The separation of powers principle has not been fully and completely realized in our constitutional structure, federal and state. The general principle has been qualified by a number of exceptions. Thus, the right conferred upon the President of the United States and the Governors of the several states to veto legislation gives to the executive branch of the government a share in the processes of legislation. Furthermore, the President may make treaties (which often lay down norms of law) with the consent of the Senate. The Senate, which is essentially a legislative body, exercises executive functions by participating in the appointment of many federal officials. Congressional power to pass private laws has already been mentioned. Judicial powers have been vested in many federal and state administrative agencies, and such agencies also frequently issue rules and regulations which are legislative in character. The Senate acts as a judicial body when it tries impeachments of public officers. Courts have promulgated codes of pleading and procedure, which are manifestly legislative in character, and often fashion case law which governs future cases just as clearly as would explicit acts of legislation. Courts also engage in executive functions when they supervise the administration of estates in bankruptcy, appoint guardians, and make decisions in uncontested probate cases. Some of these departures from the principle of the separation of governmental powers have been sanctioned directly by constitutional mandate; others have developed in governmental practice and might be viewed as a form of customary law.

Questions

(1) One author has taken the position that "any power, whatever its nature, necessarily takes its character from the department to which it is assigned by the constitution or the legislature." Whatever proceeds from a court of justice, he maintains, is judicial, and whatever power or duty is imposed upon the executive department is executive, and therefore free from interference by the other branches of the

4. Prentis v. Atlantic Coast Line Co., supra.

government. For example, the power to try contested elections, when vested in the courts, is judicial; when it is assumed by the legislature, it is legislative and may not be controlled by the courts.[5]

What objections may be raised against this theory?

(2) Suppose Congress confers the Congressional Medal of Honor upon a distinguished war hero. Is this a legislative or executive act?

(3) President Reagan appointed Sandra Day O'Connor to the United States Supreme Court. The appointment was concurred in by the Senate. How should these actions be characterized?

(4) A number of years ago, the Supreme Court of Wisconsin issued a decree setting up an integrated bar. This meant that in the future every lawyer qualified to practice law in Wisconsin was obligated to become a member of the state bar association. Was this action of the court judicial, legislative, or executive in character?

(5) During the term of President Kennedy, the United States entered into a treaty with the Soviet Union, pursuant to which both countries would refrain from testing atomic weapons above the ground. Was this action legislative or executive?

THE LEGISLATIVE VETO AND THE CHADHA CASE

Congress has frequently delegated rule-making (i.e. legislative) power to the executive departments and administrative agencies of the government. In a number of instances Congress has required such departments or agencies to submit the rules and regulations made by them, or even individual decisions reached by them, to Congress for purposes of surveillance. Congress also has empowered one of the branches of Congress (the Senate or the House of Representatives), or even a Congressional committee, to nullify such rules or decisions. This procedure was called the "legislative veto." In Immigration and Naturalization Service v. Chadha, 462 U.S. 919, 103 S.Ct. 2764, 77 L.Ed. 2d 317 (1983), the U.S. Supreme Court struck down an exercise of the legislative veto as being violative of the Constitution, and the reasoning used by the Court puts in question the constitutionality of the entire practice.

Zagdish Chadha was an East Indian who was born in Kenya and held a British passport. He was lawfully admitted to the United States in 1966 on a nonimmigrant student visa. His visa expired on June 30, 1972. On October 11, 1973, the District Director of the Immigration and Naturalization Service (INS) ordered Chadha to show cause why he should not be deported for having "remained in the United States for a longer period than permitted." Chadha conceded that he was deportable for overstaying his visa, but requested suspension of deportation under section 244(a)(1) of the Immigration and Naturalization Act (INA). This section permits the Attorney General of the United States

---

5. W. Bondy, *The Separation of Governmental Powers: Its History, in Theory, and* *in the Constitution* (1896, republished in 1967), pp. 80–81.

to suspend deportation of an otherwise deportable alien if: (1) he has been physically present in the United States for seven years, (2) he is of good moral character, and (3) his deportation would result in extreme hardship. The INS judge who heard Chadha's case pursuant to a delegation of authority from the Attorney General suspended his deportation, on the ground that all of the requirements for suspension were met in Chadha's case. A report of the suspension was transmitted to Congress.

Section 244(c)(2) of the INA provides for a veto by either the Senate or the House of Representatives of INS decisions which allow a deportable alien to remain in the United States. On December 12, 1975, Representative Eilberg, Chairman of the Judiciary Subcommittee on Immigration, introduced a resolution in the House of Representatives opposing the granting of permanent residence in the United States to six aliens, including Chadha. The resolution was referred to the House Committee on the Judiciary which, without granting a hearing to Chadha and the other five aliens concerned, submitted the resolution to the House of Representatives for a vote. The resolution had not been printed and was not made available to the members of the house prior to the time it was voted on. The House consideration of the resolution was based solely on Representative Eilberg's statement on the floor that "it was the feeling of the Committee, after reviewing 340 cases, that the aliens named in the resolution did not meet the statutory requirements," particularly the requirement of hardship. The resolution was passed without debate or recorded vote, and it was not presented to the President of the United States for his approval.

After the House veto of the INS decision allowing Chadha to remain in the United States, the immigration judge reopened the INS proceedings and ordered the deportation of Chadha pursuant to the action of the House of Representatives. Chadha filed a petition for review of the deportation order in the United States Court of Appeals for the Ninth Circuit. That court held that the House of Representatives was without constitutional authority to order Chadha's deportation; accordingly, it directed the Attorney General "to cease and desist from taking any steps to deport this alien based upon the resolution enacted by the House of Representatives." The United States Supreme Court affirmed this judgment.

The majority opinion was written by Chief Justice Burger and joined by Justices Brennan, Marshall, Blackmun, Stevens, and O'Connor. The opinion was grounded in the main on an interpretation of Article I, sections 1 and 7, of the Constitution. Article I, section 1, declares that "All legislative Powers herein granted shall be vested in a Congress of the United States, which shall consist of a Senate and House of Representatives." Article I, section 7, states that "Every bill which shall have passed the House of Representatives and the Senate, shall, before it becomes a law, be presented to the President of the United States; if he approve he shall sign it, but if not he shall return it, with his objections to that House in which it shall have originated * * *." (The provision then sets forth the procedure by which the bill, in order to become a law, must be repassed by a two-thirds majority of both houses.) The same section also provides that "Every Order, Resolution, or Vote to which the Concurrence of the Senate and House of Representatives may be necessary * * * shall be presented to the President of the United States; and before the Same shall take Effect, shall be approved by him, or being disapproved by him, shall be repassed by two thirds of the Senate and House of Representatives, according to the Rules and Limitations prescribed in the Case of a Bill."

The majority took the position that section 244(c)(2) of the INA, authorizing a veto by either the Senate or the House of Representatives of INS decisions allowing a deportable alien to remain in the United States, and any actions taken by either the House or Senate pursuant to this section, were repugnant to the provisions of the Constitution set forth above. In reaching this conclusion, the majority assumed that the resolution of the House vetoing the decision of the INS in the *Chadha* case pursuant to section 244(c)(2) was *legislative* in character. Whether actions taken by either House are an exercise of legislative power, said the Chief Justice, depends not on their form but upon " 'whether they contain matter which is properly to be regarded as legislative in its character and effect.' " (462 U.S. 919, at 952.) The Chief Justice asserted that "the House took action that had the purpose and effect of altering the legal rights, duties and relations of persons, including the Attorney General, Executive Branch officials, and Chadha." (Id.) Finally, the Chief Justice argued that the veto constituted legislative action because it enabled Congress to make a determination of policy. Because of its legislative character, the veto could have been implemented only by passage of a resolution in both houses of Congress and presentment to the President of the United States for his approval or disapproval.

Justice Powell wrote a concurring opinion. He argued that the Congressional veto of the executive decision to suspend Chadha's deportation was unconstitutional not because it was a legislative act, but because it amounted to an exercise of judicial power in violation of the principle of separation of powers. "The House did not enact a general rule; rather it made its own determination that six specific persons did not comply with certain statutory criteria." (462 U.S., at 964–65.) In his opinion, the action of the House amounted to a trial by a branch of Congress devoid of constitutional authorization.

Justice White and Justice Rehnquist dissented from the decision. Justice White, in an elaborate opinion, agreed with Justice Powell that the exercise of the Congressional veto was not an act of lawmaking. But he made it clear that he would have upheld the validity of INA section 244(c)(2) and actions taken under this provision even if the resolution of the House of Representatives ordering Chadha's deportation could be characterized as legislative. He considered the Congressional veto, as recognized in the INA and about 200 other statutes, as a valid exercise of Congressional surveillance power over administrative actions. "If Congress," he said, "may delegate lawmaking power to independent and Executive agencies, it is most difficult to understand Art. I as forbidding Congress from also reserving a check on legislative power for itself." (462 U.S. 919, at 986.) Justice White also questioned the assumption of the majority that all lawmaking must observe the requirements of Article I of the Constitution (bicameral approval and presentment to the President of the United States). He pointed out that a great deal of law is today made by executive departments and administrative agencies without compliance with the provisions of Article I.

The *Chadha* decision has been severely criticized by many authors. Can you see some basis for criticism on separation of powers grounds?

NOTE ON FOREIGN RELATIONS AND THE SEPARATION OF POWERS

In the case of United States v. Curtiss-Wright Export Corp., 299 U.S. 304, 57 S.Ct. 216, 81 L.Ed. 255 (1936), the United States Supreme Court declared:

> The broad statement that the federal government can exercise no powers except those specifically enumerated in the Constitution, and such implied powers as are necessary and proper to carry into effect the enumerated powers, is categorically true only in respect of our internal affairs. * * * As a result of the separation from Great Britain by the colonies acting as a unit, the powers of external sovereignty passed from the Crown not to the colonies severally, but to the colonies in their collective and corporate capacity as the United States of America. * * * When, therefore, the external sovereignty of Great Britain in respect of the colonies ceased, it immediately passed to the Union.

> * * *

> Not only, as we have shown, is the federal power over external affairs in origin and essential character different from that over internal affairs, but participation in the exercise of the power is significantly limited. In this vast external realm, with its important, complicated, delicate and manifold problems, the President alone has the power to speak or listen as a representative of the nation. He *makes* treaties with the advice and consent of the Senate; but he alone negotiates. Into the field of negotiation the Senate cannot intrude; and Congress itself is powerless to invade it. As Marshall said in his great argument of March 7, 1800, in the House of Representatives, "The President is the sole organ of the nation in its external relations, and its sole representative with foreign nations."

[299 U.S. at 315–316, 319, 57 S.Ct. at 218–219, 220–221.]

The sweeping breadth of some of the statements in *Curtiss-Wright* has been criticized. Mr. Justice Jackson, in his concurring opinion in the famous case of Youngstown Sheet & Tube Co. v. Sawyer, 343 U.S.

579, 72 S.Ct. 863, 96 L.Ed. 1153 (1952) (in which the Supreme Court invalidated President Truman's attempted nationalization of steel mills closed by strikes in the midst of the Korean War), declared that much of the Court's opinion in *Curtiss-Wright* had been *dictum* (that is, not necessary for the determination of the particular issue before the Court.) The precise ruling of the Court in *Curtiss-Wright* was a narrow one, namely, that Congress had power to delegate to the President authority to declare an arms embargo against Bolivia and Paraguay then engaged in the Chaco War. The decision throws little light on the general distribution of foreign affairs powers between the President and Congress under the Constitution. During the hearings on the Iran-Contra Affair conducted by a joint Congressional committee in 1987, it was argued by some that the President has virtually unlimited powers in the foreign policy area. This position was, however, rejected by the United States Supreme Court in Dames & Moore v. Regan, 453 U.S. 654, 101 S.Ct. 2972, 69 L.Ed.2d 918 (1981), in an opinion written by Justice Rehnquist.

TREATIES AND EXECUTIVE AGREEMENTS

The *Youngstown* case contained a broad statement to the effect that "in the framework of our Constitution, the President's power to see that the laws are faithfully executed refutes the idea that he is to be a lawmaker." 343 U.S. 579, at 587. The question is to what extent this statement is applicable to the field of international relations.

According to Article II, section 2, of the Constitution, the President has power to negotiate treaties with foreign nations. Such treaties often establish a scheme of mutual rights and obligations on a generalized basis and thus partake of the nature of law. This explains the fact that a treaty made by the President, according to the Constitution, will not become valid unless sustained by two-thirds of the membership of the Senate, i.e., of a lawmaking body. Presidents have, however, entered into many international agreements on their own responsibility and without Senate approval. The question arises under what circumstances such agreements may be deemed to be within the President's constitutional power. Unfortunately, this question has not as yet been answered by any decision of the United States Supreme Court.

Those members of the Constitutional Convention who were lawyers were quite familiar with the writings of a Swiss international jurist, Emmerich de Vattel. Vattel had distinguished between treaties and executive agreements as follows:

> Sec. 152. A treaty, in Latin, *foedus*, is a compact entered into by sovereigns for the welfare of the State, either in perpetuity or for a considerable length of time.

> Sec. 153. Compacts which have for their object matters of temporary interest are called agreements, conventions, arrangements. They are fulfilled by a single act and not by a continuous performance of acts. When the act in question is performed these compacts are executed

once and for all; whereas treaties are executory in character and the acts called for must continue as long as the treaty lasts.

A similar position was taken by Attorney General (later Supreme Court Justice) Robert Jackson. He concluded that international arrangements consisting of single, executed acts (such as mutual transfers of property), entailing no promises or obligations continuing in time, were within the confines of Presidential executive power.[6] According to this view, international agreements which go beyond the performance of single acts and establish general rules for the future international conduct of the signatories require Senatorial consent. It must be realized, however, that the borderline between general regulation and individual action often becomes indistinct and blurred when concrete situations have to be faced.

THE WAR POWERS RESOLUTION

Historically the conduct of foreign affairs by United States Presidents has been characterized by a far-reaching assumption of power, and the judiciary has been reluctant to find constitutional fault with this practice in the face of Congressional acquiescence. In 1973, however, Congress reasserted its prerogatives in the foreign field by passing the War Powers Resolution (87 Stat. 555). The initial impetus for this legislation was produced by the Cambodian invasion of 1970. In section 2, which is headed "Purpose and Policy," it is provided that "the constitutional powers of the President as Commander-in-Chief to introduce United States Armed Forces into hostilities, or into situations where imminent involvement in hostilities is clearly indicated by the circumstances, are exercised only pursuant to (1) a declaration of war, (2) specific statutory authorization, or (3) a national emergency created by attack upon the United States, its territories or possessions, or its armed forces." The Resolution requires the President in every possible instance to consult with Congress before introducing United States forces into hostilities and to submit a written report within 48 hours of utilizing American forces in certain military activities absent a declaration of war. (Article I, section 8, of the Constitution vests Congress with the power to declare war.) The Resolution requires further that within sixty days of the expiration of the 48–hour reporting period the President must terminate the deployment of forces unless Congress has affirmatively authorized such use or extended the sixty-day period. The Resolution also provides that at any time Congress can direct the President by concurrent resolution to remove United States forces from hostilities. Concurrent resolutions are not subject to the Presidential veto.

In the light of the *Chadha* case, are there grounds for challenging the constitutionality of the War Powers Resolution? For a discussion of this question, see Carter, "The Constitutionality of the War Powers

6. Opinion of Attorney General of August 27, 1940, 39 Op.Atty.Gen. 484 (1941).

Resolution," 70 Virginia Law Review 101 (1984); Comment, "Congressional Control of Presidential Warmaking Under the War Powers Act: The Status of a Legislative Veto after *Chadha*," 132 University of Pennsylvania Law Review 1217 (1984).

Further References

Chayes, A., "The Role of the Judge in Public Law Litigation," 89 Harvard Law Review 1281 (1976).

Dainow, J., "The Civil Law and the Common Law," 15 American Journal of Comparative Law 419 (1967).

Farnsworth, E.A., *An Introduction to the Legal System of the United States*, 2d ed. (1983).

Henkin, L., *Foreign Affairs and the Constitution* (1972).

Jolowicz, H.F., "The Civil Law in Louisiana," 29 Tulane Law Review 491 (1955).

Kurland, P.B., "The Rise and Fall of the 'Doctrine' of Separation of Powers," 85 Michigan Law Review 592 (1986).

Vanderbilt, A.T., *The Doctrine of the Separation of Powers* (1953).

Zweigert, K., and Kötz, H., *An Introduction to Comparative Law* (1977), Vol. I, pp. 260–274.

Chapter II

COMMON LAW, EQUITY, AND THE DEVELOPMENT OF THE ANGLO-AMERICAN COURT SYSTEM

A. THE COMMON LAW COURTS AND THE WRIT SYSTEM

1. COMMON LAW COURTS

We learned in Chapter I that the common law is a system which had its roots in medieval England, was shaped in the courts of the English king, and was applied throughout the English realm. Its development as a distinct body of national law began during the reign of Henry II (1154–1189), who was successful in expanding the jurisdiction of the royal courts. Before his time, the bulk of the law was local customary law, which was administered in local or regional courts and in the private manorial courts of the feudal lords. Afterwards, three royal courts emerged. One of them, the Court of Exchequer, continued to exercise the jurisdiction of the earliest king's court over matters pertaining to the king's property and revenue. The other two competed with the local, regional and manorial courts: the Court of King's Bench asserted jurisdiction over criminal cases and civil actions involving a breach of the peace, while the Court of Common Pleas heard all other civil disputes. The following excerpt details the development of these three courts and describes the competition that ultimately arose between them for jurisdiction over civil actions.

SCOTT AND KENT, CASES AND OTHER MATERIALS ON CIVIL PROCEDURE

pp. 26–32 (1967) [Footnotes omitted].*

A. THE EARLIER ENGLISH COURTS

In England there have always been local courts, which are inferior courts of limited jurisdiction. It is unnecessary to enumerate them.

---

* Reprinted by permission of authors and publishers, Little, Brown & Co. Copyright ©1967 by Austin W. Scott and Robert B. Kent.

They included county courts, courts-baron, hundred courts, and others. Blackstone gives an account of them in the fourth chapter of his third book.

Of much greater importance are the royal courts, the superior courts of justice. The courts which prior to 1875 had come to have jurisdiction over actions at law were three in number, the Common Pleas, the King's Bench, and the Exchequer. In addition, there was the Court of Chancery, which had jurisdiction over suits in equity.

Common Pleas. The Court of Common Pleas, or Common Bench as it was sometimes called, was early established as a permanent court, with jurisdiction to determine controversies between the King's subjects. In Magna Carta (1215) it was provided that this court should not follow the King from place to place but should be held in some fixed place, and this place was established in Westminster Hall. The court had jurisdiction to hear and determine civil controversies. It was composed in Blackstone's day of four judges, the Chief Justice of the court and three puisne (pronounced *puny*) justices. It had jurisdiction of actions originally brought in the court and actions removed to the court from some of the local courts. It had jurisdiction over "common pleas," that is, controversies between individuals, as distinguished from "pleas of the crown," that is, criminal proceedings. Its jurisdiction over private controversies, however, was not exclusive, since, as we shall see, the Court of King's Bench had jurisdiction over some private controversies, and gradually assumed jurisdiction over other private controversies, as did also the Court of Exchequer. The Court of Common Pleas, however, always had exclusive jurisdiction of certain actions to recover land, known as real actions, until those actions were finally abolished in the nineteenth century.

King's Bench. The Court of King's Bench was established probably in the early part of the thirteenth century. It had jurisdiction over criminal cases. It also had jurisdiction over civil actions involving a breach of the peace. It had jurisdiction also over other actions brought against a person in the custody of the King's marshal of the Marshalsea Prison. It did not, however, have jurisdiction in the case of other civil actions, as, for example, an action of debt. By the use of a fiction it acquired such jurisdiction. If a plaintiff desired to sue a defendant for debt in the King's Bench he might first sue him for trespass, have him arrested and committed to the Marshalsea, and thereafter the court could entertain an action of debt against him. The proceeding would be begun, not by an original writ but by what was known as a "bill of Middlesex," a process directing the sheriff to arrest the defendant to answer a charge of trespass and also (ac etiam) of debt. The charge of trespass was a sufficient ground for arresting the defendant and committing him to the custody of the marshal, and the Court of King's Bench thus acquired jurisdiction to determine the question of the indebtedness of the prisoner. Since the court was anxious to extend its jurisdiction, it came to be held that it was not necessary that the defendant should be actually arrested; it was held that an allegation by the plaintiff that the defendant had been arrested was sufficient and the defendant would not be permitted to deny the allegation. Thus, the Court of King's Bench acquired concurrent jurisdiction over all kinds of civil controversies except real actions. Later it came to be held that a proceeding in the court could be begun by an original writ as well as by a bill of Middlesex. The court was composed of four judges, the Chief Justice of England and three puisne justices.

Exchequer. The Court of Exchequer originally had jurisdiction over controversies affecting the King's property and his revenue. By an ingenious device the jurisdiction of this court was enlarged. If a plaintiff wished to bring an ordinary personal action against the defendant in the Court of Exchequer, he would allege that he, the plaintiff, was indebted to the King, and that the defendant had refused to discharge a liability to the plaintiff, whereby he is the less able (quo minus) to pay the King. The writ by which the proceeding was begun was known as a "writ of Quominus." Thus, the question of the royal revenues being involved, the Court had jurisdiction over the private controversy. This court, like other courts, was only too ready to extend its jurisdiction, and therefore it became unnecessary for the plaintiff to prove his allegation of his indebtedness to the King. It might seem to be a dangerous thing for a plaintiff to admit such an indebtedness if it did not in fact exist, but the King never appears to have taken advantage of the admission. Indeed, it came to be recognized that the allegation was purely fictitious and that its purpose was merely to confer jurisdiction upon the court over the private controversy. The court was composed of a Chief Baron of the Exchequer and three puisne barons.

Thus gradually it came about that the three superior courts of common law had concurrent jurisdiction over actions between subject and subject, except those actions relating to land which were known as real actions, as to which the Court of Common Pleas retained its exclusive jurisdiction until they were finally abolished. In ordinary personal actions, whether they involved tort or contract, the plaintiff might select any of the three courts as the tribunal to determine the litigation. From the point of view of logic and practical convenience it would seem better to have had a single tribunal, but the development of legal institutions is not governed altogether by logic or convenience. It is curious, also, to see how the whole matter was developed through the use of fictions; but fictions have played a great part in the development of the law, both on the procedural and on the substantive side. The notion that fictions are foolish at best and dishonest at worst is a comparatively modern and sophisticated notion and is by no means undebatable. It is fairly arguable that the employment of fictions has been an admirable device when properly used to improve the juridical system.

Exchequer Chamber. The judgment of one of these three courts did not necessarily end a case. It was possible by a writ of error to carry the case to a higher court. To do this it was necessary for the losing party to obtain from the Court of Chancery a writ of error. The party who lost in the court below became the "plaintiff in error," and the party who won in the court below became the "defendant in error." Originally the court of error from the Common Pleas was the Court of King's Bench, the court of error from the King's Bench was the House of Lords, and the court of error from the Court of Exchequer was the Court of Exchequer Chamber, composed at first of the Chancellor and the Treasurer, and later of the Chancellor alone, with the judges of the King's Bench and Common Pleas sitting as assessors. In the reign of Queen Elizabeth (1585) it was provided that a case could be carried from the Court of King's Bench to another Court of Exchequer Chamber, composed of the judges of the Common Pleas and Exchequer. Ultimately, in 1830, it was provided that from each of the three courts of original jurisdiction a case could be carried to a new Court of Exchequer Chamber, and the two older courts of that name were abolished. That court thus came to be composed of the judges of the three superior courts, but when a case was carried up from one of the courts the judges of the other two courts alone sat. From the Court of Exchequer Chamber the case could be carried to the House of Lords. Thus, there came to be an intermediate appellate court and a court of final appeal.

House of Lords. The House of Lords was the final appellate tribunal. Originally the theory seems to have been that Parliament, as the highest court of England, had power to correct errors in the judgments of any lower court, and that the Commons as well as the Lords were entitled to participate in the decision of cases in error. In practice, however, the appellate jurisdiction of Parliament came to be exercised by the Lords alone in the later Middle Ages. But for centuries appeals were dealt with by the House of Lords in the same manner as any other matters coming before the House. As late as 1783, judgments of the Common Pleas and King's Bench were reversed by a bare majority in a House composed almost entirely of bishops and lay peers. But it was finally established in 1844 that, as a convention of the English constitution, only the members of the House learned in the law are entitled to take part in the hearing of appeals. Accordingly the House of Lords, for judicial business, consisted of the Lord Chancellor, ex-Lord Chancellors, and other peers who held or had held high judicial office as chose to attend. In 1876 the House was increased by the creation of salaried peers for life, called Lords of Appeal in Ordinary, to assist the hereditary peers learned in the law.

The Nisi Prius system. The history of the development of the judicial system in England is the history of a contest between the King and the local authorities. Before the Norman Conquest there was a division of authority between the local tribunals on the one hand and the King and his council of advisers which was called the Witan on the other. After the Norman Conquest it became the purpose of the Kings to extend the limits of the royal justice and to limit the power of the local authorities. The purpose of the Kings was to establish a strong centralized government, and to carry out this purpose it was necessary to have strong central courts. If justice was to be administered by the royal courts, however, it was impracticable to compel suitors and witnesses to resort to the King's capital in order to obtain justice. England was much too large for that, particularly before the days of easy communication. How could the King have his centralized court and yet bring justice to every man's door? The problem was solved by the creation of courts which sat at the King's capital, at the same time sending the judges of those courts and others bearing the royal commission at intervals on circuit throughout the realm.

It is of great importance that the student should understand the method by which in England the administration of justice by the royal courts was brought to every man's door. Each of the three superior courts of common law, the King's Bench, the Common Pleas, and the Exchequer, sat as a court at Westminster. The year was divided into four terms, the Hilary Term, the Easter Term, the Trinity Term, and the Michaelmas Term. Each of these terms lasted for only a few weeks. During these terms each of the courts sat on the bench, in banc. Before the court thus sitting were brought for its determination all questions arising in the course of an action, except such as arose at the trial. Thus, the full bench sitting at Westminster in term time determined questions as to the legal sufficiency of the pleadings, such as those which arose on a demurrer. The full bench of the court would also determine questions arising after the trial. It was the full bench which gave judgment on the verdict. It was to the full bench that the party against whom a verdict was given might apply for a new trial. The party against whom the verdict had been given might also make a motion before the full court in arrest of judgment, on the ground that the pleadings of the opposite party were insufficient in law, or he might move for judgment notwithstanding the verdict.

As we have seen, each of the three superior courts of common law sat at Westminster only during four comparatively brief periods during the year. Between these terms of court there were periods of vacation. It was during the vacations that the trials of issues of fact arising in these courts were held. Except in a few cases where the trial was held before the full bench at Westminster in term time, the trials would be held before one or two judges in the various towns in England. For the purpose of conducting the trials, the judges of the superior courts and others commissioned by the King for the purpose would go on circuit. It was the function of the judges on circuit to try the issues of fact raised by the proceedings taken at Westminster.

2. MODES OF TRIAL

One reason for the growing popularity of the royal courts was the fact that they used trial by jury in an ever-increasing number of cases. By contrast, the chief modes of trial used in the early period of English law were wager of law (compurgation), battle, and the ordeal. Wager of law will be described later, in section B.2(e) of this chapter. Battle was a combat or duel between the plaintiff and the defendant, in which the defeated party lost the case. The ordeal (used primarily in criminal cases in the early Middle Ages) was an appeal to the Deity to show by a sign or miracle who was guilty and who was innocent. The accused had to perform a task imposed upon him by the judges. If he performed it to their satisfaction, it was assumed that God was on his side, and that he was innocent. In the ordeal by fire, for example, the accused had to carry a piece of hot iron in his hand for a number of steps, or he was required to pick a stone out of boiling water. After the wound was inflicted, a priest bound up the injured hand or arm. If it healed cleanly after three days, the person in question was deemed innocent. If there was a blister as large as half a walnut or more, he was convicted.

In the course of time, these older modes of trial were supplanted by trial by jury. But it should be noted that the function of the jury during the formative period of the common law differed from that of the jury in our time. Today, the jurors hear the evidence in a trial, listen to the witnesses, look at the documents, and then decide questions of fact on the basis of the evidence. They are supposed to be impartial people who come into court with an open mind. Personal knowledge of the case is grounds for disqualification. The jurors in medieval England, on the other hand, were primarily witnesses who were called in order to tell what they knew about a case. They were a body of neighbors summoned by the king's officials (not only by judges) to give answers to questions under oath. Hence, in its origins, the jury system was less a bulwark of popular liberties than an exercise of the royal prerogative. It was a device used by a strong king to collect information from anyone he pleased in his kingdom.

Henry II introduced jury trial into civil litigation, especially to determine questions of ownership and possession of land. The jurors were usually neighbors of the litigants who were well acquainted with the facts underlying the controversy. If they lacked the requisite knowledge, they were sometimes sent back to the local community to obtain additional information. Unlike the earliest jurors, they were used not only as witnesses but also as judges of the facts who decided whether the plaintiff or the defendant had the better right.

3. THE WRIT SYSTEM

When a litigant wanted a royal court to take jurisdiction of a case, he asked the king (or more precisely, the king's chancellor) to issue a writ. The chancellor was an ecclesiastic. He kept the king's great seal and supervised a staff of clerks who prepared all the documents that were issued in the name of the king. The following excerpts describe and illustrate the common law writ system.

BLACKSTONE, COMMENTARIES ON THE LAWS OF ENGLAND (1765)

Ed. by W.D. Lewis, Book 3, pp. 272–273.

First, then of the original, or original writ: which is the beginning or foundation of the suit. When a person hath received an injury, and thinks it worth his while to demand a satisfaction for it, he is to consider with himself, or take advice, what redress the law has given for that injury; and thereupon is to make application or suit to the crown, the fountain of all justice, for that particular specific remedy which he is determined or advised to pursue. * * * To this end he is to sue out, or purchase by paying the stated fees, an original, or original writ, from the court of chancery, which is the *officina justitiae,* the shop or mint of justice, wherein all the king's writs are framed. It is a mandatory letter from the king, on parchment, sealed with his great seal, and directed to the sheriff of the county where injury is committed, or supposed to be committed, requiring him to command the wrong-doer or party accused either to do justice to the complainant or else to appear in court and answer the accusation against him. Whatever the sheriff does in pursuance of this writ, he must return or certify to the court of common pleas, together with the writ itself; which is the foundation of the jurisdiction of that court, being the king's warrant for the judges to proceed to the determination of the cause. For it was a maxim introduced by the Normans, that there should be no proceedings in common pleas before the king's justices without his original writ; because they held it unfit that those justices, being only the substitutes of the crown, should take cognizance of anything but what was thus expressly referred to their judgment.

EXAMPLES OF EARLY WRITS

Pound and Plucknett, Readings on the History and System of the Common Law (1927), pp. 62–63.

(1) William King of England to the Abbot of Peterborough, Greeting: I command and require you that you permit the Abbot of St. Edmund to receive sufficient stone for his church, as he has had hitherto, and that you cause him no more hindrance in drawing stone to the water, as you have heretofore done. Witness the Bishop of Durham (c. 1070–1080 A.D.).

(2) Henry, King of England, to Nigel of Oilly and William Sheriff of Oxford, Greeting: I command you that you do full right to the Abbot of Abingdon concerning his sluice which the men of Stanton broke, and so that I hear no more complaint thereof for defect of right, and this

under penalty of ten pounds. Witness Ralph the Chancellor, at Westminster (c. 1105–1107 A.D.).

(3) Henry King of England to Jordan de Sackville, Greeting. I command you to do full right to Abbot Faritius and the church of Abingdon concerning the land which you took from them, which Ralph of Cainesham gave to the church in alms; and unless you do this without delay, I command that Walter Giffard do it, and if he shall not have done it, that Hugh of Bocheland do it, that I may hear no complaint thereof for defect of right. Witness, Goisfrid of Magnavill, at Woodstock (c. 1108 A.D.).

(4) The King to the Sheriff, Health. Command A that, without delay, he render to B one hyde of land, in such a vill, of which the said B complains that the aforesaid A hath deforced him; and unless he does so, summon him by good summoners, that he be there, before me or my Justices * . * * to show wherefore he has failed; and have there the summoners and this writ (c. 1187–1189 A.D.).

Note that these writs were, either wholly or in part, executive orders issued by the King. They were not, or at least not in the first place, devices for instituting litigation. The first writ is simply an order commanding a certain person to do a certain act and refrain from doing another act. The second writ moves a little closer to the use of judicial rather than executive power by setting a fine in case of noncompliance with the King's command. The third writ shows that the King, instead of decreeing a penalty, could simply order that the act be done by a third person. This delegation of power to enforce the law was a precursor of injunctive relief. The fourth writ initiates litigation before royal judges, but only as an alternative to compliance with the King's command to A, transmitted by the sheriff, to give up a piece of land.

At the end of the twelfth century, a new form of writ made its appearance. It did not begin with a demand for restitution, but simply contained an order to the sheriff, combined with a brief statement of the essential facts, that he should summon the defendant to come before the royal court and show why he had done a particular act. This later form of writ tended to become the prevailing form used to institute proceedings in the royal courts.

Such writs had to be obtained from the King's Chancery. They were called "original writs" to distinguish them from writs issued by a court of law during a judicial proceeding.[1]

In its beginning, the original writ was a special license from the King to litigate in the King's court some controversy which would

1. Blackstone, in the excerpts set forth above, states that the original writs were issued by the "court of chancery." The judicial "court" of this name did not come into existence until 1474, i.e., several centuries after the practice of issuing original writs had begun. Blackstone means by the "court of chancery" to refer to the offices of the clerks of the King's Chancellor. The chancery clerks issued original writs not in a judicial capacity but in the form of a "mandatory letter from the King," as Blackstone puts it.

otherwise be litigated in a local or manorial court. It was evidence of an exceptional privilege, a mark of royal favor. Such a writ, since it contained a special permission for one case only, was executive in nature.

But writs soon ceased to be mere favors. They became transformed into writs *de cursu,* routine writs issued as a matter of course. Royal justice was placed at the disposal of anyone who could bring his case within a formula found in one of the existing writs.

Writs *de cursu* were entered into a Register of Writs kept in the Chancery. If a person found himself aggrieved by the action of another, his lawyer went to the Chancery and examined the Register. If he found a writ fitting the facts of his case, he asked that it be issued to him upon payment of a fee. If none fitted his case, he was without a remedy unless the Chancellor was willing to make a new writ for him.

Whether or not the Chancellor was willing to extend the scope of royal jurisdiction by granting new writs in novel situations depended very much upon whether or not the king whom he served was a strong or a weak king. The feudal lords of England viewed the writ-making power of the Crown with grave suspicion. Every new writ tended to enlarge the jurisdiction of the royal courts at the expense of the private courts of the lords. Hence, the lords had an interest in keeping down the number of writs by which litigation could be instituted in the courts of the king.

Henry II was a strong king able to stand his ground against the pressures of the feudal aristocracy. Under his reign, many new writs were issued, and the common law grew by leaps and bounds. After his death, however, the Crown suffered a number of setbacks and defeats in its attempt to build up a royal justice for the entire country. Under Henry III, a weak king, the King's Council (the predecessor of Parliament) enacted the Provisions of Oxford in 1258, which laid it down that the Chancellor should seal no writs except the existing ones without the sanction of the king and his Council. This enactment secured the control of the King's Council, consisting mostly of feudal dignitaries, over the issuance of new writs and crippled the writ-making power of the Chancery.

In 1285, under the rule of a strong king, Edward I, a part of the writ-making power was restored to the Chancery by virtue of the Statute Westminster II, set forth below. The Chancery was authorized to issue writs in cases similar to those covered by a pre-existing writ. True innovations in writ-making, however, were reserved to Parliament.

STATUTE WESTMINSTER II
13 Edw. I, c. 24 (1285).

Whenever henceforth it shall happen in the Chancery that in one case a writ is found and in a like case falling under the same law and requiring a like remedy no writ is found, then the clerks of the Chancery shall agree in making the writ, or they may adjourn the plaintiffs until the next parliament, and let them write the cases in which they cannot agree and refer them to the next parliament, and let the writ be made with the consent of the wise men of the law; and from henceforth, let it not happen that the court any longer fail complainants seeking justice.

Questions

(1) Maitland, a distinguished English legal historian, has stated that "the granting of a newly worded writ was no judicial act" (2 *Collected Papers* 123 (1911)). Consider that under the Statute of Westminster II the clerks of the Chancery were authorized to present writs similar to existing writs to Parliament for approval. You may also have noted that entirely new writs, according to the Provisions of Oxford, required the sanction of the King and his Council (the predecessor of Parliament). At an earlier time, the Chancellor issued original writs as a representative of the King, who at that time possessed legislative, executive, and judicial powers. Could it be argued that the evolution of the common law forms of actions occurred by a procedure akin to legislation?

(2) Can you see some good reason why, according to the historical record, hardly any legal system has left the making of new law entirely to its judges?

B. THE FORMS OF ACTION AT COMMON LAW

1. INTRODUCTION

The "forms of action" at common law were part and parcel of the writ system. There were many different writs, and each writ embodied one particular form of action. If the name of a writ is likened to the title of a song, the related form of action functioned as the writ's words and music. The forms of action seem arcane in retrospect due to the subtle differences between the tunes and the unique procedural dance that became associated with each. As writs proliferated and came to serve somewhat overlapping purposes, it became easy for unwary counsel to call the wrong tune for a particular occasion, or to make a procedural misstep that halted the litigation in its tracks.

Blackstone points out in the excerpt set forth in Section A that the writs were returned by the sheriff to the Court of Common Pleas, which was the chief court of civil jurisdiction. But when the other two courts of the common law also acquired some measure of civil jurisdiction, the system of original writs was extended to them. Each writ stated briefly the substance of the plaintiff's claim. For each writ there was a particular mode of pleading and a particular type of judgment. The plaintiff's choice of a writ was irrevocable. In the words of Maitland, "he must play the rules of the game he has chosen." The plaintiff had to identify his action as one in trespass or trover. If he chose an inappropriate writ, he lost the case and had to start all over again by purchasing a different kind of writ.

The forms of action were abolished in England and the United States in the second half of the nineteenth century. Section 307 of the California Code of Civil Procedure provides: "There is in this state but one form of civil action for the enforcement or protection of private rights and the redress or prevention of private wrongs." Identical or similar provisions are found in the codes of virtually all states. The wording of the provision seems to suggest that the multitude of actions at the common law (and, for that matter, in equity) has given way to the creation of one unitary form of action.

If this is a correct description of the present state of the law, that is, if the forms of action have actually and fully been done away with, why should it be necessary to engage in any further study of them? The answer to this question is hinted at in the following statement by the English legal historian, F.W. Maitland: "The forms of action we have buried, but they rule us from their graves." What did Maitland mean by this statement?

He meant that the statutes declaring that henceforth there shall be one form of action only refer to form rather than substance. Today, in order to obtain relief in trespass or trover, it is no longer necessary for the plaintiff to label his action correctly, to obtain a writ describing the essential elements of the action, and to go through a special system of pleading appropriate to the form of action chosen. If the plaintiff's attorney makes a mistake in describing the action as one of detinue, while in fact it is one of trespass, he may prevail in the suit in spite of the mislabeling. But he will prevail only if the substance of his contentions establishes a good case in trespass. As the California Supreme Court pointed out in Philpott v. Superior Court, 1 Cal.2d 512, 515, 36 P.2d 635, 636–637 (1934), the legislature's abolishing the *forms* of action did not mean to destroy the essential characteristics of the common law actions, that is, of the rights people had to legal relief from the common law courts of England. In a similar vein, the New York Court of Appeals in Goulet v. Asseler, 22 N.Y. 225, 228 (1860) made the following observations: "Although the Code has abolished all distinctions between the mere forms of action, * * * yet actions vary in their nature, and there are intrinsic differences between them which no law can abolish. * * * The mere formal differences between such actions are abolished. The substantial differences remain as before." The statements made by these two courts are representative of the position taken by courts throughout the United States.

The truth is that the whole substance of the common law was shaped and molded by the forms of action. Their abolition did not, as such, create any new rights or remedies. Hence, as a general rule, a common law action can be maintained only in those cases where some kind of action was available under the old system. Only in a limited number of situations has the modern law provided new remedies or enlarged the scope of old ones. In the light of these facts, it may be said that the forms of action at common law constitute the genetic material out of which most of the modern law has evolved. Only by digging among the fossils of the forms of action can one gain a full understanding of the strange bends and fractures in the skeleton of the common law today.

The survey of the most important forms of action at common law which follows is quite concise and general. The beginning student will learn more about common law actions in his or her courses in torts, contracts, and property.

2. A SUMMARY OF THE CHIEF FORMS OF ACTION AT COMMON LAW

(a) Replevin

This action had its roots in the ancient remedy of distress, and for several hundred years it was used for no other purpose than to restore to the owner chattels that had been wrongfully distrained. Distress was used in medieval England by feudal lords to enforce the feudal services owed to them by their tenants. If the tenant defaulted in his services, or if he failed to pay his rent when due, the lord could seize his cattle or other personal goods without a court order and keep them until the tenant performed.

The purpose of replevin was to restore to the tenant chattels that had been unlawfully distrained. If the tenant wished to challenge the seizure, he would obtain a writ of replevin which would direct the sheriff to locate the chattels and redeliver them to the plaintiff before the action was tried. The plaintiff was required, however, to give bond or security for the return of the chattels if the decision should be for the defendant. This unusual procedure had its reason in the fact that the goods distrained by the landlord usually consisted of cattle or agricultural tools which were indispensable to the husbandry of the tenant, that is, his ability to run his farm and feed his family.

In the course of time, the action was extended to cover all cases of unlawful taking of chattels. If the chattel itself could not be recovered, its value could be obtained. It also became possible for the defendant, upon giving a counter-bond, to keep possession of the chattel during the litigation.

(b) Detinue

Originally, this action was limited to cases of bailment. Where a person had delivered goods to another to keep them for him, and the bailee refused to return the goods at the termination of the bailment, the bailor could bring detinue. The action was gradually extended to any case of unlawful detention of a chattel, no matter how the defendant had obtained possession. As a result of this development, detinue became an alternative to replevin in those cases in which the defendant had taken a chattel unlawfully from the plaintiff and later refused to return it to the plaintiff.

The judgment in detinue was that the plaintiff recover the chattel or its value, at the option of the defendant. Thus the defendant in detinue could not be forced to give up the chattel itself, if he refused to surrender it. Damages could be recovered for the injury suffered by plaintiff because of the unlawful withholding.

(c) Debt

Debt was an action for the recovery of a specific sum of money. The amount to be recovered had to be fixed and certain, that is, the exact amount of the debt had to be stated in the complaint.

The action split off into four varieties: (1) Debt on a Record was brought to recover money due on a judgment of a domestic court of record. A court of record is one whose acts and proceedings are recorded, and which has the power to fine or imprison for contempt. (2) Debt on a Statute lay where the plaintiff was seeking to recover a definite sum due from the defendant as a penalty or forfeiture under a statute. The action could not be used when the statute provided for unliquidated (i.e., undetermined) damages rather than a fixed sum. (3) Debt on a Specialty could be used where the defendant had promised in a document under seal to pay a sum certain. (4) Debt on a Simple Contract was available to enforce a defendant's unsealed promise to pay a sum of money, provided that the *quid pro quo* (consideration) promised by the plaintiff (such as goods or services) had already been received by the defendant. The action could also be used to recover on an obligation imposed upon the defendant by law, other than statute or record, to pay a liquidated sum, as, for example, on a foreign judgment, or on a judgment of a domestic court not of record, or for money received and kept by defendant under such circumstances that the law imposed a duty on him to pay it over to the plaintiff.

For many centuries, the requirement that the amount sued upon must be a sum certain was rigidly interpreted by the courts. As Ames points out, "if [plaintiff] demanded a debt of 20 pounds and proved a debt of 19 pounds, he failed as effectually as if he had declared in detinue for the recovery of a horse and could prove only the detention of a cow." In the course of the nineteenth century, the requirement was gradually relaxed in England as well as in the United States.

(d) Covenant

The province of covenant was the recovery of damages due for the breach of a sealed contract, whether the damages were liquidated or unliquidated. When the damages were liquidated upon breach of a sealed instrument, debt and covenant were concurrent remedies. When the damages were unliquidated, covenant was the only common law remedy. (Later, special assumpsit developed as a remedy for the recovery of unliquidated damages for breach of an unsealed contract.)

(e) Trespass

The term "trespass" is a translation of the Latin word *transgressio,* and it denotes an act which transcends, or passes beyond, the bounds of legal right and invades the rights of another person. The action of trespass is in its nature a tort, or an action *"ex delicto,"* arising from an act made wrongful by law, as opposed to an action on a contract, or *"ex contractu,"* arising from an act made wrongful only by agreement.

The writ of trespass came into use in the thirteenth century. The writ averred that defendant's act had been committed *vi et armis et contra pacem Domini Regis* —with force and arms and against the peace of the Lord King. The requirement of a forcible act was the cause of the rule that a plaintiff, in order to prevail in trespass, had to show a direct and immediate injury. An indirect injury was not actionable in trespass.

There were three major subdivisions of the action of trespass. Trespass to the person lay when the defendant had committed an act of battery, assault, or false imprisonment against the plaintiff. Trespass *de bonis asportatis* involved the carrying away, destruction, or damaging by the defendant of a chattel in plaintiff's possession, or to the possession of which the plaintiff was immediately entitled. Trespass *quare clausum fregit* allowed recovery for an unlawful intrusion upon plaintiff's land. Relief in trespass was limited to damages.

Trial in trespass was by jury, which made the action very popular. In some of the other common law actions, such as debt and detinue, the defendant could wage his law, that is, swear that he was innocent of the charge and win the case by having twelve oath-helpers (compurgators) confirm the truthfulness of his oath. This mode of trial was obviously very unsatisfactory from the point of view of the plaintiff, but it was not abolished in England until 1833.

(f) Trespass on the Case

It has been pointed out that trespass could be maintained only for harms to persons or property that were directly and immediately caused by a forcible act of the defendant (although insistence on the use of force decreased as time went on). Trespass could not be maintained for indirect or consequential injuries. If the defendant threw a log at the plaintiff traveling on the highway, trespass would lie. If he wrongfully left a log on the highway and the plaintiff stumbled over it, the defendant was not responsible in trespass.

In the course of time—probably by virtue of the authorization to grant "similar writs" contained in the Statute of Westminster II—a form of action developed which was designed to give redress for indirect and consequential injuries to the person, goods, or land of the plaintiff. This action was called trespass on the case, or simply case. It lay for various kinds of negligent acts, for the commission of a nuisance, for malicious prosecution, fraud and deceit, libel and slander. It also became the remedy for injuries to non-possessory interests in property, such as easements. Trial in trespass on the case was by jury.

One difference between trespass and case—which has survived into the modern common law of torts—was that nominal damages were deemed proper in simple trespass, so that the action could be used for the sole purpose of vindicating a right. Actual, material damages had to be proved in trespass on the case.

(g) Trover

Trover began its career as a subdivision of trespass on the case, but it gradually developed into an independent action. Originally it lay only where the plaintiff had lost a chattel and the defendant had found it and converted it to his own use. Subsequently, the scope of the action was enlarged so as to cover any act constituting a conversion, that is, unlawful appropriation of plaintiff's chattel by the defendant. The plaintiff could recover the full value of the chattel plus damages for the withholding of possession.

Trover became more or less concurrent with detinue, but it was more popular than detinue since the plaintiff in trover had a right to a jury trial.

(h) Special Assumpsit

The action of assumpsit was originally a subdivision of trespass on the case. It split off from case and became a separate action about 1500. It assumed two distinct forms, Special Assumpsit and General Assumpsit. Trial for both forms of assumpsit was by jury.

Special assumpsit lay against persons engaged in a particular calling who had undertaken (assumpsit) to do certain work for the plaintiff and had performed it so unskillfully as to cause a loss to the plaintiff. The earliest cases of assumpsit were suits against surgeons who had undertaken to cure the plaintiff but had treated him inexpertly; against contractors who had agreed to build well but built unskillfully so that the house collapsed; and against barbers who had undertaken to shave the plaintiff with a clean razor but had used a dirty one which caused an infection.

In these cases, the plaintiff sought to recover damages for a physical injury to his person or property attributable to the active misconduct of the defendant. The breach of promise by the defendant was merely incidental. The action thus sounded in tort rather than contract. (This situation is consistent with the finding of legal anthropologists that tort actions have been a regular feature of legal orders from their early beginnings, while contracts play a subordinate role in the legal systems of pre-commercial civilizations.)

While special assumpsit originally required a misfeasance on the part of the defendant, it was later extended to cases of mere nonfeasance. Thus, when the defendant agreed to build a house for the plaintiff and failed to live up to his promise, he would be held liable in damages. Special assumpsit would also lie for a breach of contract to sell goods, for failure to pay the purchase price for goods, and for failure to pay compensation for the performance of services. This development, which coincided with the rise of a commercial class in England, turned special assumpsit into the most important action for breach of contract. The plaintiff in assumpsit could not, however, enforce compliance with the terms of the contract, such as performance of the promise to build a house; he could only claim damages for nonperformance or faulty performance. Furthermore, special assumpsit was restricted to the breach of unsealed promises.

(i) General Assumpsit

General assumpsit originated in the seventeenth century and became an action for the enforcement of promises implied in fact and promises implied in law, as distinguished from express promises. A promise implied in fact arises out of a transaction which had not been reduced to the form of a distinct bargain. Examples are services rendered by a tailor or innkeeper or common carrier without any specific agreement as to the amount of compensation. For many centuries, there was no action by which a reasonable compensation could be recovered. When general assumpsit became available in these types of cases, it appeared in two varieties: (a) *quantum meruit* ("as much as he deserved"), an action by which reasonable compensation for services could be recovered if the services were rendered under circumstances in which a remuneration was to be normally expected; (2) *quantum valebant* ("as much as they are worth"), an action by which, in the absence of a specific agreement to the price, the reasonable value of goods sold to the defendant could be recovered.

Having taken the step of implying promises in fact and enforcing them, the courts went one step further. They also implied promises "in law." For example, if the defendant, by mistake, received a payment intended for the plaintiff, he was held responsible to the plaintiff under an implied promise to pay over the money erroneously received. Here the promise was purely fictitious, since there was no agreement between the parties, and the courts used the term "quasi-contract" for the purpose of classifying the promise. General assumpsit in this area developed into an action for the recovery of money or other property in situations where the defendant was deemed unjustly enriched at the expense of the plaintiff.

General assumpsit was also allowed as an alternative to the action of debt, for the purpose of collecting a simple contract debt resulting from an unsealed contract. The reason was that trial by jury was the exclusive mode of trial in general assumpsit, while the defendant could wage his law in an action of debt. This variety of the action was called *indebitatus assumpsit*. If a contract had been fully executed by the plaintiff and nothing remained to be done but the payment of the price for goods or services by the defendant, the plaintiff could declare either in special assumpsit on the express contract or in general assumpsit on an implied (fictitious) promise to pay.

(j) Ejectment

At the early common law, a person who claimed a freehold interest in land, such as an estate in fee simple (full ownership and disposition) or an estate for life, could bring one of the real actions (writ of right, assize of novel disseizin, writ of entry) in order to vindicate his right and title against an intruder. These actions, which fell into disuse at a relatively early period of time, were called "real actions" because the plaintiff, if successful, recovered the "res" or thing itself for which suit was brought rather than damages. A lessee for years was not considered to have a freehold interest in land, and he could therefore not use the real actions if he was ousted from the land during the term.

In the thirteenth century, certain writs were invented to enable a lessee for years to recover the possession of land. These writs developed out of the writ for trespass on the case and eventually became merged in the action of ejectment.

The action of ejectment could be maintained to recover a leasehold interest, but not to recover a freehold interest. But this limitation— inasmuch as ejectment soon proved to be an expeditious and popular action triable by jury—was circumvented by the invention of certain fictions. The history of ejectment is in fact the history of fictions used for the purpose of making the action available to *any* holder of land— whether freeholder or leaseholder—who had been ousted from the possession of land. The courts of King's Bench and Exchequer were particularly eager to wink at the use of sham devices to circumvent the limitations of ejectment, since the real actions were the monopoly of the Court of Common Pleas and the other two courts were anxious to expand their jurisdiction at the expense of Common Pleas. However, the latter court, too, used the fictions, its judges feeling perhaps that an open and above-board extension of the action was not within the judicial function.

In order to make the action available to a freeholder it was necessary for the freeholder to create a lease for years. Hence, when A claimed a freehold interest in land in the possession of B, A first had to execute a lease to X. X then went on the land and made himself comfortable on it until he was ejected. If he was not ejected, the courts said that if he was "spied" by the occupant, this should be deemed a disturbance of his peaceful possession equivalent to an ouster. After ejectment, X maintained an action against B. If he recovered possession of the land, he handed it over to A, the real party in interest.

After a while, a new trick was practiced. A proceeded as before, that is, he delivered a lease to X who then went on the land. Then A immediately procured a second friend, Y, who also went upon the land

and ousted X. This second friend was called the "casual ejector." X would then sue Y for recovery of possession. Of course, it would be unfair to allow recovery without notice to the actual occupant, B, so the courts refused to give judgment unless B was given an opportunity to defend his possession.

The action of ejectment continued in this condition for several centuries. Then, between 1650 and 1660, Chief Justice Rolle of the Common Pleas hit upon an ingenious idea. Why was it necessary to insist that X and Y be men of flesh and blood? Why couldn't they be converted into figments of the imagination? This idea was adopted. The two friends of the person ousted became fictitious persons called John Doe and Richard Roe, or John Goodtitle and Richard Shamtitle. The action was purported to be brought by Doe, who was alleged to be a tenant of the real party in interest, A. It was brought against Roe, who was alleged to have ousted Doe. Attached to the declaration was a letter by Roe to B, the person in possession, notifying B that he could come in and defend the action, inasmuch as Roe had no intention of doing so. The courts would permit B to defend the action only if he entered into the so-called "consent rule," that is, if he admitted the fictitious lease, entry, and ouster in writing. The declaration was then changed making him the real defendant. This sham procedure was used in England and the United States until the latter half of the nineteenth century.

3. PROBLEMS

In the following cases, A sued B at a time when the common law forms of action were still in effect. What action or actions could be maintained by A?

(1) B used a steamroller for repairs on a highway. After working hours, he parked it at the side of the highway, but part of it protruded into the driving lane. In the dark of a foggy night, A drove his automobile into the steamroller and was severely injured.

(2) B entered A's land without A's permission and appropriated some timber stacked up on the land. A made a demand for the return of the timber, but B refused to comply with the demand.

(3) A and B made a contract not under seal by which A was to sell and deliver a horse to B for a price of $100. A delivered the horse and B accepted delivery, but B refused to pay for it.

(4) A entered into a written contract under seal with B, whereby B promised to install a steam boiler in the basement of A's house for a stated compensation. B failed to install the steam boiler.

(5) A loaned an expensive watch to B for a few days. B dropped the watch and damaged it. He returned the watch, but refused to pay for the repair.

(6) A owns Blackacre. B ousts A under a claim of title and takes possession of Blackacre.

(7) A purchases an apartment building from B. C, one of the tenants, mistakenly sends a current rent payment of $500 to B, the former owner. B refuses to return the money to C or to turn it over to A, and C, lacking other funds, is in breach of the lease.

C. EQUITABLE JURISDICTION AND THE COURT OF CHANCERY

1. EQUITY AND JUSTICE

The system of equity originated in the late Middle Ages as a rival of the common law. The chief agency responsible for its development was the Court of Chancery. The first two excerpts expound the notion of equity, as interpreted by Aristotle and a famous English barrister of the sixteenth century. The note which follows deals with the development, functions, and jurisdiction of the Court of Chancery.

ARISTOTLE, THE NICOMACHEAN ETHICS

Trans. by H. Rackham (Everyman's Library ed., 1947), pp. 313–317.

We have next to speak of Equity and the equitable, and of their relation to Justice and to what is just respectively. For upon examination it appears that Justice and Equity are neither absolutely identical nor generically different. Sometimes, it is true, we praise equity and the equitable man, so much so that we even apply the word equitable as a term of approval to other things besides what is just, and use it as the equivalent of "good," denoting by "more equitable" merely that a thing is better. Yet at other times, when we think the matter out, it seems strange that the equitable should be praiseworthy if it is something other than the just. * * *

These then are the considerations, more or less, from which the difficulty as to the equitable arises. Yet they are all in a manner correct, and not really inconsistent. For equity, while superior to one sort of justice, is itself just: it is not superior to justice as being generically different from it. Justice and equity are therefore the same thing, and both are good, though equity is the better.

The source of the difficulty is that equity, though just, is not legal justice, but a rectification of legal justice. The reason for this is that law is always a general statement, yet there are cases which it is not possible to cover in a general statement. In matters therefore where, while it is necessary to speak in general terms, it is not possible to do so correctly, the law takes into consideration the majority of cases, although it is not unaware of the error this involves. And this does not make it a wrong law; for the error is not in the law nor in the lawgiver, but in the nature of the case: the material of conduct is essentially irregular. When therefore the law lays down a general rule, and thereafter a case arises which is an exception to the rule, it is then right, where the lawgiver's pronouncement because of its absoluteness is defective and erroneous, to rectify the defect by deciding as the lawgiver would himself decide if he were present on the occasion, and would have enacted if he had been cognizant of the case in question. Hence, while the equitable is just, and is superior to one sort of justice, it is not superior to absolute justice, but only to the error due to its absolute statement. This is the essential nature of the equitable: it is a rectification of law where law is defective because of its generality. In fact this is the reason why things are not all determined by law: it is because there are some cases for which it is impossible to lay down a law, so that a special ordinance becomes necessary.

ST. GERMAIN, THE DOCTOR AND THE STUDENT
pp. 45–46 (1532).

[St. Germain agrees with Aristotle that equity is an exception from the law in cases where the law is deficient because of its generality. He continues:]

* * * Wherefore it appeareth, that if any law were made by man without any such exception expressed or implied, it were manifestly unreasonable, and were not to be suffered: for such cases might come, that he that would observe the law should break both the law of God and the law of reason. As if a man make a vow that he will never eat white-meat, and after it happeneth him to come there where he can get no other meat: in this case it behoveth him to break his avow, for the particular case is excepted secretly from his general avow by his equity or *epieikeia*, as it is said before. Also if a law were made in a city, that no man under pain of death should open the gates of the city before the sun-rising; yet if the citizens before that hour flying from their enemies, come to the gates of the city, and one for saving of the citizens openeth the gates before the hour appointed by the law, he offendeth not the law, for that case is excepted from the said general law by equity, as is said before. And so it appeareth that equity rather followeth the intent of the law, than the words of the law. And I suppose that there be in like wise some like equities grounded on the general rules of the law of the realm.

Stud. Yea verily; whereof one is this. There is a general prohibition in the laws of England, that it shall not be lawful to any man to enter into the freehold of another without authority of the owner or the law: but yet it is excepted from the said prohibition by the law of reason, that if a man drive beasts by the highway, and the beasts happen to escape into the corn of his neighbor, and he, to bring out his beasts, that they should do no hurt, goeth into the ground, and setteth out his beasts, there he shall justify that entry into the ground by the law. Also notwithstanding the statute of Edw. 3, made the 14th year of his reign, whereby it is ordained, that no man, upon pain of imprisonment, should give any alms to any valiant beggar, that is well able to labour; yet if a man meet with a valiant beggar in so cold a weather, and so light apparel, that if he have no clothes, he shall not be able to come to any town for succour, but is likely rather to die by the way, and he therefore giveth him apparel to save his life, he shall be excused by the said statute, by such an exception of the law by reason as I have spoken of.

2. THE COURT OF CHANCERY AND THE DEVELOPMENT OF EQUITY *

The common law, in its early period, had exhibited considerable flexibility. There was a great deal of equity in it. Under Henry II, many new writs were granted, and the Register of Writs expanded rapidly. Then, as shown in Section A, the development of the common law was to a large extent arrested by the passage of the Provisions of Oxford. The Statute of Westminster II restored a part of the writ-making power of the Chancery, but the clerks of the Chancery did not make expansive use of the powers granted to them. There were many situations in which the plaintiff could get no relief, or where the relief which was afforded was clearly inadequate. To give an example: The plaintiff bought a house from the defendant and asked for a conveyance. The defendant refused to convey. The plaintiff was determined to get that particular house, but all the common law courts would give him was damages.

It was this condition of relative sterility and inflexibility which caused the rise of equity jurisprudence. Litigation at common law was also very expensive, and a poor litigant could hardly afford it. What could be done by an impecunious litigant or one who felt that the highly technical rules of the common law prevented him from getting relief?

The common law courts were the chief instruments of the king in dispensing justice. But their jurisdiction was not exclusive. The king, in delegating to the common law courts his power to do justice, reserved to himself the power to do justice extralegally, by executive fiat. Thus the king himself, as a member of his council, could hear and determine a case. Many people took advantage of this residual power of the king. If they felt they deserved relief, and if the common law courts were unable or unwilling to grant it, they might present a petition to the king and his council and ask for a remedy, not as a matter of right, but of grace ("For the love of God and by way of Charity," as the customary invocation read.)

Many of these petitions were dismissed as frivolous on the ground that there was an adequate remedy at the common law. But a certain number of them were entertained, and such petitions, if they alleged a defect or inadequacy in the common law, were referred to the Chancellor, who was a member of the council. First, the Chancellor, in hearing these petitions and rendering decisions on them, acted only as a delegate of the council. But even before the close of the fourteenth

* The text of this section is based on Radcliffe and Cross, *The English Legal System* (6th ed. 1977), Ch. VIII.

century we find petitioners addressing the Chancellor directly, and beginning with the fifteenth century, the decree was made in his name. Thus equitable remedies, like the legal remedies they supplemented, came over time to be bureaucratized. Equitable relief always retained, however, the flexible, relatively non-technical nature which was its original *raison d'etre*.

At first, the jurisdiction of the Chancellor was very vaguely defined. The Chancellors of the early period were almost invariably bishops or other high ecclesiastical dignitaries. They intervened in order to correct the harshness of the common law on grounds of conscience and morality. Furthermore, they were concerned much more with the facts of the individual case than with laying down any general principles which their successors might follow. Nevertheless, there were certain types of cases in which it came to be recognized that the Chancellor would grant relief. Here are some of these types of cases:

First, the Chancellor recognized and protected the so-called "uses." If the legal estate in any property was held by A "to the use" of B, the Chancellor would give effect to the "equitable" rights of B, while fully recognizing that the legal title to the property was in A. This enforcement of uses as equitable rights gave rise, in the course of time, to a whole new body of law known as the law of trusts.

Secondly, the Chancellor often gave relief in cases where a contract or other legal transaction had come into existence through fraud, mistake, or duress. The common law granted very limited redress in such cases and was unable to order the cancellation of fraudulent instruments.

Thirdly, the Chancellor generally took a far broader view of contracts than the common law courts did in the Middle Ages. He was ready to enforce an obligation that had been created by the mere fact of mutual agreement. The common law courts, on the other hand, demanded either that the obligation be created in a document under seal, or that there be performance by one party to the contract. (These were the limitations of the two types of action designed to enforce contracts at the early common law—the actions of covenant and debt.) Even when the common law courts interfered in contract matters, they would only grant damages. The Court of Chancery, on the other hand, would sometimes enforce the contract directly, by compelling the defendant to perform the exact obligation stipulated by him. This remedy applied by the Chancery is known as specific performance.

The procedure which the Chancellor used in exercising his jurisdiction was very different from the procedure of the common law courts. The common law judge was like a referee at a fight. He saw to it that the rules were observed and awarded points to the parties, but he could not develop new rules of procedure as the fight developed before him. The Chancellor, on the other hand, had complete discretion in procedural matters. He intervened in the proceeding whenever he deemed it desirable. He summoned the defendant before him by the writ of subpoena and subjected him personally to an examination. The object of this examination was defined in ecclesiastical language. It was "to ascertain the condition of the defendant's conscience and to purge it by an appropriate prescription, if necessary." In doing this, the Chancellor had full power to subject the defendant to an oath, which forced him to disclose the secrets of his case. There was no jury in equity proceedings.

The Chancellor did not always hear a case personally. He often delegated authority to an official known as the Master of the Rolls. The losing party had the right, however, to apply to the Chancellor for a rehearing.

In time, the Chancellor extended his jurisdiction into more and more fields in which the common law claimed a monopoly, and strained relations ensued between the common law courts and the Chancery. In the sixteenth century, the common lawyers' jealousy of the Chancery had grown to considerable proportions. This feeling of animosity was accentuated by the conduct of Chancellor Wolsey, who made it a practice to issue injunctions prohibiting parties from suing in the common law courts on the ground, for example, that the defendant had an equitable defense which the common law court would not recognize, and who also sometimes prevented parties from enforcing a judgment which they had obtained from a common law court on the ground that it was inequitable.

The common law courts struck back. On several occasions they held that imprisonments by the Chancellor for disobedience of injunctions were unlawful, and they released the prisoners upon writs of habeas corpus. Finally, in 1616, Chief Justice Coke of the King's Bench caused a defendant in a common law action who had dared to apply to Lord Chancellor Ellesmere for an injunction against a judgment allegedly obtained by gross fraud and imposition to be indicted criminally. This action brought matters to a head, and the conflict was submitted to the Crown for a decision. King James I decided in favor of the Chancery and dismissed Lord Coke from office.

Following the period of the Commonwealth and the restoration of the monarchy in the seventeenth century, relations between the common law courts and the Court of Chancery improved. One important reason for this betterment in their mutual relations was a change in the character of equity. As we have seen, equity started out as a discretionary jurisdiction based on the moral ideas of the individual chancellors who exercised it. John Selden, who lived in the early seventeenth century, objected to the system of equity then administered by the Chancellor as a "roguish thing," because it varied with each Chancellor's type of conscience. The equity of the later seventeenth and of the eighteenth century, on the other hand, was discretionary only in theory. In practice, it developed into a system of formulated rules, and precedents were followed by the Chancellor as they were by the common law judges. In its new form, equity was not so much a correction of, or departure from, the common law, but a body of rules supplementing it. It should be noted, however, that many of the rules of equity were formulated in a more flexible and elastic manner than most of the rules of the common law. This left a margin of discretion in the judges in equity which enabled them—to a larger degree than was possible at the common law—to adapt the rule to the facts of the individual case.

The change in the general character of equity was accompanied by a change in the type of person administering it. The practice of appointing ecclesiastics as Chancellor ended with Wolsey, who died in 1530. With few exceptions, all Chancellors after him were secular officials. They were, however, not necessarily lawyers. Some of the early secular chancellors were statesmen or politicians. Only after 1675 did it become a practice to appoint only lawyers to the post of Chancellor.

D. ESTABLISHMENT OF THE COMMON LAW IN THE UNITED STATES

WALSH, A HISTORY OF ANGLO–AMERICAN LAW (2d ed. 1932)

pp. 85–96 * [footnotes omitted except as indicated].

§ 45. **English common law in the American colonies.**—The task of tracing in detail the development of American law has never been attempted. Nevertheless, the outlines of this development in colonial times have been sketched based on sufficient original evidences to give a very fair representation of the ways in which laws were established and enforced prior to the Revolution. In Massachusetts in 1636 a resolution of the general court after entreating the governing officers "to make a draft of laws agreeable to the word of God," directed the magistrates to hear and determine all causes "according to the laws now established, and where there is no law, then as near the law of God as they can." * * * The subsidiary law, in the absence of local statute, was the law of God. The magistrates administered a rude justice dependent on their interpretation of the divine law, based largely on their discretion in cases not expressly covered by enacted laws. There was no reception of the common law in these enactments. It was ignored.

In the actual practice of this early law in the courts, the common law was not followed or applied.

* * * The terms of the common law were used, as were common-law forms of action, but very loosely and informally, with wide variations. Common-law forms of deeds and contracts were followed, but the

* Reprinted by permission of the publisher, Bobbs–Merrill Co. Copyright ©1932 by William F. Walsh.

authority of the English common law was always denied except as the rule had been adopted by colonial statute.

The magistrates and judges during the early period were not trained lawyers. The first judge who was a professional lawyer was made chief justice in 1712. From that time until the Revolution, the common law was drawn on more extensively, but its binding authority was not recognized except as it was specifically adopted by statute or decision in specific instances. John Adams said: "Our ancestors were entitled to the common law of England when they emigrated; that is to say to so much of it as they pleased to adopt and no more. They were not bound or obliged to submit to it unless they chose."

In the early Connecticut and New Haven colonies we have very much the same colonial law as in Massachusetts, with nothing like reception or adoption of the common law.

In New York the reception of the common law was more complete than in the other colonies. The royal governors accustomed the people to the use of the common law. But prior to 1700 there were probably very few trained lawyers and judges, and though law actions ostensibly were conducted according to the English law, it was necessarily a kind of layman's law in fact, departing in many ways from common-law rules. * * * In 1700 a trained lawyer became chief justice, and he undertook to establish definitely the rules and practice of the common law in New York. A court of Chancery was established prior to 1727. In Governor Tyron's report, 1774, he said: "The common law of England is the fundamental law of the province, and it is a received doctrine that all the statutes enacted before the province had a legislature are binding upon the colony."

In Maryland we find the earliest recognition in the colonies of the common law as a subsidiary system. The first laws of 1642 provided for the trial of civil causes according to the law and usage of the province, and in cases where they failed, then according to equity and good conscience, "not neglecting (so far as the judge shall be informed thereof and shall find no inconvenience in the application to this province) the rules by which right and justice useth and ought to be determined in England," indicating that the common law might be looked to for guidance and illustration rather than as positive law. In 1662 it was enacted that where the laws of the province had no provision, justice should be administered according to the laws and statutes of England—"All courts shall judge of the right pleading and the inconsistency of the said laws with the good of the province according to the best of their judgment." * * * In Virginia and the Carolinas, we find the enactment of codes of law based on the common law and made necessary by the absence of lawyers and law books, the establishment of layman courts and administration necessarily involving a rude kind of natural justice worked out in the discretion of the judges in cases not expressly covered by the statutes. * * *

It seems clear, therefore, that in colonies which formally adopted the common law—Maryland, Virginia, the Carolinas—as in colonies which ignored it as a subsidiary law, substituting the divine law, or reason and equity, the law actually administered was a popular law without lawyers or trained judges, differing radically from the contemporary common law of England, and that in some of the colonies, notably in New York, considerable development in this law had taken place during a period just preceding the Revolution, and that the groundwork had been laid for the actual reception of the common law of England as part of our legal system, which in fact took place through developments in the law in the different states after the Revolution.

* * *

§ 46. **Special characteristics of colonial law.**—From the standpoint of the legal historian, a very interesting characteristic of this early colonial law is its popular informal character, with courts of laymen generally consisting of several persons administering customary law according to the general sense of reason and justice of the community as expressed in the sense of reason and justice of the magistrates or judges who decided the cases. The special needs of a newly-settled country with a homogeneous population in each colony equal in most respects socially and economically, without lawyers or English law books, demanded this type of court, which resembled the popular courts of the earlier time in England rather than the developed contemporary common-law courts. But more important than this are the special characteristics of American law by which it is distinguished from the common law of England, which had their origin and historical explanation in the colonial period. The most prominent characteristic of this kind is the strong tendency to codification. In nearly every colony most of the law under which the people lived was expressed in codes more or less elaborate and complete, the codes of Pennsylvania, as we have seen, foreshadowing in many ways the New York Code of Civil Procedure which has been copied in a large majority of the other states. Though in several of the colonies the English common law was formally adopted as the fundamental subsidiary law subject to local statutes and modifications to meet special local conditions as determined by the courts, as a practical matter, it was quite impossible to give it effect without lawyers trained in it or English law books from which it might be acquired. This practical reason was, no doubt, the immediate occasion for the enactment of codes as complete as possible in these colonies. In New England and New Jersey where the common law was not so adopted, codes of law were even more necessary, as the law outside of the statutes was left to the discretion of the judges and magistrates in their interpretation of reason and justice. The American tendency to codification, therefore, rests on this well-established historical foundation.

* * *

§ 47. **Relation of English common law to law in the United States.**—Judge Story said in a leading case: "The common law of England is not to be taken in all respects to be that of America. Our ancestors brought with them its general principles, and claimed it as their birthright; but they brought with them and adopted only that portion which was applicable to their condition."

Kent said:—"The common law, so far as it is applicable to our situation and government, has been recognized and adopted, as one entire system, by the constitutions of Massachusetts, New York, New Jersey and Maryland. It has been assumed by the courts of justice, or declared by statute, with the like modifications, as the law of the land in every state. It was imported by our colonial ancestors, as far as it was applicable, and was sanctioned by royal charters and colonial statutes. It was also the established doctrine, that English statutes, passed before the emigration of our ancestors, and applicable to our situation, and in amendment of the law, constitute a part of the common law of this country."

There can be no doubt that the New England colonies and New Jersey did not adopt the common law except as they expressly adopted parts of it in their statutes and their customary law as decided by their courts. New York actually applied the English law more fully than any other colony, and developed courts trained in common-law principles at an earlier date and more completely than did any other colony, and the leadership of New York in the development of American law in the last century was aided to a considerable degree by that early development. Maryland and the southern colonies formally adopted the common law, but it seems clear that its actual application by courts trained in that law had not progressed very far until a comparatively short time prior to the Revolution. It is clear, of course, that such law as the colonists were acquainted with was English law, that they brought with them and used the language and general principles and the forms of action of that law, but in most of the colonies the binding effect of English law was not recognized. They adopted similar law, but with extensive changes and modifications to meet their special needs. This law, even when it coincided with English law, bound them because they had enacted it or established it by their own decisions, not because it had been decided by English courts. Nevertheless, the common law as a general system of legal principles was adopted by the states after the Revolution and in most of the new states thereafter, as stated by Kent.[32] What is this common law? It seems clear that no rule of the English law became law in the United States until the question of

32. New York Const. Kent–Radcliff Rev. 1802, I, 15. "And this convention doth * * * ordain, determine and declare, that such parts of the common law of England, and of the statutes of England and Great Britain, and of the acts of the legislature of the colony of New York, as together did form the law of the said colony" on April 19, 1775, "shall be and continue the law of this state."

Declaration of Rights, Continental Congress, 1774:

"5. That the respective colonies are entitled to the common law of England, and more especially to the great and inestimable privilege of being tried by their peers of the vicinage, according to the course of that law.

"6. That they are entitled to the benefit of such of the English statutes as existed at the time of their colonization; and which they have, by experience, respectively found to be applicable to their several local and other circumstances."

whether it was "applicable to our situation and government," as stated by Kent, or "applicable to their condition," as stated by Story, had first been determined either by legislation or decision. Whether any specific part of that law was so applicable or not had to be determined by the law-making power of each state, whether legislative or judicial. By constitutional provision or by statute, we have, at least, adopted the common-law system as distinguished from any other, such as the civil law. We have established a common law in each state, agreeing on most points but varying in different ways on many others, each with its own system of courts, practice, and procedure.

In determining the rule to be applied in any case in which the law has not been settled either by statute or former decisions, it is the duty of the court to apply the common-law rule, but in determining what that rule is, the court is not limited to English decisions prior to American independence. It is free to consider English decisions of a later date, and decisions on the same question in other American states. From all of these decisions the court decides what principle of law applies to the case and how the application should be made. As between conflicting decisions in England and in different states, the court decides what rule shall be applied, based on sound reason and policy. The court is simply exercising the judicial function of declaring the law, a function as old as the common law and of its essence from the beginning. The change from the early colonial law is in the development of the courts, from laymen doing justice of a rude, popular sort, with scant knowledge of legal principles, to judges who are professional lawyers trained in the common-law system of jurisprudence. The decisions of the courts of any state establish the law of that state, and those decisions establish rules often differing from the English law, ancient or modern, or from decisions in other states arrived at after a like process. In this way is developed a common law of each state, based on the principles of the English common law, but varying from it in many cases, and varying as between the different states. There can be no doubt, therefore, that the "reception" of the common law after the Revolution was a continuation, fundamentally, of what had taken place in the colonial period. In both periods the English common law was adopted only in detail, as each rule was made the law by statute or by decisions.

E. THE MERGER OF LAW AND EQUITY

The development of equity outside of the common law resulted in many inconveniences and had many confusing aspects. There were two systems of law with different rules. There were two sets of courts. The systems of pleading and procedure were entirely different. Cases could not be transferred from a common law court to the Court of Chancery, and vice versa. A party seeking relief in the wrong court had to start all over again. Equitable defenses could not be set up in actions at law. In many cases, a controversey would be decided entirely differently, depending on whether it was settled in a court of law or equity.

Because of these shortcomings of the dual system of courts (to which reasons of economy might be added), the demand for reform became strong in England as well as the United States. The same 19th century wave of reform that led to the putative abolition of the forms of action also resulted in English and American trial courts generally receiving a unified jurisdiction over all civil actions, regardless of whether the relief sought was formerly within the exclusive competence of courts of common law or equity. A single mode of pleading and procedure in civil cases was instituted; in the United States this was called "Code pleading," and was pioneered by New York's adoption of David Dudley Field's innovative Code of Civil Procedure in 1848. The large majority of the states, including the State of California, followed the example of New York.

The question remains, however: How complete is the merger? Does the abolition of the separate courts of law and equity and the concurrent administration of these two branches of the law mean that there is no longer a distinction between law and equity? The answer to this question is that the procedural merger of law and equity has not done away with the distinction between the substantive rules of "law" (meaning the rules applied by the common law courts prior to the merger of law and equity) and "equity" (meaning the equitable remedies formerly applied by the Chancery and other courts of equity). The substantive rules of the two systems remain, to a large extent, intact. The respective types of relief given under each system also remain unaffected by the fusion. We speak of legal and equitable estates, of legal and equitable ownership. The common law action for damages is basically different from the equitable action for specific performance. And we still have to familiarize ourselves with the complex rules under which courts of equity granted injunctions. Furthermore, the facts that must be pleaded and proved in order to obtain equitable relief are largely the same as before the merger, including proof that the remedy at law (meaning the common law) is inadequate.

In one important respect, there remains a general disparity in the procedure for trying civil cases on "equitable" as opposed to "legal" causes of action. Generally, disputed facts in equitable cases are decided by the trial judge rather than a jury. This reflects the fact that the federal Constitution and most state constitutions guarantee the right to jury trial in civil cases only when a common law remedy is sought.[1] When equitable relief is sought, there is no right to a jury

---

1. The federal Constitution guarantees the right to jury trial both in criminal cases (the Sixth Amendment) and in civil cases (the Seventh Amendment). Although the Sixth Amendment right to jury trial in criminal cases applies to trials in state as well as federal courts, the Seventh Amendment right to jury trial in civil cases applies only to trials in federal courts. Thus the question whether the parties to a state civil case have a right to jury trial depends solely on whether the state constitution or a state statute provides such a right.

trial. Legislatures have been reluctant to provide for jury trials except as constitutionally required, because they are a cumbersome and expensive means of resolving disputes. Thus the use of jury trials in equitable cases has generally been left to the discretion of the trial court, which may in extraordinary circumstances empanel a jury to decide questions of fact on an advisory basis. If the case raises some legal issues and others of an equitable nature, a party is generally entitled to a jury trial on the legal issues only.

The continuing significance of the distinction between law and equity is emphasized by cases in which the legislature has created a new statutory remedy, and the courts are asked to determine whether a person claiming relief under the statute is entitled to a jury trial. The general rule in such instances is that when the statutory remedy "cannot be classified by looking to its counterpart in English practice, the nature of the remedy must be examined to determine if it more clearly resembles a traditional legal, or a traditional equitable, remedy." Southern Pacific Transportation Co. v. Superior Court, 58 Cal. App.3d 433, 129 Cal.Rptr. 912 (1976). Thus the Supreme Court of the United States held that the Seventh Amendment right to jury trial applied to an action for damages for housing discrimination created by the Civil Rights Act of 1968, because "the relief sought here—actual and punitive damages—is the traditional form of relief offered in the courts of law." Curtis v. Loether, 415 U.S. 189, 196, 94 S.Ct. 1005, 1009, 39 L.Ed.2d 260 (1974).

Often this mode of analysis leads to inconclusive results, and the final determination whether the remedy gives rise to a right to jury trial turns on the solicitude of particular courts for jury trials as a matter of social policy. In general, the federal courts have been more receptive to claims of a right to jury trial than have the state courts. Compare Ross v. Bernhard, 396 U.S. 531, 90 S.Ct. 733, 24 L.Ed.2d 729 (1970), with C & K Engineering Contractors v. Amber Steel Co., 23 Cal.3d 1, 151 Cal.Rptr. 323, 587 P.2d 1136 (1978); Abner A. Wolf, Inc. v. Walch, 385 Mich. 253, 188 N.W.2d 544 (1971); Hiatt v. Yergin, 152 Ind.App. 497, 284 N.E.2d 834 (1972). When a statute creates a cause of action to be adjudicated by an administrative tribunal rather than a conventional court, however, even the federal courts have not insisted on jury trials. See Atlas Roofing Co., Inc. v. Occupational Safety and Health Review Comm., 430 U.S. 442, 97 S.Ct. 1261, 51 L.Ed.2d 464 (1977).

F. MODERN ENGLISH AND AMERICAN COURTS

1. MODERN ENGLISH COURTS

(a) Jurisdiction

SCOTT AND KENT, CASES AND OTHER MATERIALS ON CIVIL PROCEDURE
pp. 33–34 (1967) *

The judicial system of England was completely reorganized in 1875. Shortly before that time the conclusion had come to be generally accepted that the system of separate courts was unnecessarily cumbersome and that the court organization should be simplified by merging the courts into a single court, with a trial branch and an appellate branch. This complete merger was not, however, effected. By the Judicature Act, 1873, 36 & 37 Vict., c. 66, which went into effect in 1875, and by subsequent acts amending it, a new system of court organization was established. The local courts were not wholly abolished, and the county courts were retained. Moreover, the House of Lords continued to be the highest court of appeal. The three superior courts of law, the Court of Common Pleas, the Court of King's Bench, the Court of Exchequer, and the Court of Chancery and the High Court of Admiralty and the Court of Probate, together with the Court of Exchequer Chamber, were merged into a single court called the Supreme Court of Judicature. That court was divided into a lower branch, called the High Court of Justice, and an upper branch, called the Court of Appeal. The High Court of Justice is now divided into three divisions, namely the King's Bench Division, the Chancery Division, and the Probate, Divorce and Admiralty Division. For a time there was also a Common Pleas Division and an Exchequer Division. These were abolished in 1880.

The Court of Appeal in practice consists of the Master of the Rolls and eight Lords Justices of Appeal. It ordinarily sits in two divisions of three judges each, and has general appellate jurisdiction. In the House of Lords appeals are now heard by at least three, and quite usually five, of the members who are eligible for such duty. Those who are eligible comprise the Lord Chancellor, the Lords of Appeal in Ordinary, and peers who have held high judicial office. The highest court of appeal for the dominions and colonies is the Judicial Committee of the Privy Council. Such appeals have been eliminated with respect to Canada and most other dominions.

(b) Diagrams of Court Structure

W. FRYER & H. ORENTLICHER, CASES AND MATERIALS ON LEGAL METHOD AND LEGAL SYSTEM 680 (1967)

Copyright © West Publishing Co., 1967.

(1) ORGANIZATION OF ENGLISH COURTS IN 1873

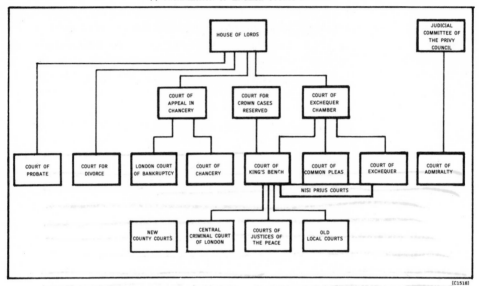

(2) MODERN ENGLISH COURTS

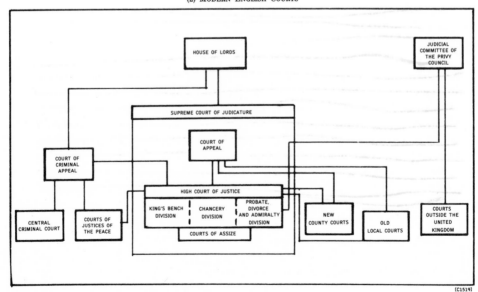

2. MODERN AMERICAN COURTS

(a) Note on the Dual System of State and Federal Courts

By definition, the "federal" system of government entails two levels of authority to make and administer law. In the United States, the competence to regulate most aspects of the day-to-day lives of citizens and the basic institutions of daily life remains with state governments, and most civil and criminal cases are accordingly heard in state courts and decided by rules of law created according to state constitutional processes. By their ratification of the federal Constitution, however, the original 13 states that had emancipated themselves from British rule in the Revolutionary War relinquished part of their sovereignty and subordinated themselves to the constitutional authority of a national government composed of a federal union of states. The federal government was endowed with the power to regulate matters thought likely to create friction among the states if left to state regulation. Certain of the federal government's powers, particularly with respect to the regulation of commerce and the conduct of foreign affairs, have been expansively interpreted in response to the pressures of the industrial revolution, the Civil War, the two World Wars, and the atomic age. With this federal law-making has grown an extensive system of federal courts.

The dual system of state and federal courts in the United States would not be so confusing if each system of courts were concerned only with its own system of law. However, each system of courts is constantly confronted with questions which arise under the law created by the other system of government.

Federal law is the supreme law of the land, and state court cases constantly raise issues of federal law. Indeed, some federal laws create rights and duties which are expressly left for their enforcement to cases that plaintiffs may choose to bring either in federal or state courts, and state courts have no privilege under the Constitution to refuse to entertain such suits on federal rights. More frequently, federal issues of a collateral or defensive nature arise in the course of state litigation, as when a defendant in a state criminal prosecution claims that the state police proceeded against him or her in some way which was in violation of the federal Constitution. State courts are obliged to decide all these issues of federal law in good faith, as they think a federal court would under the guiding precedent of the United States Supreme Court. If a federal issue is erroneously decided by a state court, the aggrieved party must pursue the issue to the highest state court in which review can be had before seeking further review from the United States Supreme Court.

The federal "diversity" jurisdiction presents a converse case of interaction between one system of courts and another system of law. Some cases governed solely by state law may nevertheless be brought in federal court because the parties to the cases are citizens of different states, or are aliens. In these cases, it is the federal courts that must attempt, in good faith, to decide how state courts would rule on disputed issues of state law. This decisional process is complicated by the fact that federal courts sitting in diversity cases are dealing with the separate legal systems of 50 different states, and there is no provision for review of their decisions by the supreme courts of those states.

We are going to describe the basic structure of the state courts first, and then will discuss the structure of the federal courts as well as the basics of federal jurisdiction and federal review of state court decisions. A diagram of the federal court system appears at the end of the chapter.

(b) State Court Systems *

Each state has a hierarchy of courts with at least three layers. On the bottom are those dealing with petty cases where small monetary amounts or minor criminal penalties are involved. In a nonurban area, the judge of such a court is likely to be called a justice of the peace, and the position might be only a part-time one. In the cities, he or she is likely to be called a magistrate or a judge and might be attached to a specialized court with a name like police court, traffic court, or small claims court. These petty or "inferior" courts are generally not "courts of record"; they make no detailed record of the proceedings beyond the identification of parties, lawyers, and disposition of the case. The procedure may be rather informal. The losing party may appeal to the next level of court, but it is not an appeal in the usual sense, since it typically involves a completely new trial rather than appellate review of the record made in the lower court.

The next level of court is known as a "trial court of general jurisdiction," authorized to hear civil and criminal cases generally. Unlike the petty court, it is a court of record; its procedure is quite formal; it is not confined to, and indeed is usually prevented from entertaining, the petty sort of case. It is often called a "district" court or "circuit" court, though in some places it has such other names as "superior court" or "court of common pleas." (New York State creates a special confusion by establishing a "supreme court" that is *not* a court of last resort. The highest state court in New York is called the Court of Appeals. The New York Supreme Court operates as the state trial court of general jurisdiction, and the Appellate Division of the New York Supreme Court is that state's intermediate appellate court.) Besides the trial court of general jurisdiction—or, in some states, within this court as departments or divisions thereof—there are specialized courts like those handling probate matters, or divorce and other domestic relations issues, or juvenile problems.

The trial court of general jurisdiction exercises *some* appellate jurisdiction when it takes an "appeal" from a petty court, usually by

* Adapted from S. Mermin, *Law and The Legal System* (2d ed.), pp. 58–60, with per- mission of the author. Copyright © 1982 by S. Mermin.

conducting a completely new trial as if the case had never been brought before the petty court. (This is called a "trial de novo.") To a limited extent, the trial court of general jurisdiction also exercises the more usual form of appellate jurisdiction. For instance, it may be authorized to review *administrative agency* decisions on the record made before the administrative agency, as distinguished from holding a trial *de novo.* In such a case the agency fact-findings, while not conclusive, will be upheld by the court in the absence of arbitrariness.

Uppermost in the hierarchy are the appellate courts. In a dwindling number of states[1] there is only one appellate court, and that is the highest court of the state. It hears appeals from the judgments of the trial courts of general jurisdiction, and either affirms or reverses, or occasionally modifies, the judgment. There are some cases in which a litigant seeks to control the trial court's action not by waiting to take an appeal from its judgment, but by seeking directly in the highest court an "extraordinary writ" directing the lower court to do something (e.g., grant a change in the venue or place of trial, or justify its order holding someone in allegedly illegal custody) or refrain from doing something (e.g., from continuing to exercise jurisdiction in a case).

In 36 states there are intermediate appellate courts. Their role varies in the different states. A state may provide that the appeal from a trial court goes to this intermediate court, and that a further appeal is then permissible, after unfavorable judgment, to the highest court. The state may say that in some other classes of cases (deemed more serious) the losing party in the trial court can skip the intermediate court and appeal directly to the highest court. In still other cases, the appeal from the trial court may be allowed only to the intermediate court, and an additional appeal to the highest court is either not allowed or allowed only for special reasons, or is left to the discretion of the highest court to allow. This limited-review type of provision is being increasingly suggested as a means of coping with the overburdened dockets of the states' highest courts.

DISTRIBUTION OF INTERMEDIATE STATE APPELLATE COURTS IN 1986

States With Intermediate Appellate Courts (36)	States Without Intermediate Appellate Courts (14)
Alabama	Delaware
Alaska	Maine
Arizona	Mississippi
Arkansas	Montana
California	Nebraska
Colorado	Nevada

1. The number of states without an intermediate appellate court declined from 23 in 1978 to 14 in 1986.

States With Intermediate Appellate Courts (36)	States Without Intermediate Appellate Courts (14)
Connecticut	New Hampshire
Florida	North Dakota
Georgia	Rhode Island
Hawaii	South Dakota
Idaho	Utah
Illinois	Vermont
Indiana	West Virginia
Iowa	Wyoming
Kansas	
Kentucky	
Louisiana	
Maryland	
Massachusetts	
Michigan	
Minnesota	
Missouri	
New Jersey	
New Mexico	
New York	
North Carolina	
Ohio	
Oklahoma	
Oregon	
Pennsylvania	
South Carolina	
Tennessee	
Texas	
Virginia	
Washington	
Wisconsin	

Source: Council of State Governments, *The Book of the States 1986–87,* at pages 157–58 (1986).

(c) The Federal Court System

i. Basic Structure *

There are three layers in the federal court hierarchy: the trial courts of general jurisdiction known as the district courts, the 13 courts of appeals, and the Supreme Court. There are also a few specialized trial courts (such as the Claims Court, the Tax Court and the Court of International Trade) and appellate courts (such as the Court of Military

---

* Adapted from S. Mermin, *Law and The Legal System* (2d ed.), pp. 166–69, with permission of the author. Copyright © 1982 by S. Mermin. United States Supreme Court disposition statistics taken from "The Supreme Court, 1985 Term," 100 Harvard Law Review 1, 308 (1986).

Appeals and the Temporary Emergency Court of Appeals which deals with certain economic and energy-related cases).

About half of the states have one federal district court each. In the others, the greater volume of business has necessitated creation of additional districts within the state. Thus in California there are the eastern, northern, central and southern districts, headquartered in Sacramento, San Francisco, Los Angeles and San Diego, respectively. A number of new judgeships were created in 1978 and 1984 by adding new judgeships to existing districts in populous areas. The Central District of California now has 22 judges; the Eastern District of California has 6. Some districts, such as the Eastern District of Oklahoma, still have only one judge each; the largest district, the Southern District of New York (in Manhattan) has 27 judges.

A federal district court case is heard by a single judge (with a jury, where one has been rightfully demanded). Until 1976, special 3–judge panels were required in district court cases considering the constitutionality of statutes; such panels are now limited to certain rare types of cases. In addition, in cases of special significance, all the judges of a particular district may choose to sit together on a case. This is called hearing a case "en banc."

The 13 courts of appeals are assigned to 11 numbered "circuits" or areas into which the country is divided, plus a separate circuit for the District of Columbia and a special appellate court called the "Federal Circuit." [1] (The term circuit dates from the early days of the federal judicial system, when circuit judges literally "rode circuit," travelling throughout the area of the court and holding sessions at the major towns and cities therein.) One of the busiest is the Second Circuit, which includes the state of New York (as well as Connecticut and Vermont) and therefore handles much important commercial litigation. The District of Columbia Circuit handles more litigation involving government agencies than do the others. The District of Columbia Circuit covers the smallest area; the Ninth Circuit, the largest (Alaska, Arizona, California, Guam, Hawaii, Idaho, Montana, Nevada, the Northern Marianas, Oregon, Washington). Another large area is covered by the Fifth Circuit, which embraces Louisiana, Mississippi, Texas and the Canal Zone. It is not surprising that these two massive circuits, the Fifth and Ninth, are the busiest of all, necessitating 16 and 28 judges respectively. Judges in the other circuits range from 4 for the First Circuit (Maine, Massachusetts, New Hampshire, Puerto Rico, Rhode Island) to 15 for the Sixth Circuit (Kentucky, Michigan, Ohio, Tennessee).

The courts of appeals normally sit in panels of 3 judges—sometimes including (when the spot cannot be filled by a regular circuit judge) a

1. The Federal Circuit has jurisdiction based on subject-matter rather than geography. In brief, its jurisdiction consists of appeals in federal district court cases involving either patents or contract claims against the federal government, all appeals from the Claims Court and the Court of International Trade, and appeals in a few other special categories of cases.

district judge from within the circuit or a district or circuit judge from another circuit. Frequently these assigned judges who fill out the ranks of courts of appeals panels are "senior" circuit or district judges, that is, semi-retired judges who work less than full-time and who are not counted in the number of regular judges allotted by Congress to each circuit and district court. The assignments are made by the chief judges of the circuit courts. (Each circuit and district court has a chief judge with responsibility for administrative matters. By statute, the chief judge is simply the most senior judge of the court, not yet 65 years of age, who has served as a circuit judge for at least a year and is willing to accept the job.) In an occasional case of particular importance, all or a substantial number of the regular judges of a court of appeals will sit "en banc." The unsuccessful litigant in a district court can take an appeal, as a matter of right, to the court of appeals.

The Supreme Court of the United States has 9 members. Its annual term begins in October and usually ends late in June. Each case is handled by the entire Court rather than by a panel. A quorum is 6. In the Court year designated as October Term, 1985, the Court disposed of 4289 cases, of which 290 (6.8%) were disposed of "on the merits," i.e., by deciding the substance of the legal issues presented. There were 159 full written opinions of the Court, disposing of 172 cases; 118 cases were disposed of by cursory "per curiam" decisions,[2] and the remaining 3999 cases were disposed of by the Court simply refusing to exercise its jurisdiction, as the Court has discretion to do (and as it must do in order to have adequate time for deciding the important cases which it does choose to review).

ii. Basic Jurisdiction

Federal jurisdiction is intricate enough to require a complete course of its own. We will merely outline the most general forms of federal jurisdiction. One basic principle of federal jurisdiction should be learned now, however: for the most part, federal jurisdiction is the creation of Congress, not the Constitution, and is accordingly subject to Congressional modification.

At the top of the federal pyramid is the Supreme Court of the United States. Almost all of its business consists of reviewing the judgments of lower courts. These may be the judgments of state courts of last resort which dealt with questions of federal law, or they may be the judgments of lower federal courts. By "lower federal courts" we mean the federal circuit courts of appeals and district courts. As previously noted, the district courts are the trial courts of the federal system, and their judgments are generally appealed to the federal courts of appeals for the circuits in which they are located. In a few types of cases, which are becoming increasingly rare, the Supreme Court hears an appeal from a district court without any intermediate

---

2. The authorship of a per curiam ("by the Court") decision is not attributed to a particular Justice. Ordinarily an opinion of the Court is written by a particular Justice and concurred in by all or a majority of the other Justices.

appeal to the circuit court. For the most part, however, the Supreme Court hears only cases which have already been appealed either to a state appellate court or to one of the 13 federal circuit courts of appeals.

We have previously indicated that the Supreme Court of the United States has the discretion to refuse to hear the vast majority of the cases in which its review is sought. This was not always the case. Until 1925, the Court heard most of its cases by means of a "writ of error," which functioned largely as an appeal as of right. In 1925, the Court's jurisdiction was revised by Congress to provide not only for appeals but also for writs of "certiorari." At the time, it was intended for the Court to have discretionary control only over cases subject to review by writ of certiorari; cases which met the more stringent criteria for an appeal were cases which the Court was supposed to hear automatically. In recent years, however, the volume of appeals filed with the Court has led the Court to adopt procedures by which it disposes of most appeals just as summarily as it denies petitions for writs of certiorari, so that the distinction between review by appeal and by certiorari has been reduced to little more than a technicality.[3] Congress is currently considering a proposed revision of the Supreme Court's jurisdiction which would legitimate this development by expressly conferring upon the Court plenary discretion over its own docket.

The jurisdiction of the federal courts of appeals, or circuit courts, is much simpler.[4] It consists principally of appeals from decisions by district courts, together with appeals from decisions by federal administrative agencies, such as the Interstate Commerce Commission and the National Labor Relations Board. In almost all of these cases, the courts of appeals have mandatory jurisdiction and cannot refuse to hear properly filed appeals. The rate of filing of appeals has increased drastically in all American appellate courts in the last two decades, and lacking any significant discretionary control over their dockets, many of the federal circuit courts have fallen substantially behind in their work.

The civil jurisdiction of the district courts is the most complex part of federal jurisdiction. The nationwide system of federal law is intertwined with highly variegated systems of state law in each of the fifty states, the District of Columbia and territories such as Puerto Rico and Guam. Not all issues of federal law which arise in litigation give rise to the right to bring suit in a federal district court—of all questions of federal jurisdiction, the question of when a case "arises under" federal law for purposes of federal trial court jurisdiction is probably the most intractable. Besides these "arising under" cases, also called "federal

3. Judges of the federal courts of appeals can also "certify" questions of law for binding decisions by the Supreme Court. The Supreme Court has strongly discouraged use of the certification device in all but truly extraordinary cases. The Court has exercised its certification jurisdiction only once in each of the past three decades.

4. An exception is the rather complex jurisdictional criteria of the United States Court of Appeals for the Federal Circuit, discussed in footnote 1, supra.

question" cases, federal courts also have jurisdiction over civil cases involving maritime law (called "admiralty" jurisdiction) or involving parties from different states (called "diversity of citizenship" jurisdiction). The scope of the district courts' civil jurisdiction is further complicated by two facts: (1) most civil cases which qualify for federal jurisdiction can also be brought, at the plaintiffs' option, in the state courts; (2) some cases brought originally in state court can be "removed" to federal courts at the request of the defendants. By contrast, the district courts' criminal jurisdiction is relatively simple: with the exception of crimes by members of the military, all prosecutions for federal crimes are brought in federal district courts.[5]

iii. Jurisdictional Diagrams

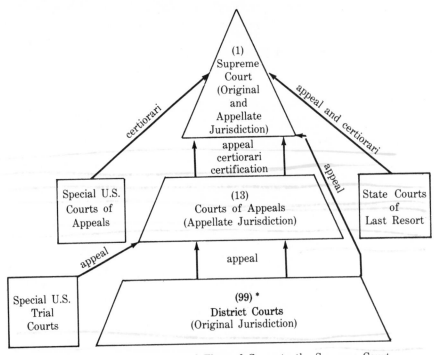

Federal Court Structure and Flow of Cases to the Supreme Court

* Includes 94 federal district courts in the 50 states, and the federal district courts for the District of Columbia, Puerto Rico, Guam, the Northern Mariana Islands, and the Virgin Islands.

[C1517]

5. Prosecutions of misdemeanors (punishable by no more than a year's imprisonment) may be tried before federal magistrates, who are parajudicial assistants appointed by the judges of a federal district court. An appeal in such a case is heard by a regular district judge. Prosecutions for violations of military law are tried before the courts-martial of the military services, with a special system of appeal to courts of military review, The United States Court of Military Appeals, and ultimately (if certiorari is granted) the United States Supreme Court.

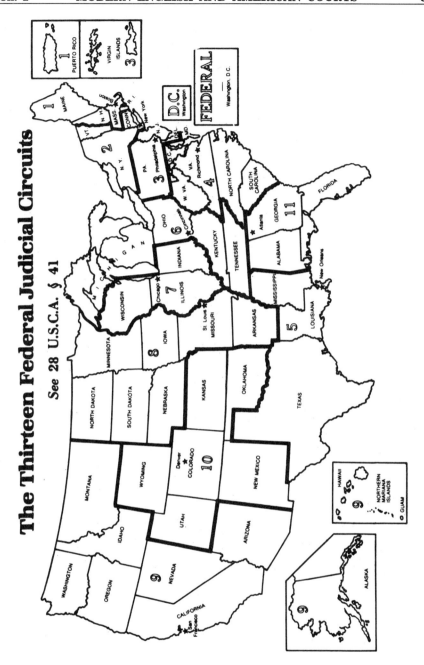

Further References

Hall, F.W., "The Common Law: An Account of Its Reception in the United States," 4 Vanderbilt Law Review 791 (1951).

Kempin, F.G., *Historical Introduction to Anglo–American Law in a Nutshell* (2d ed. 1973).

Radcliffe, G.R.Y., and Cross, G., *The English Legal System* (6th ed. 1977).

Spence, G., "The History of the Court of Chancery," 2 *Select Essays in Anglo–American Legal History* 219 (1907–1909).

Thayer, J.B., "The Older Modes of Trial," 5 Harvard Law Review 45 (1891).

Thompson, R.S., and Oakley, J.B., "From Information to Opinion in Appellate Courts: How Funny Things Happen on the Way Through the Forum," 1986 Arizona State Law Journal 1.

Chapter III

THE DOCTRINE OF PRECEDENT

A. OVERVIEW

In Chapter I you were introduced to two formal sources of law: legislation and case law. You will recall that legislation is prescribed by some formally constituted law-making body, or by popular initiative, and (in the Anglo–American legal system at least) is generally prospective in application, that is, legislation makes rules of law to be applied in the future. The most familiar form of institution for enacting legislation is simply called a *legislature,* such as the Congress of the United States, the legislatures of the fifty states, and the Parliament of Great Britain. So long as the legislature acts with the powers granted to it by the constitution which created it, its legislation is unquestionably *authoritative,* which is to say that judges have no choice but to decide lawsuits in accordance with applicable legislative rules. The application of legislative rules may raise difficult questions of statutory construction, which we will explore in Chapter VI. The constitutionality of legislation, although a matter of the greatest public significance, is a relatively rare problem for the practicing lawyer to encounter. Except for alerting you in Chapter I to the special way in which American constitutional law affects the process of legal classification, we will not attempt to present the basic principles of what American legislatures constitutionally can and cannot do.

In this chapter and the two which follow, we deal at length with the second of the formal sources of law: case law or "precedent," that is, the decisions by which judges have resolved previous lawsuits. The authoritative force of precedent is far more flexible than the authoritative force of legislation. This flexibility results from two circumstances.

First, judges do not typically decide cases with the sort of canonical language of general application which characterizes a statute. Although cases are normally decided on the basis of rules or general principles, judges will often articulate their decisions in language that focuses on the unique facts upon which the claims of the parties arise. A legislature, for instance, might provide that "any person who sells stock in an insolvent corporation without first disclosing to the purchaser that the corporation is insolvent, is liable to the purchaser of the stock for the refund of the purchase price." The decision of a court in a lawsuit for the return of the purchase price of stock bought by a purchaser who did not have the benefit of such a statute might hold only that under the circumstances of that case the sale of the stock without the disclosure to the purchaser of the fact of insolvency constituted fraud, and that under the relevant case law the commission of fraud made the seller liable to the purchaser for a refund of the purchase price of the stock. If another case arises in which the purchaser of stock in an insolvent corporation sues the seller of the stock for a refund, and the purchaser has only the previous decision, rather than a statute, to rely upon as establishing a legal right to the refund, a great deal will depend upon the analysis of the judicial ruling in the prior case. Was it held that any sale of worthless stock was fraudulent in the absence of disclosure? Or was the ruling confined to the particular kind of stock in issue in the prior case (mining stock, for instance), or to the particular kind of plaintiff in the prior case (a financially unsophisticated widow who had invested her life savings, for instance), or to the particular kind of defendant (a publicly-licensed stock broker, for instance)? There might be many other factual differences between the first case and the second.

Lawyers call reliance on these differences as a means of avoiding the authoritative effect of the prior decision the process of "distinguishing" a precedent. Because virtually all lawsuits arise on unique facts, virtually every precedent can arguably be "distinguished" from a subsequent case. Obviously some such distinctions are frivolous, because the factual difference is patently irrelevant to the legal rule announced in the prior case—as when the first case involves the operation of a red automobile in what is held to be a negligent manner, and the second case involves just the same sort of operation of a blue automobile. Equally obviously the process of determining which distinctions are relevant and which are not is frequently more difficult. Suppose a court holds that a homeowner's insurance policy which excludes coverage of fire loss caused by the "unreasonably dangerous storage of inflammables in the home" does not obligate the insurance company to cover losses from a fire caused by a homeowner's storage of a can of gasoline in the kitchen. Does this precedent control a suit to enforce a similar insurance policy for a loss caused by the storage of a can of paint thinner in the garage?

The problem of determining whether a preceding judicial decision is really "in point" and not factually distinguishable from the legal dispute in which it is cited as a precedent has two dimensions. It involves not only the question of what the facts were in the preceding case, but also which of the facts of the preceding case were actually relied upon by the court in deciding the case. It also involves the question whether the decision in the preceding case, if articulated in general terms which went beyond the facts actually then in issue, ought to be controlling in a subsequent case involving different facts. This second dimension calls for the determination of the "ratio decidendi" (a Latin phrase meaning "the reason for the decision") or the "holding" of the prior case. This problem will be discussed in detail in Chapter IV.

This leads us to the second fundamental reason for the flexibility of the authoritative force of precedent. Even when the controlling facts and "ratio decidendi" of a precedent are indisputably applicable to and dispositive of a subsequent lawsuit, an American court will not automatically follow that precedent—even if the court which decided the precedent is the very court which is later asked to follow it. This is not to say that American courts never follow precedent. They almost always do, and they frequently invoke the doctrine of "stare decisis," which seems to say they must. This makes the doctrine of stare decisis a complex problem of American law, fascinating to study but not easy to understand.

B. THE DOCTRINE OF STARE DECISIS

The term is an abbreviation of the Latin phrase "*stare decisis et non quieta movere*," which literally means "to stand by precedents and not to disturb settled points." As a legal term of art, stare decisis signifies the principle that once a disputed point of law has been settled by a judicial decision, that decision will be followed in all subsequent cases. Differently expressed, stare decisis forecloses parties to a lawsuit from rearguing a point of law which has previously been argued and resolved in some prior lawsuit within the same legal system. It does not matter that the parties to the present lawsuit are not the same as the parties who argued the case in which the precedent was established.[1]

You should understand, and emphatically remember, that the doctrine of stare decisis *is binding* to the extent that a lower court must follow the applicable precedent of a court with supervisory

1. As you will learn in Civil Procedure, "res judicata" ("a thing which has been adjudicated") is the general term for the doctrine that particular parties may not relitigate some dispute which they personally have previously had settled by a court. In its specific applications the doctrine of res judicata bars relitigation of particular issues of fact or law as well as the more general contentions of a lawsuit, such as whether one party is liable to another for having caused a particular injury. Unlike the doctrine of stare decisis, the doctrine of res judicata is generally followed quite strictly by American courts.

jurisdiction over it. Thus a federal trial court is bound to follow the case law of the federal court of appeals for the circuit in which it is located, and all federal courts must follow the case law of the United States Supreme Court, as must state courts with respect to questions of federal law.

State courts are not bound by decisions of any federal court on nonfederal matters. Nor are they bound by decisions of federal courts, other than the Supreme Court, even on federal matters, although they will usually pay close attention to such decisions.

The most significant problem of stare decisis is the treatment by a court of its own precedent. Under the American doctrine of stare decisis, no court, state or federal, is bound absolutely by its own decisions. It may overrule its decisions, except where overruling would put the court out of line with decisions of a higher court by which it is bound.

In Thomas v. Washington Gas Light Co., 448 U.S. 261, at 272, 100 S.Ct. 2647, at 2656, 65 L.Ed.2d 757 (1980), the following statement is found in the plurality opinion written by Justice Stevens:

> The doctrine of *stare decisis* imposes a severe burden on the litigant who asks us to disavow one of our precedents. For that doctrine not only plays an important role in orderly adjudication; it also serves the broader societal interests in evenhanded, consistent, and predictable application of legal rules. When rights have been created or modified in reliance on established rules of law, the arguments against their change have special force.

Justice Stevens points out in a footnote that stare decisis has a more limited application when the precedent rests on constitutional grounds, because correction of an earlier ill-advised decision through legislation is practically impossible.

E. BODENHEIMER, JURISPRUDENCE: THE PHILOSOPHY AND METHOD OF THE LAW

(Rev. ed. 1974), pp. 425–430 (footnotes omitted except as indicated).*

In a legal system where the rule of *stare decisis* is strictly and consistently applied, a precedent must not be disregarded or set aside, even though the rule or principle for which it is authority may seem archaic and wholly unreasonable to the judge called upon to apply it in a lawsuit. This element of the doctrine has frequently evoked criticism from laymen as well as from lawyers. A famous instance of lay criticism of the doctrine is an often-quoted passage from *Gulliver's Travels* by Jonathan Swift. "It is a maxim among * * * lawyers," says Gulliver, "that whatever hath been done before may legally be done again: and therefore they take special care to record all the decisions formerly made against common justice and the general reason of mankind. These, under the name of precedents, they produce as authorities to justify the most iniquitous opinions; and the judges never fail of directing accordingly." Some jurists and judges have likewise charged that the doctrine of precedent produces excessive conservatism.

Since adherence to the doctrine of precedent obviously tends to freeze the law and to preserve the *status quo,* it must be asked what the advantages and meritorious features of the doctrine are. We may list the following five positive factors in support of the *stare decisis* principle:

(1) The doctrine introduces a modicum of certainty and calculability into the planning of private and business activities. It enables people to engage in trade and arrange their personal affairs with a certain amount of confidence that they will not become entangled in litigation. It gives them some basis for predicting how other members of the community are likely to act toward them (assuming that such other members of the community comply with the law). Without this element of calculability, people would be uncertain of their rights, duties, and obligations, and they would be unable to ascertain what they might do without fear of coercive sanctions. Men would never know whether to settle or litigate a dispute if every established rule was liable to be overthrown from one day to the next, and litigation would be increased a thousandfold under such a state of affairs.

(2) *Stare decisis* provides attorneys counseling private parties with some settled basis for legal reasoning and the rendering of legal advice. A lawyer who does not have available to him the benefit of certain tools which are helpful to him in forecasting the probable outcome of litigation is of little use to his clients. In the words of Sir William Jones, "No man who is not a lawyer would ever know how to act and no lawyer would, in many instances, know how to advise, unless courts are bound by authority."

(3) The doctrine of *stare decisis* tends to operate as a curb on the arbitrariness of judges. It serves as a prop for weak and unstable judges who are inclined to be partial and prejudiced. By forcing them to follow (as a rule) established precedents, it reduces their temptation to render decisions colored by favor and bias. "If the doctrine of precedent were to be abolished in this country (where statutes have a relatively limited scope), the judges would be free to operate according to their individual whims and their private notions of right and wrong throughout the entire area of human relations not covered by statute." Such a condition would not be conducive to the maintenance of respect for the law and the preservation of public confidence in the integrity of

the judiciary. One important reason why people are willing to accept judicial decisions as binding is that they are supposed to be based on an objective body of law and on impersonal reasoning free from subjective predilections—even though this condition may not always be fully realized in the practical operation of the legal system.

(4) The practice of following prior decisions facilitates dispatch of judicial business and thereby promotes efficient judicial administration. Following precedents saves the time and conserves the energy of judges and at the same time reduces the costs of litigation for the parties. It makes it unnecessary for the court to examine a legal problem *de novo* each time the problem is presented again. "The labor of judges," said Mr. Justice Cardozo, "would be increased almost to the breaking point if every past decision could be reopened in every case, and one could not lay one's own course of bricks on the secure foundation of the courses laid by others who had gone before him."

(5) The doctrine of precedent also receives support from the human sense of justice. The force of precedent in the law is heightened, in the words of Karl Llewellyn, by "that curious, almost universal sense of justice which urges that all men are properly to be treated alike in like circumstances." If A was granted relief last month against an unwarranted interference with his privacy, it would be unjust to deny such relief to B this month if the facts shown by B are essentially the same as those that were presented by A a month ago.

In its relation to justice, however, the doctrine of precedent exhibits a weakness which has often been noted. A precedent controlling the decision of a court may be considered antiquated at the time when the problem arises again for decision. The prevailing notions of justice may have undergone a marked change in the interval between the earlier and the later decision. The first decision, reflecting perhaps the views of an earlier epoch of history, may have denied an action based on an invasion of the right to privacy. The decision may appear iniquitous to a modern judge, since our notions regarding infringement of personal privacy may in the meantime have become more sensitive and refined.

Assuming that there is a close relation between equality and justice, it must be realized that the equality contemplated by *stare decisis* is that between a *past* and a *present* decision. Justice, on the other hand, may require a modification of the standards of equality because of a change in social outlook. While *stare decisis* promotes equality in *time*, that is, equal treatment as between A litigating his case in 1760 and B obtaining a decision in a lawsuit occurring in 1960, justice may be more properly concerned with equality in *space*, with an equal treatment of two persons or two situations measured in terms of contemporary value judgments. Furthermore, the earlier decision may have been rendered by a weak or inept judge, so that considerations of justice and reasonableness might be adduced in favor of its overthrow on this ground.

What can the judge confronted with an outdated or unreasonable precedent do? May he disregard or set aside the precedent on the ground that it is repugnant to our contemporary notions of right and wrong? Or is he compelled to sacrifice justice to stability and adhere to the unwelcome precedent?

Prior to 1966, the highest courts of England and the United States took conflicting positions on this question. The British House of Lords decided in 1898 that it was absolutely bound by its own decisions. This principle was established in the case of London Street Tramways Co. v. London City Council, in which the House of Lords ruled that "a decision of this House upon a question of law is conclusive, and * * * nothing but an act of Parliament can set right that which is alleged to be wrong in a judgment of this House." In endeavoring to justify the rule, the Earl of Halsbury, who wrote the opinion in this case, made the following comments: "I do not deny that cases of individual hardship may arise, and there may be a current of opinion in the profession that such and such a judgment was erroneous; but what is that occasional interference with what is perhaps abstract justice as compared with the inconvenience—the disastrous inconvenience—of having each question subject to being reargued and the dealings of mankind rendered doubtful by reason of different decisions, so that in truth and in fact there would be no real final Court of Appeal?" In 1966, however, the House of Lords changed its position. Lord Chancellor Gardiner announced that "Their Lordships * * * recognize that too rigid adherence to precedent may lead to injustice in a particular case and also unduly restrict the proper development of the law. They propose, therefore, to modify their present practice and, while treating former decisions of this House as normally binding, to depart from a previous decision when it appears right to do so." [10]

In the United States, *stare decisis* has never been considered an inexorable command, and the duty to follow precedent is held to be qualified by the right to overrule prior decisions. Although the inferior courts within a certain precinct of jurisdiction are considered bound by the decisions of the intermediate or highest appellate courts, the highest courts of the states, as well as the supreme federal court, reserve to themselves the right to depart from a rule previously established by them. In the interest of legal security, however, they will not lightly make use of this prerogative. "Adherence to precedent should be the rule and not the exception," said Mr. Justice Cardozo. Mr. Justice Brandeis observed: "*Stare decisis* is usually the wise policy, because in most matters it is more

10. See [1966] Weekly Law Reports 1234, 110 Solicitor's Journal 584 (1966); W. Barton Leach, "Revisionism in the House of Lords," 80 Harvard Law Rev. 797 (1967).

important that the applicable rule be settled than that it be settled right." Nevertheless, the court will sometimes overrule its own decisions when it is necessary to avoid the perpetuation of pernicious error or where an earlier decision is wholly out of step with the exigencies of the time. On the whole, the United States Supreme Court will be less inclined to set aside a precedent which has become a well-established rule of property or commercial law than to overrule a case involving the validity of legislation under the federal Constitution. In the words of Chief Justice Stone, "The doctrine of *stare decisis,* however appropriate or even necessary at times, has only a limited application in the field of constitutional law." In this area, it is particularly important to keep the law in accord with the dynamic flow of the social order, since correction of constitutional decisions by means of legislation is practically impossible.

It would seem that the American attitude toward precedents is preferable to the policy followed by the English House of Lords prior to 1966. Since the maintenance of stability is not the only goal of the legal order, the judges should be given authority to set aside former decisions which are hopelessly obsolete or thoroughly ill-advised and contrary to the social welfare. "If judges have woefully misinterpreted the mores of their day or if the mores of their day are no longer those of ours, they ought not to tie, in helpless submission, the hands of their successors." The same elasticity should be allowed to the judges with respect to precedents which represent an anomaly, do not fit into the structure of the legal system as a whole, or are at odds with some of its guiding principles. This last point was emphasized by Justice Frankfurter in Helvering v. Hallock, where he wrote: "We recognize that *stare decisis* embodies an important social policy. It represents an element of continuity in law and is rooted in the psychological need to satisfy reasonable expectations. But *stare decisis* is a principle of policy and not a mechanical formula of adherence to the latest decision, however recent and questionable, when such adherence involves collision with a prior doctrine more embracing in its scope, intrinsically sounder, and verified by experience." In granting courts the right to overrule their decisions, it should be made clear, however, that in exercising this right they should make certain that less harm will be done by rejecting a previous rule than by retaining it, even though the rule may be a questionable one. In every case involving the abandonment of an established precedent, the interest in a stable and continuous order of law must be carefully balanced against the advantages of improvement and innovation.

RODRIGUEZ v. BETHLEHEM STEEL CORP.

Supreme Court of California, 1974.
12 Cal.3d 382, 115 Cal.Rptr. 765, 525 P.2d 669 (footnotes
omitted except as indicated).

[Richard and Mary Anne Rodriguez were married in 1969. Both were gainfully employed. They wanted children and planned to raise a large family. Sixteen months after their marriage, their young lives were shattered by a grave accident. While at work, Richard was struck on the head by a falling pipe weighing over 600 pounds. The blow caused severe spinal cord damage which left him totally paralyzed in both legs and in his body below the midpoint of the chest. He lost his bladder and bowel control and his capacity for sexual intercourse. Because he needed assistance in virtually every activity of daily living, Mary Anne gave up her job and undertook his care on a 24–hour basis. She sued Richard's employer for loss of consortium, i.e., for loss of conjugal fellowship and sexual relations.

The trial court dismissed the complaint on the authority of Deshotel v. Atchison T. & S.F. Ry. Co., 50 Cal.2d 664, 328 P.2d 449 (1960). In that case, the California Supreme Court held that a married person whose spouse had been injured by the negligence of a third party had no cause of action for loss of consortium. The court stated that "the granting of relief to the wife for loss of consortium caused by negligent injury to her husband would constitute an extension of common law liability, and the courts are justifiably reluctant to depart from established limitations on recovery." This and other reasons advanced by the *Deshotel* court in favor of its ruling are discussed in the following excerpts from Justice Mosk's opinion for the California Supreme Court in *Rodriguez*:]

STARE DECISIS AND THE ROLE OF THE LEGISLATURE

The principal reliance of the *Deshotel* court was on two related arguments broadly applicable to any proposed change in judge-made law. In the light of recent legal history it will be seen that both arguments have outlived their time.

First and foremost, the *Deshotel* court emphasized that the "overwhelming weight of authority" supports the common law rule, and "the courts are justifiably reluctant to depart from established limitations on recovery." (50 Cal.2d at pp. 667, 669, 328 P.2d at p. 451.) In the 16 years since *Deshotel* was decided, however, there has been a dramatic reversal in the weight of authority on this question. At the time of *Deshotel* the majority of the states denied the wife the right to recover for loss of consortium, while that right was recognized in only five jurisdictions. Today those 5 have grown in number to at least 31. In 26 of these jurisdictions the change was brought about by judicial decision, while in 5 it was accomplished by statute. Four states appear to have taken no definitive position on the question. There remain 2 states with statutes which have been construed to deny by implication the right of the wife to recover for loss of consortium, and only 13 which, like California, reached that result by judicial decision. The authority of these 13, moreover, is considerably weakened by two factors: a number of the courts express support for the rule allowing recovery by the wife but thus far feel bound to await legislative action on the subject, while others rely heavily on a long line of decisions of their sister jurisdictions which have since been overruled.

* * *

As the Massachusetts court observed, "We should be mindful of the trend although our decision is not reached by a process of following the crowd." (Diaz v. Eli Lilly and Company (Mass.1973), supra, 302 N.E.2d 555, 561.) Quantitative at first, the trend took a qualitative leap when the American Law Institute reversed its position on the subject not long ago. Consonant with prior law, section 695 of the first Restatement of Torts, published in 1938, had declared that a wife was not entitled to recover for any harm caused to any of her marital interests by one who negligently injured her husband. In 1969, however, at a time when the weight of authority was still slightly against such recovery—although the trend was running in its favor—the institute adopted a new section 695, declaring in relevant part that "One who by reason of his tortious conduct is liable to a husband for illness or other bodily harm is also subject to liability to his wife for resulting loss of his society, including any impairment of his capacity for sexual intercourse. * * *" (Rest.2d Torts (Tent.Draft No. 14, Apr. 15, 1969) § 695, adopted May 21, 1969 (Proceedings of American Law Inst. (46th Annual Meeting, 1969) pp. 148–157).[13]

In these circumstances we may fairly conclude that the precedential foundation of *Deshotel* has been not only undermined but destroyed. In its place a new common law rule has arisen, granting either spouse the right to recover for loss of consortium caused by negligent injury to the other spouse. Accordingly, to adopt that rule in California at this time would not constitute, as the court feared in *Deshotel* (50 Cal.2d at p. 667, 328 P.2d 449), an "extension" of common law liability, but rather a *recognition* of that liability as it is currently understood by the large preponderance of our sister states and a consensus of distinguished legal scholars.

The second principal rationale of the *Deshotel* opinion (at pp. 668–669 of 50 Cal.2d, 328 P.2d 449, 452) was that any departure from the then-settled rule denying the wife recovery for loss of consortium

---

13. Section 693 of both the first and second Restatements recognizes an identical right of the husband to recover for loss of his wife's consortium, but includes liability for loss of her services as well.

"should be left to legislative action," and defendants in the case at bar echo that plea. But in the years since *Deshotel* the argument has fared badly in our decisions. As we summarized in People v. Pierce (1964), supra, 61 Cal.2d 879, 882, 40 Cal.Rptr. 845, 847, 395 P.2d 893, 895, "In effect the contention is a request that courts of law abdicate their responsibility for the upkeep of the common law. That upkeep it needs continuously, as this case demonstrates."

The judicial responsibility to which we referred in *Pierce* arises from the role of the courts in a common law system. In California as in other jurisdictions of Anglo–American heritage, the common law "is not a codification of exact or inflexible rules for human conduct, for the redress of injuries, or for protection against wrongs, but is rather the embodiment of broad and comprehensive unwritten principles, inspired by natural reason and an innate sense of justice, and adopted by common consent for the regulation and government of the affairs of men.

* * *

"The inherent capacity of the common law for growth and change is its most significant feature. Its development has been determined by the social needs of the community which it serves. It is constantly expanding and developing in keeping with advancing civilization and the new conditions and progress of society, and adapting itself to the gradual change of trade, commerce, arts, inventions, and the needs of the country." (Fns. omitted.) (15 Am.Jur.2d, Common Law, §§ 1, 2, pp. 794–796.)

* * *

While the courts of California have long exercised this power to insure the just and rational development of the common law in our state (see, e.g., Katz v. Walkinshaw (1903), 141 Cal. 116, 123–124, 70 P. 663, 74 P. 766), it is perhaps since *Deshotel* that the independence of the judicial branch in this regard has been most firmly asserted.

* * *

[The court summarizes the post-*Deshotel* cases in which it abolished several long-standing common law tort rules, including the doctrine of governmental immunity and the rules limiting a landowner's duty of care for dangerous conditions on the premises.]

* * *

The rule denying the wife recovery for loss of consortium is no less a judicial creation than any of the foregoing. Recognizing this fact, the highest courts of our sister states have time and again rejected, since *Deshotel,* the argument that the rule can be changed only by legislative action.

* * *

Thus in Montgomery v. Stephan (1960), supra, 359 Mich. 33, 101 N.W.2d 227, 229, the Michigan Supreme Court observed that "Were we to rule upon precedent alone, were stability the only reason for our being, we would have no trouble with this case. We would simply tell the woman to begone, and to take her shattered husband with her, that we need no longer be affronted by a sight so repulsive. In so doing we would have vast support from the dusty books. But dust the decision would remain in our mouths through the years ahead, a reproach to law and conscience alike. Our oath is to do justice, not to perpetuate error." The court rejected the precedents denying recovery for loss of consortium as "out of harmony with the conditions of modern society. They do violence to our convictions and our principles. We reject their applicability. The reasons for the old rule no longer obtaining, the rule falls with it. The obstacles to the wife's action were judge-invented and they are herewith judge-destroyed." (Id. at p. 235.)

* * *

We agree with this reasoning. Whatever may have been the correct approach at the time of *Deshotel*, the question today is whether the rule against recovery for loss of consortium should survive on its merits as a judicially declared principle of our tort law. If upon further analysis it appears the remaining reasons given in *Deshotel* no longer support that rule—no new reasons are suggested by the parties to this appeal—we shall have no hesitation in abrogating it. Such a step would not be a usurpation of legislative authority, but a reaffirmation of our high responsibility to renew the common law of California when it is necessary and proper to do so.

* * *

The final argument advanced in *Deshotel* is that a judicial recognition of the wife's cause of action for loss of consortium would operate retroactively and "might work hardship upon persons who, in reliance upon the common law rule, have made settlement with the husband, believing that the wife could not sue." (50 Cal.2d at p. 668, 328 P.2d at p. 451.) This argument, too, has been rejected in many of the post-*Deshotel* decisions allowing recovery for loss of consortium.

The solution of the majority of the other courts, which we adopt, is simply to declare that for reasons of fairness and sound administration a spouse will not be permitted to initiate an action for loss of consortium—even though not barred by the statute of limitations—when the action of the other spouse for the negligent or intentional injury giving rise to such loss was concluded by settlement or judgment prior to the effective date of this decision. (Deems v. Western Maryland Railway Company (1967), supra, 247 Md. 95, 231 A.2d 514, 525; Diaz v. Eli Lilly and Company (Mass.1973), supra, 302 N.E.2d 555, 564; Ekalo v. Constructive Serv. Corp. of Am. (1965), supra, 46 N.J. 82, 215 A.2d 1, 8; Millington v. Southeastern Elevator Co. (1968), supra, 22 N.Y.2d 498, 293 N.Y.S.2d 305, 312, 239 N.E.2d 897, 902; but see Kotsiris v. Ling

(Ky.1970), supra, 451 S.W.2d 411, 413; Shepherd v. Consumers Cooperative Association (Mo.1964), 384 S.W.2d 635, 638–640.) [30]

We therefore overrule Deshotel v. Atchison, T. & S.F. Ry. Co. (1958), supra, 50 Cal.2d 664, 328 P.2d 449, and West v. City of San Diego (1960), supra, 54 Cal.2d 469, 475–478, 6 Cal.Rptr. 289, 353 P.2d 929, and declare that in California each spouse has a cause of action for loss of consortium, as defined herein, caused by a negligent or intentional injury to the other spouse by a third party.

It follows that the court below erred in sustaining the general demurrers to the second cause of action of the complaint, and the judgment of dismissal as to Mary Anne must be reversed.

WRIGHT, C.J., and TOBRINER, BURKE, SULLIVAN and CLARK, JJ., concur.

McCOMB, JUSTICE (dissenting).

I dissent. I adhere to the view that any change in the law denying the wife recovery for loss of consortium should be left to legislative action. (Deshotel v. Atchison, T. & S.F. Ry. Co., 50 Cal.2d 664, 669, 328 P.2d 449.)

NOTE BY THE EDITORS

In the subsequent trial of Richard and Mary Anne Rodriguez's cases, the jury returned a verdict of $500,000 in Mary Anne's action for loss of consortium and a verdict of $4,235,996 in Richard's action for his personal injuries.

C. THE PROBLEM OF RETROACTIVITY

When a court is persuaded that one of its own precedents would be unjust or irrational to apply in the current state of affairs, it may find itself facing a new dilemma of justice. Ordinarily a court does not sit back and review its accumulated precedents, discarding those found obsolete or unwise. The continuing authority of a precedent is an issue raised in the course of litigation, and the litigant who asks a court to overrule its precedent is, in effect, asking for the rules to be changed while the game is in progress. At least where a change in law prejudices a private individual rather than the government or some public entity, the moral and political tradition of Western civilization condemns most instances of the retrospective application of law as

---

30. It is probable that few if any such claims exist in any event, as serious injury cases are rarely settled or brought to judgment within one year after the occurrence of the injury, the governing period of limitations (Code Civ.Proc., § 340, subd. 3). With the exception of such cases, all claims for loss of consortium not barred by the statute of limitations may now be asserted: for the reasons persuasively stated in Fitzgerald v. Meissner & Hicks, Inc. (1968), supra, 38 Wis.2d 571, 157 N.W.2d 595, 598–599, our decision herein is to be given normal retroactive effect within the limits of the statute of limitations.

fundamentally unfair. People should, in principle, have the opportunity to inform themselves of the law and to conform their conduct to it in advance of incurring any liability.

This tradition is strongest with regard to rules of the criminal law, and the "ex post facto" clauses of Article I of the federal Constitution forbid either the federal or the state governments from giving criminal laws retroactive (also called retrospective) application. The constitutional constraints on retroactive application of laws affecting civil liabilities are somewhat weaker, but (as noted earlier) it nonetheless remains a general feature of legislation that it is enacted for prospective effect only—that is, it regulates only conduct which occurs after the date of enactment (or later effective date if the statute so specifies).

The decisions of judges may, of course, surprise the parties in many cases which do not overrule prior case law, but rather reach a decision on a particular subject for the first time, thereby filling in a gap in the pre-existing web of legislation and case law. In this situation, where the adverse parties to the law suit cannot have acted in reliance on the sort of authoritative pronouncement of the law which would have existed had there been a judicial precedent squarely in point, there has been little consternation among judges in applying their gap-filling decision retroactively; this means disposing of the case at hand even though that case involves conduct previous to their articulation of the authoritative and dispositive rule of law.

The truly difficult dilemma occurs when there is already an authoritative and dispositive rule of law in the form of a judicial precedent, but when that precedent is no longer just or rational given subsequent developments in the legal system and the society it serves. On the one hand, injustice will occur if the disfavored precedent is applied to dispose of the case at hand; on the other hand, a different sort of injustice will occur if the disfavored precedent is discarded and new law is applied retroactively to penalize individual conduct which was legally proper under the prior rule.

The traditional judicial solution to this problem consisted of giving overruling decisions retroactive application in fact, while avowing in principle that the law was not being applied retroactively at all. The central proposition of this solution was that the overruled precedent was mistaken, was never the law, and was therefore mistakenly relied upon by the losing litigant.

THE GRAVES CASE

This solution is well illustrated by People ex rel. Rice v. Graves, 242 A.D. 128, 273 N.Y.S. 582 (1934). In 1928, the United States Supreme Court had decided that a state had no right to tax income from copyright royalties. Long v. Rockwood, 277 U.S. 142, 48 S.Ct. 463, 72 L.Ed. 824 (1928). In 1932, this decision had been overruled. Fox

Film Corp. v. Doyal, 286 U.S. 123, 52 S.Ct. 546, 76 L.Ed. 1010 (1932). During the years 1928–1932, Elmer Rice, a dramatist living in New York, had received large royalties from his plays on which he had paid no New York income tax. In *People v. Graves*, the New York authorities demanded three years' back taxes from Mr. Rice on these royalties. The New York court, supporting the tax authorities, held Mr. Rice liable not only for the back taxes, but also for the payment of interest at six percent for being late. The court justified its decision on the following basis:

> The effect to be given to the action of a court of last resort, when it reverses itself, is a subject which has given rise to prolific litigation and has for centuries furnished a theme for philosophical discussion by jurists and text-writers. Out of the age-old discussion there have been developed two fundamentally opposing theories. According to one theory the decisions of the courts are always conclusive evidence of what the law is. Followers of the other school assert that the decisions are evidence, but not conclusive evidence, of the law. * * *

> A natural desire for stability in the law gave rise to a reliance on decided cases as far back as Bracton and the early Year Books of the fourteenth century. According to the orthodox theory of Blackstone, which still claims at least the nominal allegiance of most courts, a judicial decision is merely evidence of the law, not law itself; and when a decision is overruled, it does not become bad law; it never was the law, and the discredited decision will be viewed as if it had never been and the reconsidered pronouncement regarded as law from the beginning. Despite the expressed disapproval of some courts of repute and certain eminent writers, the prevailing doctrine is not that the law is changed by the overruling decision, but that the court was mistaken in its former decision, and that the law is, and always was, as expounded in the later decision. It should be said, however, that many leading English and American writers on jurisprudence characterize this theory of law as childish fiction and champion the doctrine that the rules which the judicial organs of the state lay down in deciding cases constitute law. However, according to the great weight of authority the theory that courts make law is unsound. The courts do not make law, but simply declare law. A judicial decision is but evidence of the law. An overruling decision does not change law, but impeaches the overruled decision as evidence of law. Adopting the theory that courts merely declare preexisting law, it logically follows that an overruling decision operates retroactively. Courts have generally given retroactive effect to decisions which have overruled earlier precedents.

* * *

> Salmond, in his work on Jurisprudence (8th Ed.) p. 197, in discussing the retrospective effect of a later decision said: "The overruling of a precedent is not the abolition of an established rule of law; it is an authoritative denial that the supposed rule of law has ever existed. The precedent is so treated not because it has made bad law, but

because it has never in reality made any law at all. Hence it is that the overruling of a precedent, unlike the repeal of a statute, has retrospective operation. The decision is pronounced to have been bad ab initio. A repealed statute, on the contrary remains valid and applicable as to matters arising before the date of its repeal. The overruling of a precedent is analogous not to the repeal of a statute, but to the judicial rejection of a custom as unreasonable or as otherwise failing to conform to the requirements of customary law. * * *"

* * *

We have not overlooked the relator's contention that a retrospective application of the decision in the Fox Film Case works an apparent hardship as to him. We concede as much. The answer to that argument, however, is that the hardship in question is no greater on the relator than was that suffered by the state by the erroneous decision in Long v. Rockwood. The ruling in that case deprived the state of revenue to which it was justly entitled. The construction in the instant case involves no hardship upon the relator beyond the payment of those taxes which he would have been required to pay in any event had the discredited decision in Long v. Rockwood never have [sic] been made.

[242 A.D. 130–133, 134–135, 273 N.Y.S. 586, 587, 588, 591.]

THE SUNBURST CASE

The converse approach to People v. Graves, one of complete prospectivity rather than complete retroactivity, was adopted by the Montana Supreme Court in the contemporaneous cases of Montana Horse Products Co. v. Great Northern Rwy. Co., 91 Mont. 194, 7 P.2d 919 (1932), and Sunburst Oil and Refining Co. v. Great Northern Rwy. Co., 91 Mont. 216, 7 P.2d 927 (1932). In both of these cases the shipper had paid freight charges which were later established, upon the shipper's complaint to the Montana Railroad Commission, to have been unreasonably high. The Commission, which under state law had the power to control railroad tariffs, in each case had ordered the rates reduced. The shippers had then filed suit in state court for refunds of the difference between the rates they had paid and the new rates established by the Commission. The trial courts had awarded the refunds on the authority of the Montana Supreme Court's decision in Doney v. Northern Pacific Rwy. Co., 60 Mont. 209, 199 P. 432 (1921), which had expressly held that shippers could sue for refunds of freight charges paid to railroads which were later held by the Commission to have been excessive. On Great Northern's appeals of these two judgments awarding refunds, the Supreme Court of Montana held that *Doney*'s rule of law regarding refunds was ill-advised, and *Doney* was pro tanto overruled. (The Latin phrase "pro tanto" literally means "by so much"; in this context it means "in this respect.") The chief reason for overruling *Doney* was that the railroad commission's act of establishing new and lower rates was deemed to be a quasi-legislative act operative only in the future, so that the excess paid by the shippers in the past was not subject to refund.

Because the shippers had relied upon the *Doney* refund rule in paying rates subject to a later suit for a refund, and because *Doney* had similarly put railroads on notice that they might have to make refunds of charges subsequently found by the Commission to have been unreasonable, the Montana Supreme Court decided to make its decision to overrule the *Doney* refund rule purely prospective. In both cases the trial court's award of the refund was affirmed. Although the *Doney* rule was abrogated, that change in the law was not applied to the cases in which the change was announced.

For reasons that are not known, only one of these Montana cases was appealed to the United States Supreme Court. In Great Northern Rwy. Co. v. Sunburst Oil and Refining Co., 287 U.S. 358, 53 S.Ct. 145, 77 L.Ed. 360 (1932), the railroad argued that the traditional rule of complete retroactivity (such as applied in *People v. Graves*) was constitutionally required as part of the "due process of law" required of the states by the 14th Amendment to the federal Constitution. The Court rejected this argument in an opinion by Mr. Justice Cardozo which can now be seen as the beginning of the modern trend away from unlimited retroactivity of case law.

* * * This is not a case where a court in overruling an earlier decision has given to the new ruling a retroactive bearing, and thereby has made invalid what was valid in the doing. Even that may often be done, though litigants not infrequently have argued to the contrary. This is a case where a court has refused to make its ruling retroactive, and the novel stand is taken that the constitution of the United States is infringed by the refusal.

We think the federal constitution has no voice upon the subject. A state in defining the limits of adherence to precedent may make a choice for itself between the principle of forward operation and that of relation backward. It may say that decisions of its highest court, though later overruled, are law none the less for intermediate transactions. Indeed there are cases intimating, too broadly, that it *must* give them that effect; but never has doubt been expressed that it *may* so treat them if it pleases, whenever injustice or hardship will thereby be averted. On the other hand, it may hold to the ancient dogma that the law declared by its courts had a Platonic or ideal existence before the act of declaration, in which event the discredited declaration will be viewed as if it had never been, and the reconsidered declaration as law from the beginning. The alternative is the same whether the subject of the new decision is common law or statute. The choice for any state may be determined by the juristic philosophy of the judges of her courts, their conceptions of law, its origin and nature. We review not the wisdom of their philosophies, but the legality of their acts. The

State of Montana has told us by the voice of her highest court that with these alternative methods open to her, her preference is for the first. In making this choice, she is declaring common law for those within her borders. The common law as administered by her judges ascribes to the decisions of her highest court a power to bind and loose that is unextinguished, for intermediate transactions, by a decision overruling them. As applied to such transactions we may say of the earlier decision that it has not been overruled at all. It has been translated into a judgment of affirmance and recognized as law anew. Accompanying the recognition is a prophecy, which may or may not be realized in conduct, that transactions arising in the future will be governed by a different rule. If this is the common law doctrine of adherence to precedent as understood and enforced by the courts of Montana, we are not at liberty, for anything contained in the constitution of the United States, to thrust upon those courts a different conception either of the binding force of precedent or of the meaning of the judicial process.

[287 U.S. at 363–366, 53 S.Ct. at 148–149 (citations and footnotes omitted).]

THE LINKLETTER CASE

The problem with the doctrine of complete retroactivity articulated in *People v. Graves* is that it ignores what may have been quite legitimate reliance on the existing law as authoritatively declared by the courts—as might occur, for instance, if people lent money to a child, or a corporation, or a state agency, in reliance on an authoritative decision, later overruled, that such a loan gave rise to an enforceable debt. The opposite problem with the doctrine of complete prospectivity found constitutional in *Sunburst* is that a litigant who has succeeded in showing that a prior decision was wrong gets only the cold comfort that future litigants will not suffer the injustice of having the bad precedent applied to their detriment—the overruled case is applied, one last time, to the very litigant who has demonstrated its injustice. In a case like *Sunburst*, where the railroad was likely to be the future litigant most benefitted by the prospective overruling of *Doney*, the railroad cannot be said to have suffered any great harm. But in a more typical sort of case where the litigant incurs substantial personal expense in successfully demonstrating why a precedent should be overruled, the only incentive for doing so is the hope of reaping the immediate benefit of the change in law.

This has led the federal courts, and many state courts, to adopt an intermediate rule of limited retroactivity, whereby the successful litigant in the case in which prior law is overruled does get the benefit of that decision, but the retroactive effect of the overruling on other litigants is not automatic. Generally the change in law is also made applicable to all other lawsuits still in the process of litigation at the time the change in law is announced, and the hard question then becomes whether the change in law is also applicable to litigation already terminated. This is principally a problem with respect to the constitutional rights of persons convicted of crimes, because criminal convictions, unlike judgments of civil liability, remain subject to reexamination if it can later be shown that the convictions were obtained in violation of the defendants' constitutional rights.

It was in this context that the United States Supreme Court considered, in Linkletter v. Walker, 381 U.S. 618, 85 S.Ct. 1731, 14 L.Ed.2d 601 (1965), whether state prisoners convicted through the use of illegally seized evidence were all entitled to new trials, even if their convictions had become final before the United States Supreme Court held, in Mapp v. Ohio, 367 U.S. 643, 81 S.Ct. 1684, 6 L.Ed.2d 1081 (1961), that illegally seized evidence was inadmissible in state criminal prosecutions. As the following excerpts show, Mr. Justice Clark's opinion for the Court in *Linkletter* sought to place the problem of *Mapp*'s retroactivity in jurisprudential perspective before describing the elements of a balancing test to determine questions of retroactivity.

Initially we must consider the term "retrospective" for the purposes of our opinion. A ruling which is purely prospective does not apply even to the parties before the court. See, e.g., England v. Louisiana State Board of Medical Examiners, 375 U.S. 411 (1964). See also Great Northern R. Co. v. Sunburst Oil & Refining Co., 287 U.S. 358 (1932). However, we are not here concerned with pure prospectivity since we applied the rule announced in *Mapp* to reverse Miss Mapp's conviction. That decision has also been applied to cases still pending on direct review at the time it was rendered. Therefore, in this case, we are concerned only with whether the exclusionary principle enunciated in *Mapp* applies to state court convictions which had become final before rendition of our opinion.

While to some it may seem "academic" it might be helpful to others for us to briefly outline the history and theory of the problem presented.

At common law there was no authority for the proposition that judicial decisions made law only for the future. Blackstone stated the rule that the duty of the court was not to "pronounce a new law, but to maintain and expound the old one." 1 Blackstone, Commentaries 69 (15th ed. 1809). This Court followed that rule in Norton v. Shelby County, 118 U.S. 425 (1886), holding that unconstitutional action "confers no rights; it imposes no duties; it affords no protection; it creates no office; it is, in legal contemplation, as inoperative as though it had never been passed." At 442. The judge rather than being the creator of the law was but its discoverer. Gray, Nature and Sources of the Law 222 (1st ed. 1909). In the case of the overruled decision, Wolf v. Colorado, supra, here, it was thought to be only a failure at true discovery and was consequently never the law; while the overruling one, *Mapp*, was not "new law but an application of what is, and thereto fore had been, the true law." Shulman, Retroactive Legislation, 13 Encyclopaedia of the Social Sciences 355, 356 (1934).

On the other hand, Austin maintained that judges do in fact do something more than discover law; they make it interstitially by filling in with judicial interpretation the vague, indefinite, or generic statutory or common-law terms that alone are but the empty crevices of the law. Implicit in such an approach is the admission when a case is overruled that the earlier decision was wrongly decided. However, rather than being erased by the later overruling decision it is considered as an existing juridical fact until overruled, and intermediate cases finally decided under it are not to be disturbed.

The Blackstonian view ruled English jurisprudence and cast its shadow over our own as evidenced by Norton v. Shelby County, supra. However, some legal philosophers continued to insist that such a rule was out of tune with actuality largely because judicial repeal ofttime did "work hardship to those who [had] trusted to its existence." Cardozo, Address to the N.Y. Bar Assn., 55 Rep.N.Y. State Bar Assn. 263, 296–297 (1932). The Austinian view gained some acceptance over a hundred years ago when it was decided that although legislative divorces were illegal and void, those previously granted were immunized by a prospective application of the rule of the case. Bingham v. Miller, 17 Ohio 445 (1848). And as early as 1863 this Court drew on the same concept in Gelpcke v. Dubuque, 1 Wall. 175 (1863). The Supreme Court of Iowa had repeatedly held that the Iowa Legislature had the power to authorize municipalities to issue bonds to aid in the construction of railroads. After the City of Dubuque had issued such bonds, the Iowa Supreme Court reversed itself and held that the legislature lacked such power. In *Gelpcke,* which arose after the overruling decision, this Court held that the bonds issued under the apparent authority granted by the legislature were collectible. "However we may regard the late [overruling] case in Iowa as affecting the future, it can have no effect upon the past." At 206. The theory was, as Mr. Justice Holmes stated in Kuhn v. Fairmont Coal Co., 215 U.S. 349, 371 (1910), "that a change of judicial decision after a contract has been made on the faith of an earlier one the other way is a change of the law." And in 1932 Mr. Justice Cardozo in Great Northern R. Co. v. Sunburst Oil & Refining Co., 287 U.S. 358, applied the Austinian approach in denying a federal constitutional due process attack on the prospective application of a decision of the Montana Supreme Court. He said that a State "may make a choice for itself between the principle of forward operation and that of relation backward." At 364. Mr. Justice Cardozo based the rule on the avoidance of "injustice or hardship" citing a long list of state and federal cases supporting the principle that the courts had the power to say that decisions though later overruled "are law none the less for intermediate transactions." At 364. Eight years later Chief Justice Hughes in Chicot County Drainage Dist. v. Baxter State Bank, 308 U.S. 371 (1940), in discussing the problem made it clear that the broad statements of *Norton,* supra, "must be taken with qualifications." He reasoned that the actual existence of the law prior to the determination of unconstitutionality "is an operative fact and may have consequences which cannot justly be ignored. The past cannot always be erased by a new judicial declaration." He laid down the rule that the "effect of the subsequent ruling as to invalidity may have to be considered in various aspects." At 374.

* * *

Under our cases it appears (1) that a change in law will be given effect while a case is on direct review, *Schooner Peggy,* supra, and (2) that the effect of the subsequent ruling of invalidity on prior final judgments when collaterally attacked is subject to no set "principle of absolute retroactive invalidity" but depends upon a consideration of "particular relations * * * and particular conduct[,] * * * of rights claimed to have become vested, of status, of prior determinations deemed to have finality"; and "of public policy in the light of the nature both of the statute and of its previous application." Chicot County Drainage Dist. v. Baxter State Bank, supra, at 374.

That no distinction was drawn between civil and criminal litigation is shown by the language used not only in *Schooner Peggy,* supra, and *Chicot County,* supra, but also in such cases as State v. Jones, 44 N.M. 623, 107 P.2d 324 (1940) and James v. United States, 366 U.S. 213 (1961). In the latter case, this Court laid down a prospective principle in overruling Commissioner v. Wilcox, 327 U.S. 404 (1946), "in a manner that will not prejudice those who might have relied on it." At 221. * * * Thus, the accepted rule today is that in appropriate cases the Court may in the interest of justice make the rule prospective. And "there is much to be said in favor of such a rule for cases arising in the future." Mosser v. Darrow, 341 U.S. 267, at 276 (dissenting opinion of Black, J.).

While the cases discussed above deal with the invalidity of statutes or the effect of a decision overturning long-established common-law rules, there seems to be no impediment—constitutional or philosophical—to the use of the same rule in the constitutional area where the exigencies of the situation require such an application. It is true that heretofore, without discussion, we have applied new constitutional rules to cases finalized before the promulgation of the rule. Petitioner contends that our method of resolving those prior cases demonstrates that an absolute rule of retroaction prevails in the area of constitutional adjudication. However, we believe that the Constitution neither prohibits nor requires retrospective effect. As Justice Cardozo said, "We think the federal constitution has no voice upon the subject."

Once the premise is accepted that we are neither required to apply, nor prohibited from applying, a decision retrospectively, we must then weigh the merits and demerits in each case by looking to the prior history of the rule in question, its purpose and effect, and whether retrospective operation will further or retard its operation. We believe that this approach is particularly correct with reference to the Fourth Amendment's prohibitions as to unreasonable searches and seizures. Rather than "disparaging" the Amendment we but apply the wisdom of Justice Holmes that "[t]he life of the law has not been logic: it has been experience." Holmes, The Common Law 5 (Howe ed. 1963).

* * *

Nor can we accept the contention of petitioner that the *Mapp* rule should date from the day of the seizure there, rather than that of the judgment of this Court. The date of the seizure in *Mapp* has no legal significance. It was the judgment of this Court that changed the rule and the date of that opinion is the crucial date. In the light of the cases of this Court this is the better cutoff time. See United States v. Schooner Peggy, supra.

All that we decide today is that though the error complained of might be fundamental it is not of the nature requiring us to overturn all final convictions based upon it. After full consideration of all the factors we are not able to say that the *Mapp* rule requires retrospective application.

[381 U.S. at 621–625, 627, 628–629, 639–640, 85 S.Ct. at 1733–1735, 1736–1738, 1743–1744.]

DEVELOPMENTS SINCE LINKLETTER

A close reading of *Linkletter* suggests that the flexible rule on retroactivity enunciated by the Court was meant to apply only to situations where the judgment of a court had become final[2] and was subsequently challenged on collateral attack, perhaps by way of a habeas corpus petition presenting newly-discovered evidence tending to show the use of perjured testimony at the trial. The Court seemed to say, on the other hand, that a new rule of constitutional law changing the previous law should be applied to all cases on direct review that had not become final at the time the change of law was made.

However, in Johnson v. New Jersey, 384 U.S. 719, 86 S.Ct. 1772, 16 L.Ed.2d 882 (1966), the Court decided that the flexible *Linkletter* test should be used to determine the retroactivity of a new ruling to final as well as nonfinal decisions. The *Linkletter* test was reformulated so as to require the Court, in making a decision on retroactivity, to consider three factors: (1) the purpose to be served by the new standards, (2) the extent of reliance by law enforcement officers on the old standards, and (3) the effect on the administration of justice of a retroactive application of the new standards. 384 U.S. at 727, 86 S.Ct. at 1777; see also Stovall v. Denno, 388 U.S. 293, at 297, 87 S.Ct. 1967, at 1970 (1967). This test was subsequently referred to by the Court as the "three-pronged test."

In United States v. Johnson, 457 U.S. 537, 102 S.Ct. 2579, 73 L.Ed. 2d 202 (1982), the Court returned to its original *Linkletter* position, according to which the three-pronged test was to be applied only to the question whether a new ruling should be made retroactive to final decisions. A change in law, on the other hand, was to be given effect

2. "Final" means that a judgment has been rendered, the availability of appeal has been exhausted, and the time for a petition for certiorari has elapsed (or a petition for certiorari has been denied).

while a case was on direct review. This latter rule was, however, made subject to an exception. If a new rule could be classified as a "clear break with the past," it was to be applied only prospectively, except that it would be applied to the parties in the lawsuit which produced the new rule. This exception was repealed by the Court in Griffith v. Kentucky, ___ U.S. ___, 107 S.Ct. 708, 93 L.Ed.2d 649 (1987), on the grounds that the exception obviates an evenhanded administration of the retroactivity rule to defendants who are in an essentially similar position. The rule presently in effect was stated by the Court as follows: "A new rule for the conduct of criminal prosecutions is to be applied retroactively to all cases, state or federal, pending on direct review or not yet final, with no exception for cases in which the new rule constitutes a 'clear break with the past.'" 107 S.Ct. at 716.

Although *Linkletter* stated that no distinction has been drawn by the Court between civil and criminal litigation, Justice Blackmun pointed out in *United States v. Johnson,* supra, that questions of civil retroactivity are governed by the standard announced in Chevron Oil Co. v. Huson, 404 U.S. 97, at 106–107, 92 S.Ct. 349, at 355, 30 L.Ed.2d 296 (1971). According to this decision, three factors will be considered in dealing with retroactivity questions in civil litigation. First, the decision to be applied nonretroactively must establish a new principle of law, either by overruling clear past precedent on which litigants may have relied, or by deciding an issue of first impression whose resolution was not clearly foreshadowed. Second, the merits and demerits of each case must be weighed by looking to the prior history of the rule in question, its purpose and effect, and whether retrospective operation will further or retard its operation. (This was the language used in *Linkletter* to determine retroactivity in criminal procedure cases.) Finally a decision should be made nonretroactive if retroactivity would produce substantial inequities.

Problems

The Supreme Court has held that, in determining the retroactivity of new rulings in criminal procedure with respect to final judgments, particular weight should be given to the question whether "the new rule affected the very integrity of the fact-finding process and the clear danger of convicting the innocent." *Johnson v. New Jersey,* supra. Using this test in conjunction with the "three-pronged" test, do you think that the following two decisions should be given complete retroactive effect, so that even convictions that had become final by the time of the decision would be rendered invalid?

(1) In Gideon v. Wainwright, 372 U.S. 335, 83 S.Ct. 792, 9 L.Ed.2d 799 (1963), the Supreme Court recognized a right to the appointment of counsel for indigent defendants in felony cases. An earlier decision had held that the states were under an obligation to assign counsel to such defendants only under special circumstances, taking into account particularly the gravity of the crime and the complexity of the legal

issues. Assume that the large majority of states, including the most populous ones, had recognized, prior to the Supreme Court decision, a right to the appointment of counsel for indigents under their state constitutions.

(2) In Griffin v. California, 380 U.S. 609, 85 S.Ct. 1229, 14 L.Ed.2d 106 (1965), the Supreme Court struck down a rule, accepted in a handful of states, that allowed prosecutors and judges to comment on the failure of the defendant in a criminal trial to take the stand and testify.

Further References

Cardozo, B.N., *The Nature of the Judicial Process* (1921), pp. 142–167.

Douglas, W.O., "Stare Decisis," 49 Columbia Law Review 735 (1949).

Dworkin, R.M., *Taking Rights Seriously* (1977), Chapters 2–4.

Reynolds, W.L., *Judicial Process* (1980), pp. 73–191.

Schaefer, W.V., "Prospective Rulings: Two Perspectives," 1982 *Supreme Court Review* 1.

Schauer, F., "Precedent," 39 Stanford Law Review 571 (1987).

Chapter IV

THE RATIO DECIDENDI
OF A CASE

A. OVERVIEW

The permutations of the doctrine of stare decisis and the problem of the retroactivity of decisions overruling precedent bear directly upon the rigor with which courts will examine a prior case to determine if it arose upon distinguishable facts, and upon the expansiveness or restrictiveness with which courts will construe the ratio decidendi of a purported precedent. The manipulation of factual distinctions and the holdings attributed to prior cases provides a covert way of affirming the authoritative force of case law in principle while evading it in practice. In this chapter and the next we accordingly complement our discussion of the doctrine of stare decisis with materials on the determination of the ratio decidendi of a case, and on the role of logic and policy in the way judges reason from the ratio decidendi of a precedent to their decision of the case before them.

BODENHEIMER, JURISPRUDENCE: THE PHILOSOPHY AND METHOD OF THE LAW
pp. 432–435 (Rev. ed. 1974).*

[N]ot every statement made in a judicial decision is an authoritative source to be followed in a later case presenting a similar situation. Only those statements in an earlier decision which may be said to constitute the *ratio decidendi* of that case are held to be binding, as a matter of general principle, in subsequent cases. Propositions not partaking of the character of *ratio decidendi* may be disregarded by the judge deciding the later case. Such nonauthoritative statements are usually referred to as *dicta* or (if they are quite unessential for the determination of the points at issue) *obiter dicta*.

Unfortunately, the question as to what are the constituent elements and the scope of the *ratio decidendi* of a case is far from being settled. In the case of Northwestern Life Ins. Co. v. Wright,[1] the Supreme Court of Wisconsin stated its conception of the *ratio decidendi* of a case in the following language: "The key note of an adjudication is the ruling principle. The details showing the particular facts ruled by some particular principle are helpful; but, in the end, it is the principle, not the detail circumstances, commonly evidentiary only, which is the important feature as to whether an existing adjudication is a safe guide to follow in a case." It is widely conceded, however, that not every proposition of law formulated by a court in the course of a judicial opinion—even though it may have been the basis of the decision—possesses the authority belonging to the *ratio decidendi*. The principle of law enunciated by the court may have been much broader than was required for the decision of the case before it; and it is well established that in such situations the surplus not necessary to sustain the judgment must be regarded as a *dictum*. This qualification of the theory which identifies *ratio decidendi* with the ruling principle of a case is aptly brought out in the discussions of the problem by Sir John Salmond and Professor Edmund Morgan. Salmond points out that "a precedent * * * is a judicial decision which contains in itself a principle. The underlying principle which thus forms its authoritative element is often termed the *ratio decidendi*." He then goes on to say:

> Although it is the duty of courts of justice to decide questions of fact on principle if they can, they must take care in such formulation of principles to limit themselves to the requirements of the case in hand. That is to say, they must not lay down principles which are not required for the due decision of the particular case, or which are wider than is necessary for this purpose. The only judicial principles which are authoritative are those which are thus relevant in their subject-matter and limited in their scope. All others, at the best, are of merely persuasive efficacy. They are not true *rationes decidendi*, and are distinguished from them under the name of *dicta* or *obiter dicta*, things said by the way.[2]

Morgan defined *ratio decidendi* in a similar fashion as "those portions of the opinion setting forth the rules of law applied by the court, the application of which was *required* for the determination of the issues presented."[3]

A substantially different theory as to what constitutes the *ratio decidendi* of a case was developed in England by Professor Arthur

1. 140 N.W. 1078, at 1081–1082 (1913).

2. John Salmond, "The Theory of Judicial Precedent," 16 L.Q.Rev. 376, at 387–388 (1900). See also Salmond, *Jurisprudence,* ed. G. Williams, 11th ed. (London, 1957), pp. 222–226.

3. Edmund M. Morgan, *Introduction to the Study of Law,* 2d ed. (Chicago, 1948), p.

155 (italics mine); see also John C. Gray, *The Nature and Sources of the Law,* 2d ed. (New York, 1921), p. 261; Carleton K. Allen, *Law in the Making,* 6th ed. (Oxford, 1958), p. 247; Rupert Cross, *Precedent in English Law,* 2d ed. (Oxford, 1968), pp. 35–101.

Goodhart.[4] According to him, it is not the principle of law laid down in a decision which is the controlling element under the doctrine of *stare decisis*. In his opinion, the *ratio decidendi* is to be found by taking account of the facts treated as material by the judge who decided the case cited as a precedent, and of his decision as based on these facts.[5] Goodhart submits three main reasons for rejecting the proposition of law theory of the *ratio decidendi*. First, he points out, there may be no rule of law set forth in the opinion of the court. Second, the rule formulated by the judge may be too wide or too narrow. Third, in appellate courts the rules of law set forth by different judges in their separate opinions may have no relation to one another.

Goodhart's theory was, in its basic core, adopted by Professor Glanville Williams.[6] Williams explained that in the light of the actual practice of the courts, however, the phrase "*ratio decidendi* of a case" was slightly ambiguous, because it may mean either the rule that the judge who decided the case intended to lay down and apply to the facts, or the rule that a later court concedes him to have had the power to lay down. This is so because, as Williams rightly emphasizes, "courts do not accord to their predecessors an unlimited power of laying down wide rules."[7] This undeniable fact prompted Dean Edward Levi to take issue with Professor Goodhart on the ground that the later judge may quite legitimately find irrelevant the existence or absence of facts which the prior judge considered important. In the words of Levi, "It is not what the prior judge intended that is of any importance; rather it is what the present judge, attempting to see the law as a fairly consistent whole, thinks should be the determining classification. In arriving at this result he will ignore what the past thought important; he will emphasize facts which prior judges would have thought made no difference." [8]

A more radical point of view was advanced by Professors Sidney Post Simpson [9] and Julius Stone.[10] According to their approach, it is erroneous to assume that each decided case has its distinct *ratio decidendi*. They contend that practically each case has implicit in it a whole congeries of possible principles of decision. When a case is decided, no one can be certain which of the possible principles of decision is destined eventually to become the controlling one. In Stone's opinion, if there are ten facts stated in an opinion, as many

4. See Goodhart, "Determining the *Ratio Decidendi* of a Case," 40 Yale L.J. 161 (1930). A criticism of Goodhart's article is presented by R.N. Gooderson, "*Ratio Decidendi* and Rules of Law," 30 Can.B. Rev. 892 (1952).

5. Goodhart, p. 182.

6. Williams, *Learning the Law*, 8th ed. (London, 1969), p. 72: "The *ratio decidendi* of a case can be defined as the material facts of the case plus the decision thereon."

7. Id., p. 69.

8. Edward H. Levi, *An Introduction to Legal Reasoning* (Chicago, 1949), p. 2.

9. "English Law in the Making," 4 Modern Law Review 121 (1940).

10. "Fallacies of the Logical Form in English Law," in *Interpretations of Modern Legal Philosophies*, ed. P. Sayre (New York, 1947), pp. 709–710; cf. also Stone, *Legal System and Lawyers' Reasonings* (Stanford, 1964), pp. 267–280.

general propositions will explain the decision as there are possible combinations of these facts. Only a study of a whole series of decisions on a particular problem of the law will to some extent reveal what the fate of a particular precedent has been in the dynamic process of restricting, expanding, interpreting, reinterpreting, and reformulating a prior body of doctrine in the creative work of the courts.

If we ask ourselves what the presently prevailing attitude of the American courts toward the question of determining the *ratio decidendi* is, we must probably conclude that the views of Salmond and Morgan are accepted by most American judges as representing the most satisfactory approach. In other words, most judges will hold that the *ratio decidendi* of a case is to be found in the general principle governing an earlier decision, as long as the formulation of this general principle was necessary to the decision of the actual issue between the litigants.

NOTE BY THE EDITORS

The word "necessary," as used in the prevailing formulation of the *ratio decidendi* doctrine, should not be construed to mean "absolutely necessary." If "necessary" is defined in a radically restrictive sense, a court would always be justified in carving down a rule of law found in a judicial precedent to the narrowest range consistent with the fact situation. This would not be desirable. The rule or principle of law laid down by a court should not be unduly broad, but it should be broad enough to cover all situations that cannot on any reasonable ground be distinguished from the case at hand. This position is required by a fundamental axiom of justice, referred to in Chapter III, pursuant to which equal or essentially similar situations should be treated equally by the law.

The proper handling of the *ratio decidendi* doctrine, thus conceived, demands of the judge laying down a rule in a case of first impression a great deal of resourcefulness and imagination. The judge may easily miss the mark by stating the rule too broadly or too narrowly. In that event a lower court generally bound by the decisions of the upper court is not obliged to accept the precise formulation of the rule by the upper court. It may whittle down the rule to exclude cases with different facts that are but should not be covered by the rule. Or it may expand the rule to cover situations that are not included in the rule as formulated, but should be included because they cannot be distinguished on reasonable grounds from the facts of the precedent. The Supreme Court of California has given expression to the principle implicit in the foregoing considerations by the following pronouncement: "Our statements of law remain binding on the trial and appellate courts of this state and must be applied wherever the facts of a case are not fairly distinguishable from the facts of the case in which we have declared the applicable principle of law." People v. Triggs, 8 Cal.3d 884, at 890–891, 506 P.2d 232, at 236, 106 Cal.Rptr. 408, at 412 (1973). This statement is not essentially different from the view of Morgan and Salmond, according to which the *ratio decidendi* of a case consists of the principle of law necessary to the determination of the issues before the court and, as the California Supreme Court has made clear, of issues that cannot be fairly distinguished from them.

The difficulties encountered by judges in hitting the nail on its head in a first attempt to state an adequately phrased rule or principle in an unprovided case may disappear in the course of time. After a number of groping efforts in articulating, revising, or limiting a legal prescription have been made, a properly formulated norm of law, subject perhaps to certain exceptions and qualifications, may emerge. It is often the case that such a norm will serve as a safe guide to the courts of a jurisdiction for a considerable period of time.

Problems

(1) A left a legacy of $10,000 to B in his will. B, who had been informed by A of this testamentary bequest, murdered A shortly afterwards, because he was in need of money and wished to come into possession of the legacy immediately. He was convicted of intentional and premeditated homicide and sentenced to life imprisonment. Notwithstanding his conviction, he claimed the legacy of $10,000, for the benefit of his family, in a suit against C, the executor of A's estate. B's attorney asserted that there was no statute or judicial precedent barring B from taking the legacy. The trial court agreed with this argument and awarded the legacy to B.

On appeal by the executor, the Supreme Court of the state reversed the judgment, holding that B was not entitled to the legacy. The Court stated in its opinion that considerations of fundamental justice required the recognition of a principle to the effect that "no one shall be permitted to take advantage of his own wrong."

Some time thereafter D bequeathed $12,000 to E in his will. On a foggy day, E drove his car to a neighboring city; D was a guest in his car. Although driving within the legal speed limit, E used insufficient caution to control the speed of his car in the fog. The car ran into a truck and D was instantly killed. E was sentenced to two years' imprisonment for negligent homicide.

E brought suit against the executor of D's estate to recover the legacy of $12,000. The attorney for the executor argued that E was not entitled to the legacy, since the trial court was bound by the holding of the state's Supreme Court to the effect that "no one shall be permitted to take advantage of his own wrong." He pointed out that the law had always viewed negligent homicide, just like intentional homicide, as a "wrong."

Should the trial court accept this argument? Or would the court be justified in distinguishing B's case and reaching the conclusion that E was entitled to the legacy?

(2) The Supreme Court of Calizona laid down a rule to the effect that overhanging branches of a tree may be cut off by a neighbor if they interfere with growth on his land or otherwise inconvenience him. Later a case arose in a lower court of the state in which overhanging branches of a large rhododendron bush took sunlight away from some flowers planted by the neighbor. The plaintiff invoked the authority of

the Supreme Court case, but the defendant argued that the *ratio decidendi* of that case was limited to trees. What position should the trial court take?

B. THE EVOLUTION OF PRODUCTS LIABILITY AT COMMON LAW IN NEW YORK

The following sequence of cases focuses on the development of the law governing the liability of a manufacturer to a consumer for injuries caused by a negligently-manufactured product. It illustrates the way in which a prior precedent can be narrowed or broadened, depending upon a subsequent court's formulation of the *ratio decidendi* of the earlier case. As you read these materials, write down the *ratio decidendi* of each case immediately after reading it. Then compare your formulation with that made by the courts applying the rule of the case in subsequent decisions.

WINTERBOTTOM v. WRIGHT

Court of Exchequer, 1842.
10 M. & W. 109, 11 L.J.Ex. 415, 152 Eng.Rep. 402.

[The plaintiff was a mail coach driver who was injured when the coach broke down. The defendant had contracted with the Postmaster General to supply a number of coaches, including the coach in question, for the transport of mail. Under the terms of the contract, the defendant had promised the Postmaster General to keep the coaches in good repair. The plaintiff was employed by one Atkinson who, with knowledge of the defendant's contract, had contracted with the Postmaster General to supply horses and coachmen to operate the coaches. The plaintiff's declaration alleged that the defendant negligently failed to carry out his duties of maintenance and repair under the contract, and that as a consequence the coach had become weakened and dangerous causing the plaintiff's injuries.]

LORD ABINGER, C.B. I am clearly of opinion that the defendant is entitled to our judgment. We ought not to permit a doubt to rest upon this subject, for our doing so might be the means of letting in upon us an infinity of actions. This is an action of the first impression, and it has been brought in spite of the precautions which were taken, in the judgment of this Court in the case of Levy v. Langridge, [2 M. & W. 519, 4 M. & W. 337] * to obviate any notion that such an action could be maintained. We ought not to attempt to extend the principle of that decision, which, although it has been cited in support of this action, wholly fails as an authority in its favour; for there the gun was bought

---

* [Note by the Editors] In Levy v. Langridge, 150 Eng.Rep. 1458 (1838), the court allowed a boy who had been injured when a gun exploded in his hands to recover damages against the seller, who had sold the gun to the boy's father after making false representations that the gun had been produced by a reputable maker and that it was in good condition.

for the use of the son, the plaintiff in that action, who could not make the bargain himself, but was really and substantially the party contracting. Here the action is brought simply because the defendant was a contractor with a third person; and it is contended that thereupon he became liable to everybody who might use the carriage. If there had been any ground for such an action, there certainly would have been some precedent of it; but with the exception of actions against innkeepers, and some few other persons, no case of a similar nature has occurred in practice. That is a strong circumstance, and is of itself a great authority against its maintenance. It is however contended, that this contract being made on the behalf of the public by the Postmaster-General, no action could be maintained against him, and therefore the plaintiff must have a remedy against the defendant. But that is by no means a necessary consequence—he may be remediless altogether. There is no privity of contract between these parties; and if the plaintiff can sue, every passenger, or even any person passing along the road who was injured by the upsetting of the coach, might bring a similar action. Unless we confine the operation of such contracts as this to the parties who entered into them, the most absurd and outrageous consequences, to which I can see no limit, would ensue. Where a party becomes responsible to the public, by undertaking a public duty, he is liable, though the injury may have arisen from the negligence of his servant or agent. So in cases of public nuisances, whether the act was done by the party as a servant, or in any other capacity, you are liable to an action at the suit of any person who suffers. Those, however, are cases where the real ground of the liability is the public duty, or the commission of the public nuisance. There is also a class of cases in which the law permits a contract to be turned into a tort; but unless there has been some public duty undertaken, or public nuisance committed, they are all cases in which an action might have been maintained upon the contract. Thus, a carrier may be sued either in *assumpsit* or case; but there is no instance in which a party, who was not privy to the contract entered into with him, can maintain any such action. The plaintiff in this case could not have brought an action on the contract; if he could have done so, what would have been his situation, supposing the Postmaster-General had released the defendant? that would, at all events, have defeated his claim altogether. By permitting this action, we should be working this injustice, that after the defendant had done every thing to the satisfaction of his employer, and after all matters between them had been adjusted, and all accounts settled on the footing of their contract, we should subject them to be ripped open by this action of tort being brought against him.

ALDERSON, B. I am of the same opinion. The contract in this case was made with the Postmaster-General alone: and the case is just the same as if he had come to the defendant and ordered a carriage, and handed it at once over to Atkinson. If we were to hold that the plaintiff could sue in such a case, there is no point at which such actions would stop. The only safe rule is to confine the right to recover to those who enter into the contract: if we go one step beyond that, there is no reason why we should not go fifty. The only real argument in favour of the action is, that this is a case of hardship; but that might have been obviated, if the plaintiff had made himself a party to the contract. Then it is urged that it falls within the principle of the case of Levy v. Langridge. But the principle of that case was simply this, that the father having bought the gun for the very purpose of being used by the plaintiff, the defendant made representations by which he was induced to use it. There, a distinct fraud was committed on the plaintiff; the falsehood of the representation was also alleged to have been within the knowledge of the defendant who made it, and he was properly held liable for the consequences. How are the facts of that case applicable to those of the present? Where is the allegation of misrepresentation or fraud in this declaration? It shows nothing of the kind. Our judgment must therefore be for the defendant.

GURNEY, B., concurred.

ROLFE, B. * * * The duty [with breach of which defendant is charged], therefore, is shown to have arisen solely from the contract; and the fallacy consists in the use of that word "duty." If a duty to the Postmaster–General be meant, that is true; but if a duty to the plaintiff be intended (and in that sense the word is evidently used), there was none. This is one of those unfortunate cases in which there certainly has been *damnum*, but is it *damnum absque injuria;* it is, no doubt, a hardship upon the plaintiff to be without a remedy, but, by that consideration we ought not to be influenced. Hard cases, it has been frequently observed, are apt to introduce bad law.

Judgment for the defendant.

THOMAS AND WIFE v. WINCHESTER

New York Court of Appeals, 1852.
6 N.Y. 397, 57 Am.Dec. 455.

RUGGLES, CH. J., delivered the opinion of the court. This is an action brought to recover damages from the defendant for negligently putting up, labeling and selling as and for the extract of *dandelion,* which is a simple and harmless medicine, a jar of the extract of *belladonna,* which is a deadly poison; by means of which the plaintiff Mary Ann Thomas, to whom, being sick, a dose of dandelion was prescribed by a physician, and a portion of the contents of the jar, was administered as and for the extract of dandelion, was greatly injured, etc.

The facts proved were briefly these: Mrs. Thomas being in ill health, her physician prescribed for her a dose of dandelion. Her husband purchased what was believed to be the medicine prescribed, at the store of Dr. Foord, a physician and druggist in Cazenovia, Madison County, where the plaintiffs reside.

A small quantity of the medicine thus purchased was administered to Mrs. Thomas on whom it produced very alarming effects; such as coldness of the surface and extremities, feebleness of circulation, spasms of the muscles, giddiness of the head, dilation of the pupils of the eyes, and derangement of mind. She recovered however, after some time, from its effects, although for a short time her life was thought to be in great danger. The medicine administered was *belladonna, and not dandelion*. The jar from which it was taken was labeled "½ lb. dandelion, prepared by A. Gilbert, No. 108 John-street, N.Y. Jar 8 oz." It was sold for and believed by Dr. Foord to be the extract of dandelion as labeled. Dr. Foord purchased the article as the extract of dandelion from Jas. S. Aspinwall, a druggist at New York. Aspinwall bought it of the defendant as extract of dandelion, believing it to be such. The defendant was engaged at No. 108 John-street, New York, in the manufacture and sale of certain vegetable extracts for medicinal purposes, and in the purchase and sale of others. The extracts manufactured by him were put up in jars for sale, and those which he purchased were put up by him in like manner. The jars containing extracts manufactured by himself and those containing extracts purchased by him from others, were labeled alike. Both were labeled like the jar in question, as "prepared by A. Gilbert." Gilbert was a person employed by the defendant at a salary as an assistant in his business. The jars were labeled in Gilbert's name because he had been previously engaged in the same business on his own account at No. 108 John-street, and probably because Gilbert's labels rendered the articles more salable. The extract contained in the jar sold to Aspinwall, and by him to Foord, was not manufactured by the defendant, but was purchased by him from another manufacturer or dealer.

The extract of dandelion and the extract of belladonna resemble each other in color, consistence, smell and taste; but may on careful examination be distinguished the one from the other by those who are well acquainted with these articles. Gilbert's labels were paid for by Winchester and used in his business with his knowledge and assent.

The defendant's counsel moved for a nonsuit on the following grounds:

   1. That the action could not be sustained, as the defendant was the remote vendor of the article in question: and there was no connection, transaction or privity between him and the plaintiffs, or either of them.

* * *

The case depends on the first point taken by the defendant on his motion for a nonsuit; and the question is, whether the defendant, being a remote vendor of the medicine, and there being no privity or connection between him and the plaintiffs, the action can be maintained.

If, in the labeling a poisonous drug with the name of a harmless medicine, for public market, no duty was violated by the defendant, excepting that which he owed to Aspinwall, his immediate vendee, in virtue of his contract of sale, this action cannot be maintained. If A build a wagon and sell it to B, who sells it to C, and C hires it to D, who in consequence of the gross negligence of A in building the wagon is overturned and injured, D cannot recover damages against A, the builder. A's obligation to build the wagon faithfully, arises solely out of his contract with B. The public have nothing to do with it. Misfortune to third persons, not parties to the contract, would not be a natural and necessary consequence of the builder's negligence; and such negligence is not an act imminently dangerous to human life.

So, for the same reason, if a horse be defectively shod by a smith, and a person hiring the horse from the owner is thrown and injured in consequence of the smith's negligence in shoeing; the smith is not liable for the injury. The smith's duty in such case grows exclusively out of his contract with the owner of the horse; it was a duty which the smith owed to him alone, and to no one else. And although the injury to the rider may have happened in consequence of the negligence of the smith, the latter was not bound, either by his contract or by any considerations of public policy or safety, to respond for his breach of duty to any one except the person he contracted with.

This was the ground on which the case of Winterbottom v. Wright, 10 Mees. & Welsb. 109, was decided. A contracted with the postmaster general to provide a coach to convey the mail bags along a certain line of road, and B and others also contracted to horse the coach along the same line. B and his co-contractors hired C, who was the plaintiff, to drive the coach. The coach, in consequence of some latent defect, broke down; the plaintiff was thrown from his seat and lamed. It was held that C could not maintain an action against A for the injury thus sustained. The reason of the decision is best stated by Baron Rolfe. A's duty to keep the coach in good condition, was a duty to the postmaster general, with whom he made his contract, and not a duty to the driver employed by the owners of the horses.

But the case in hand stands on a different ground. The defendant was a dealer in poisonous drugs. Gilbert was his agent in preparing them for market. The death or great bodily harm of some person was the natural and almost inevitable consequence of the sale of belladonna by means of the false label.

Gilbert, the defendant's agent, would have been punishable for manslaughter if Mrs. Thomas had died in consequence of taking the falsely labeled medicine. Every man who, by his culpable negligence, causes the death of another, although without intent to kill, is guilty of manslaughter. 2 R.S. 662, § 19. A chemist who negligently sells laudanum in a phial labeled as paregoric, and thereby causes the death of a person to whom it is administered, is guilty of manslaughter. Tessymond's case, 1 Lewin's Crown Cases, 169. "So highly does the law value human life that it admits of no justification wherever life has been lost and the carelessness or negligence of one person has contributed to the death of another." Regina v. Swindall, 2 Car & Kir. 232–3.

And this rule applies not only where the death of one is occasioned by the negligent act of another, but where it is caused by the negligent omission of a duty of that other. 2 Car & Kir. 368, 371. Although the defendant Winchester may not be answerable criminally for the negligence of his agent, there can be no doubt of his liability in a civil action, in which the act of the agent is to be regarded as the act of the principal.

In respect to the wrongful and criminal character of the negligence complained of, this case differs widely from those put by the defendant's counsel. No such imminent danger existed in those cases. In the present case the sale of the poisonous article was made to a dealer in drugs, and not to a consumer. The injury therefore was not likely to fall on him, or on his vendee who was also a dealer; but much more likely to be visited on a remote purchaser as actually happened. The defendant's negligence put human life in imminent danger. Can it be said that there was no duty on the part of the defendant, to avoid the creation of that danger by the exercise of greater caution? or that the exercise of that caution was a duty only to his immediate vendee, whose life was not endangered? The defendant's duty arose out of the nature of his business and the danger to others incident to its mismanagement. Nothing but mischief like that which actually happened could have been expected from sending the poison falsely labeled into the market; and the defendant is justly responsible for the probable consequences of the act. The duty of exercising caution in this respect did not arise out of the defendant's contract of sale to Aspinwall. The wrong done by the defendant was in putting the poison, mislabeled, into the hands of Aspinwall as an article of merchandise to be sold and afterwards used as the extract of dandelion, by some person then unknown. The owner of a horse and cart who leaves them unattended in the street is liable for any damage which may result from his negligence. Lynch v. Nurdin, 1 Ad & Ellis, N.S. 29; Illidge v. Goodwin, 5 Car. & Payne, 190. The owner of a loaded gun who puts it into the hands of a child by whose indiscretion it is discharged, is liable for the damage occasioned by the discharge. 5 Maule & Sel. 198. The defendant's contract of sale to Aspinwall does not excuse the wrong done to the plaintiffs. It was a part of the means by which the wrong was effected. The plaintiffs' injury and their remedy would have stood on the same principle, if the defendant had given the belladonna to Dr. Foord without price, or if he had put it in his shop without his knowledge, under circumstances which would probably have led to its sale on the faith of the label.

In Longmeid v. Holliday, 6 Law and Eq.Rep. 562, the distinction is recognized between an act of negligence imminently dangerous to the lives of others, and one that is not so. In the former case, the party guilty of the negligence is liable to the party injured, whether there be a contract between them or not; in the latter, the negligent party is liable only to the party with whom he contracted, and on the ground that negligence is a breach of contract.

* * *

Judgment affirmed.

LOOP v. LITCHFIELD
New York Court of Appeals, 1870.
42 N.Y. 351, 1 Am.Rep. 513.

HUNT, J. A piece of machinery already made and on hand, having defects which weaken it, is sold by the manufacturer to one who buys it for his own use. The defects are pointed out to the purchaser and are fully understood by him. This piece of machinery is used by the buyer for five years, and is then taken into the possession of a neighbor, who uses it for his own purposes. While so in use, it flies apart by reason of its original defects, and the person using it is killed. Is the seller, upon this state of facts, liable to the representatives of the deceased party? * * * [The jury's verdict for the plaintiff had been reversed by the General Term which ordered a new trial. From this the plaintiff had appealed, stipulating, as the law then required, that if the Court of Appeals agreed with the General Term, judgment absolute should be entered for the defendant.]

To maintain this liability, the appellants rely upon the case of Thomas v. Winchester, 6 N.Y. 397, 57 Am.Dec. 455. * * *

The appellants recognize the principle of this decision, and seek to bring their case within it, by asserting that the fly wheel in question was a dangerous instrument. Poison is a dangerous subject. Gunpowder is the same. A torpedo is a dangerous instrument, as is a spring gun, a loaded rifle or the like. They are instruments and articles in their nature calculated to do injury to mankind, and generally intended to accomplish that purpose. They are essentially, and in their elements, instruments of danger. Not so, however, an iron wheel, a few feet in diameter and a few inches in thickness, although one part may be weaker than another. If the article is abused by too long use, or by applying too much weight or speed, an injury may occur, as it may from an ordinary carriage wheel, a wagon axle, or the common chair in which we sit. There is scarcely an object in art or nature, from which an injury may not occur under such circumstances. Yet they are not in their nature sources of danger, nor can they, with any regard to the accurate use of language, be called dangerous instruments. That an injury actually occurred by the breaking of a carriage axle, the failure of the carriage body, the falling to pieces of a chair or sofa, or the bursting of a fly wheel, does not in the least alter its character.

* * *

Upon the facts as stated, assuming that the deceased had no knowledge of the defects complained of, and assuming that he was in the rightful and lawful use of the machine, I am of the opinion that the verdict cannot be sustained. The facts constitute no cause of action.

* * *

All concur, Judgment affirmed, and judgment absolute ordered for the defendants.

LOSEE v. CLUTE

Commission of Appeals of New York, 1873.
51 N.Y. 494, 10 Am.Rep. 638.

Appeal from judgment of the General Term of the Supreme Court in the fourth judicial district, affirming a judgment entered upon an order dismissing plaintiff's complaint on the trial.

The action was brought to recover damages caused to the property of the plaintiff by the explosion of a steam boiler while the same was owned and being used by the Saratoga Paper Company at their mill situated in the village of Schuylerville, Saratoga county and State of New York, on the thirteenth day of February, 1864, by means whereof the boiler was thrown on to the plaintiff's premises and through several of his buildings, thereby injuring and damaging the same.

The defendants, Clute, were made parties defendants to the action with the Saratoga Paper Company and Coe S. Buchanan and Daniel A. Bullard, trustees and agents of said company, on the ground that they were the manufacturers of the boiler, and made the same out of poor and brittle iron and in a negligent and defective manner, in consequence of which negligence said explosion occurred.

At the close of the evidence the complaint was dismissed as to the defendants Clute.   *   *   *

LOTT, CH.C. It appears by the case that the defendants Clute manufactured the boiler in question for the Saratoga Paper Company, in which they were stockholders, for the purposes of and uses to which it was subsequently applied by it; and the testimony tended to show that it was constructed improperly and of poor iron, that the said defendants knew at the time that it was to be used in the immediate vicinity of and adjacent to dwelling-houses and stores in a village, so that, in case of an explosion while in use, it would be likely to be destructive to human life and adjacent property, and that, in consequence of the negligence of the said defendants in the improper construction of the boiler, the explosion that took place occurred and damaged the plaintiff's property. The evidence also tended to show that the boiler was tested by the company to its satisfaction, and then accepted, and was thereafter used by it for about three months prior to the explosion, and that after such test and acceptance the said defendants had nothing whatever to do with the boiler, and had no care or management of it at the time of the explosion, but that the company had the sole and exclusive ownership, management and conduct of it.

In determining whether the complaint was properly dismissed, we must assume all the facts which the evidence tended to show as established, and the question is thereby presented whether the defendants have incurred any liability to the plaintiff. They contracted with the company, and did what was done by them for it and to its satisfaction, and when the boiler was accepted they ceased to have any further control over it or its management, and all responsibility for what was subsequently done with it devolved upon the company and those having charge of it, and the case falls within the principle decided by the Court of Appeals in the Mayor, etc., of Albany v. Cunliff, 2 Comst., N.Y. 165, which is, that the mere architect or builder of a work is answerable only to his employees for any want of care or skill in the execution thereof, and he is not liable for accidents or injuries which may occur after the execution of the work; and the opinions published in that case clearly show that there is no ground of liability by the defendants to the plaintiff in this action. They owed *him* no *duty* whatever at the time of the explosion either growing out of contract or imposed by law.

It may be proper to refer to the case of Thomas v. Winchester, 2 Selden 397, 57 Am.Dec. 455, cited by the appellant's counsel, and I deem it sufficient to say that the opinion of Hunt, J., in Loop v. Litchfield, 42 N.Y. 351, 1 Am.Rep. 513, clearly shows that the principle decided in that case has no application to this.

It appears from these considerations that the complaint was properly dismissed, and it follows that there was no case made for the consideration of the jury, and, consequently, there was no error in the refusal to submit it to them.

There was an exception taken to the exclusion of evidence to show that two persons were killed by this boiler in passing through a dwelling-house in its course, but as it is not urged on this appeal, it is, I presume, abandoned; but if not, it was matter, as the judge held at the trial, wholly immaterial to the issue between the parties in this action.

There is, for the reasons stated, no ground for the reversal of the judgment. It must, therefore, be affirmed, with costs.

All concur.

DEVLIN v. SMITH

New York Court of Appeals, 1882.
89 N.Y. 470, 42 Am.Rep. 311.

This is an appeal from a judgment of the General Term, second department, affirming a judgment entered upon an order dismissing plaintiff's complaint, at the trial. Reported below, 25 Hun 206.

This action was commenced to recover damages for the benefit of the next of kin of Hugh Devlin, deceased, who was killed through the alleged negligence of the defendants.

The deceased, at the time he was killed, was upon a scaffold erected in the rotunda of the court-house, in Brooklyn, washing off the panels of the dome preparatory to its being painted; while thus engaged the portion of the scaffold upon which the deceased was at work broke and fell, precipitating him to the ground, a distance of ninety feet, thereby causing his death.

The defendant Smith entered into a contract with the board of supervisors, of the county of Kings, whereby he agreed to paint and fresco the inside of the county court-house, and furnish all the material and labor necessary therefor. In the performance of his contract it became necessary to have a scaffold erected in the rotunda of the court-house, and he made a contract with the defendant Stevenson to erect the scaffold in question, and to furnish the material therefor.

The scaffold erected consisted of six sections, one built on top of the other, and known as a rope and pole scaffold. Planks were being laid across the ledgers, or horizontal poles, forming a flooring to enable the men to work upon the dome.

The portion of the scaffold that broke at the time of accident was not constructed like the other portions; the end of one of the top ledgers was not supported by an upright, but instead thereof, a piece of plank was used as a brace by resting the lower end upon the ledger below, the upper end being nailed to the end of the ledger in question.

The deceased, together with a fellow workman, was upon a plank resting on this ledger at the time it broke. The defendant Stevenson knew that the brace in question was nailed to the ledger as above described, he having examined it before the accident. The defendant Smith in whose employ the deceased was, had many contracts going on at the same time, and would go about each day from one job to another, remaining at each place about half an hour. The scaffold was not examined by the defendant Smith nor his superintendent until after the accident.

RAPALLO, J. Upon a careful review of all the testimony in this case, we are of opinion that there was sufficient evidence to require the submission to the jury of the question, whether the breaking down of the scaffold was attributable to negligence in its construction. * * *

[The court concluded that Smith was not at fault and therefore not liable to the plaintiff.]

If any person was at fault in the matter it was the defendant Stevenson. It is contended, however, that even if through his negligence the scaffold was defective, he is not liable in this action, because there was no privity between him and the deceased and he owed no duty to the deceased, his obligation and duty being only to Smith, with whom he contracted.

As a general rule the builder of a structure for another party, under a contract with him or one who sells an article of his own manufacture, is not liable to an action by a third party who uses the same with the consent of the owner or purchaser, for injuries resulting from a defect therein, caused by negligence. The liability of the builder or manufacturer for such defects is, in general, only to the person with whom he contracted. But, notwithstanding this rule, liability to third parties has been held to exist when the defect is such as to render the article in itself imminently dangerous, and serious injury to any person using it is a natural and probable consequence of its use. As where a dealer in drugs carelessly labeled a deadly poison as a harmless medicine, it was held that he was liable not merely to the person to whom he sold it, but to the person who ultimately used it, though it had passed through many hands. This liability was held to rest, not upon any contract or direct privity between him and the party injured, but upon the duty which the law imposes on every one to avoid acts in their nature dangerous to the lives of others. Thomas v. Winchester, 6 N.Y. 397, 57 Am.Dec. 455. In that case Mayor, etc. v. Cunliff, 2 N.Y. 165, was cited as an authority for the position that a builder is liable only to the party for whom he builds. Some of the examples there put by way of illustration were commented upon, and among others the case of one who builds a carriage carelessly and of defective materials, and sells it, and the purchaser lends it to a friend, and the carriage, by reason of its original defect, breaks down and the friend is injured, and the question is put, can he recover against the maker? The comments of Ruggles, Ch. J., upon this suppositious case, in Thomas v. Winchester, and the ground upon which he answers the question in the negative, show clearly the distinction between the two classes of cases. He says that in the case supposed, the obligation of the maker to build faithfully arises only out of his contract with the purchaser. The public have nothing to do with it. Misfortunes to third persons, not parties to the contract, would not be a natural and necessary consequence of the builder's negligence, and such negligence is not an act imminently dangerous to human life.

Applying these tests to the question now before us, the solution is not difficult. Stevenson undertook to build a scaffold ninety feet in height, for the express purpose of enabling the workmen of Smith to stand upon it to paint the interior of the dome. Any defect or negligence in its construction, which should cause it to give way, would naturally result in these men being precipitated from that great height. A stronger case where misfortune to third persons not parties to the contract would be a natural and necessary consequence to the builder's negligence, can hardly be supposed, nor is it easy to imagine a more apt illustration of a case where such negligence would be an act imminently dangerous to human life. These circumstances seem to us to bring the case fairly within the principle of Thomas v. Winchester. * * *

Loop v. Litchfield (42 N.Y. 351, 1 Am.Rep. 543) was decided upon the ground that the wheel which caused the injury was not in itself a dangerous instrument, and that the injury was not a natural consequence of the defect or one reasonably to be anticipated. Losee v. Clute (51 N.Y. 494, 10 Am.Rep. 638) was distinguished from Thomas v. Winchester, upon the authority of Loop v. Litchfield.

We think there should be a new trial as to the defendant Stevenson, and that it will be for the jury to determine whether the death of the plaintiff's intestate was caused by negligence on the part of Stevenson in the construction of the scaffold.

The judgment should be affirmed, with costs, as to the defendant Smith, and reversed as to the defendant Stevenson, and a new trial ordered as to him, costs to abide the event.

MACPHERSON v. BUICK MOTOR CO.

New York Court of Appeals, 1916.
217 N.Y. 382, 111 N.E. 1050.

Appeal, by permission, from a judgment of the Appellate Division of the Supreme Court in the third judicial department, entered January 8, 1914, affirming a judgment in favor of plaintiff entered upon a verdict. * * *

CARDOZO, J. The defendant is a manufacturer of automobiles. It sold an automobile to a retail dealer. The retail dealer re-sold to the plaintiff. While the plaintiff was in the car, it suddenly collapsed. He was thrown out and injured. One of the wheels was made of defective wood, and its spokes crumbled into fragments. The wheel was not made by the defendant; it was bought from another manufacturer. There is evidence, however, that its defects could have been discovered by reasonable inspection, and that inspection was omitted. There is no claim that the defendant knew of the defect and wilfully concealed it. The case, in other words, is not brought within the rule of Kuelling v. Lean Mfg. Co., 183 N.Y. 78, 75 N.E. 1098, 2 L.R.A., N.S., 303, 111 Am. St.Rep. 691, 5 Ann.Cas. 124. The charge is one not of fraud, but of negligence. The question to be determined is whether the defendant owed a duty of care and vigilance to any one but the immediate purchaser.

The foundations of this branch of the law, at least in this state were laid in Thomas v. Winchester, 6 N.Y. 397, 57 Am.Dec. 455. A poison was falsely labeled. The sale was made to a druggist, who in turn sold to a customer. The customer recovered damages from the seller who affixed the label. "The defendant's negligence," it was said, "put human life in imminent danger." A poison falsely labeled is likely to injure any one who gets it. Because the danger is to be foreseen, there is a duty to avoid the injury. Cases were cited by way of illustration in which manufacturers were not subject to any duty irrespective of contract. The distinction was said to be that their conduct, though negligent, was not likely to result in injury to any one except the purchaser. We are not required to say whether the chance of injury was always as remote as the distinction assumes. Some of the illustrations might be rejected today. The principle of the distinction is for present purposes the important thing.

Thomas v. Winchester became quickly a landmark of the law. In the application of its principle there may at times have been uncertainty or even error. There has never in this state been doubt or disavowal of the principle itself. The chief cases are well known, yet to recall some of them will be helpful. Loop v. Litchfield, 42 N.Y. 351, 1 Am. Rep. 513, is the earliest. It was the case of a defect in a small balance wheel used on a circular saw. The manufacturer pointed out the defect to the buyer, who wished a cheap article and was ready to assume the risk. The risk can hardly have been an imminent one, for the wheel lasted five years before it broke. In the meanwhile the buyer had made a lease of the machinery. It was held that the manufacturer was not answerable to the lessee. Loop v. Litchfield was followed in Losee v. Clute, 51 N.Y. 494, 10 Am.Rep. 638, the case of the explosion of a steam boiler. That decision has been criticised (Thompson on Negligence, 233, Shearman & Redfield on Negligence [6th ed.], § 117); but it must be confined to its special facts.

* * * It was put upon the ground that the risk of injury was too remote. The buyer in that case had not only accepted the boiler, but had tested it. The manufacturer knew that his own test was not the final one. The finality of the test has a bearing on the measure of diligence owing to persons other than the purchaser. Beven, Negligence (3rd ed.), pp. 50, 51, 54; Wharton, Negligence (2nd ed.) § 134.

These early cases suggest a narrow construction of the rule. Later cases, however, evince a more liberal spirit. First in importance is Devlin v. Smith, 89 N.Y. 470, 42 Am.Rep. 311. The defendant, a contractor, built a scaffold for a painter. The painter's servants were injured. The contractor was held liable. He knew that the scaffold, if improperly constructed, was a most dangerous trap. He knew that it was to be used by the workmen. He was building it for that very purpose. Building it for their use, he owed them a duty, irrespective of his contract with their master, to build it with care.

From Devlin v. Smith we pass over intermediate cases and turn to the latest case in this court in which Thomas v. Winchester was followed. That case is Statler v. Ray Mfg. Co., 195 N.Y. 478, 480, 88 N.E. 1063. The defendant manufactured a large coffee urn. It was installed in a restaurant. When heated, the urn exploded and injured the plaintiff. We held that the manufacturer was liable. We said that the urn "was of such a character inherently that, when applied to the purposes for which it was designed, it was liable to become a source of great danger to many people if not carefully and properly constructed."

It may be that Devlin v. Smith and Statler v. Ray Mfg. Co. have extended the rule of Thomas v. Winchester. If so, this court is committed to the extension. The defendant argues that things imminently dangerous to life are poisons, explosives, deadly weapons—things whose normal function it is to injure or destroy. But whatever the rule in Thomas v. Winchester may once have been, it has no longer that restricted meaning. A scaffold (Devlin v. Smith, supra) is not inherently a destructive instrument. It becomes destructive only if imperfectly constructed. A large coffee urn (Statler v. Ray Mfg. Co., supra) may have within itself, if negligently made, the potency of danger, yet no one thinks of it as an implement whose normal function is destruction.

What is true of the coffee urn is equally true of bottles of aerated water, Torgeson v. Schultz, 192 N.Y. 156, 84 N.E. 956, 18 L.R.A., N.S. 726, 127 Am.St.Rep. 894. We have mentioned only cases in this court. But the rule had received a like extension in our courts of intermediate appeal. In Burke v. Ireland, 26 A.D. 487, 50 N.Y.S. 369, in an opinion by Cullen, J., it was applied to a builder who constructed a defective building; in Kahner v. Otis Elevator Co., 96 A.D. 169, 89 N.Y.S. 185, to the manufacturer of an elevator; in Davies v. Pelham Hod Elevating Co., 65 Hun 573, 20 N.Y.S. 523, affirmed in this court without opinion, 146 N.Y. 363, 41 N.E. 88, to a contractor who furnished a defective rope with knowledge of the purpose for which the rope was to be used. We are not required at this time either to approve or to disapprove the application of the rule that was made in these cases. It is enough that they help to characterize the trend of judicial thought.

* * *

We hold, then, that the principle of Thomas v. Winchester is not limited to poisons, explosives, and things of like nature, to things which in their normal operation are implements of destruction. If the nature of a thing is such that it is reasonably certain to place life and limb in peril when negligently made, it is then a thing of danger. Its nature gives warning of the consequences to be expected. If to the element of danger there is added knowledge that the thing will be used by persons other than the purchaser, and used without new tests, then, irrespective of contract, the manufacturer of this thing of danger is under a duty to make it carefully. That is as far as we are required to go for the decision of this case. There must be knowledge of a danger, not merely possible, but probable. It is possible to use almost anything in a way that will make it dangerous if defective. That is not enough to charge the manufacturer with a duty independent of his contract. Whether a given thing is dangerous may be sometimes a question for the court and sometimes a question for the jury. There must also be knowledge that in the usual course of events the danger will be shared by others than the buyer. Such knowledge may often be inferred from the nature of the transaction. But it is possible that even knowledge of the danger and of the use will not always be enough. The proximity or remoteness of the relation is a factor to be considered. We are dealing now with the liability of the manufacturer of the finished product, who puts it on the market to be used without inspection by his customers. If he is negligent, where danger is to be foreseen, a liability will follow. We are not required at this time to say that it is legitimate to go back of the manufacturer of the finished product and hold the manufacturers of the component parts. To make their negligence a cause of imminent danger, an independent cause must often intervene; the manufacturer of the finished product must also fail in his duty of inspection. It may be that in those circumstances the negligence of the earlier members of the series is too remote to constitute, as to the ultimate user, an actionable wrong. Beven on Negligence (3rd ed.) 50, 51, 54; Wharton on Negligence (2nd ed.) § 134; Leeds v. N.Y. Tel. Co.,

178 N.Y. 118, 70 N.E. 219; Sweet v. Perkins, 196 N.Y. 482, 90 N.E. 50; Hayes v. Hyde Park, 153 Mass. 514, 516, 27 N.E. 522, 12 L.R.A. 249. We leave that question open. We shall have to deal with it when it arises. The difficulty which it suggests is not present in this case. There is here no break in the chain of cause and effect. In such circumstances, the presence of a known danger, attendant upon a known use, makes vigilance a duty. We have put aside the notion that the duty to safeguard life and limb, when the consequences of negligence may be foreseen, grows out of contract and nothing else. We have put the source of the obligation where it ought be. We have put its source in the law.

From this survey of the decisions, there thus emerges a definition of the duty of a manufacturer which enables us to measure this defendant's liability. Beyond all question, the nature of an automobile gives warning of probable danger if its construction is defective. This automobile was designed to go fifty miles an hour. Unless its wheels were sound and strong, injury was almost certain. It was as much a thing of danger as a defective engine for a railroad. The defendant knew of the danger. It knew also that the car would be used by persons other than the buyer. This was apparent from its size; there were seats for three persons. It was apparent also from the fact that the buyer was a dealer in cars, who bought to resell. The maker of this car supplied it for the use of purchasers from the dealer just as plainly as the contractor in Devlin v. Smith supplied the scaffold for use by the servants of the owner. The dealer was indeed the one person of whom it might be said with some approach to certainty that by him the car would not be used. Yet the defendant would have us say that he was the one person whom it was under a legal duty to protect. The law does not lead us to so inconsequent a conclusion. Precedents drawn from the days of travel by stage coach do not fit the conditions of travel today. The principle that the danger must be imminent does not change, but the things subject to the principle do change. They are whatever the needs of life in a developing civilization require them to be.

*   *   *

In this view of the defendant's liability there is nothing inconsistent with the theory of liability on which the case was tried. It is true that the court told the jury that "an automobile is not an inherently dangerous vehicle." The meaning, however, is made plain by the context. The meaning is that danger is not to be expected when the vehicle is well constructed. The court left it to the jury to say whether the defendant ought to have foreseen that the car, if negligently constructed, would become "imminently dangerous." Subtle distinctions are drawn by the defendant between things inherently dangerous and things imminently dangerous, but the case does not turn upon these verbal niceties. If danger was to be expected as reasonably certain, there was a duty of vigilance, and this whether you call the danger inherent or imminent. In varying forms that thought was put before the jury. We do not say that the court would not have been justified in ruling as a matter of law that the car was a dangerous thing. If there was any error, it was none of which the defendant can complain.

We think the defendant was not absolved from a duty of inspection because it bought the wheels from a reputable manufacturer. It was not merely a dealer in automobiles. It was a manufacturer of automobiles. It was responsible for the finished product. It was not at liberty to put the finished product on the market without subjecting the component parts to ordinary and simple tests. Richmond & Danville R.R. Co. v. Elliott, 149 U.S. 266, 272, 13 S.Ct. 837, 37 L.Ed. 728. Under the charge of the trial judge nothing more was required of it. The obligation to inspect must vary with the nature of the thing to be inspected. The more probable the danger, the greater the need of caution. There is little analogy between this case and Carlson v. Phoenix Bridge Co., 132 N.Y. 273, 30 N.E. 750, where the defendant bought a tool for a servant's use. The making of tools was not the business in which the master was engaged. Reliance on the skill of the manufacturer was proper and almost inevitable. But that is not the defendant's situation. Both by its relation to the work and by the nature of its business, it is charged with a stricter duty.

Other rulings complained of have been considered, but no error has been found in them.

The judgment should be affirmed with costs.

Further References

Cross, R., *Precedent in English Law* (3rd ed. 1977), pp. 38–102.

Levi, E.H., *An Introduction to Legal Reasoning* (1949), pp. 1–19.

Note, "Diverse Views of What Constitutes the Principle of Law of a Case," 36 University of Colorado Law Review 377–390 (1964).

Williams, G., *Learning the Law* (11th ed. 1982), pp. 67–79.

Chapter V

LOGIC AND POLICY IN LEGAL REASONING

A. THEORETICAL PERSPECTIVES

Under the doctrine of stare decisis each judicial decision forms a precedent to be followed in subsequent cases. Judicial opinions are therefore often characterized as syllogisms. The previously-established precedent is the major premise, the proposition stating the crucial facts in the case before the court is the minor premise, and the judge's decision is the conclusion. The first excerpt in this chapter demonstrates how judicial opinions can be cast into syllogistic form.

TREUSCH, "THE SYLLOGISM", IN: HALL, READINGS IN JURISPRUDENCE

(1938), pp. 539–548 * [footnotes omitted].

I. THE CATEGORICAL SYLLOGISM

1. Proposition Defined.

Legal rules, findings of fact, and decisions may be stated in the form of propositions. A proposition is the verbal expression of a thought. Grammatically, it is a sentence in which something (the "predicate") is asserted or denied of something else (the "subject"). Where this relation is unconditionally asserted or denied the proposition is said to be in "categorical" form. The subject (S) and the predicate (P) are known as the "terms", and the relation between them is always expressed by some form of the verb "to be," called the "copula" (C). Thus the rule, An oral conveyance of real estate (S) is (C) invalid (P), is a proposition in categorical form, as is the finding of fact, This conveyance of real estate (S) is (C) oral (P). Similarly, if a decision is taken as asserting or denying that a legal consequence should be applied to a given fact situation, the legal consequence may be stated as the predicate, and the given fact situation to which such conveyance is held applicable or inapplicable may be stated as the subject of a categorical proposition; e.g., This conveyance of real estate (S) is (C) invalid (P).

* * *

2. *Syllogism Defined.*

Suppose it becomes necessary to decide whether a given conveyance of real estate is valid or not. The conveyance is an oral one. Moreover, there is a rule of law in the jurisdiction to the effect that all oral conveyances of real estate are invalid. An opinion might then appear in the form of the syllogism:

Oral conveyances of real estate are invalid

This conveyance is an oral conveyance of real estate

Therefore, this conveyance is invalid.

Here the term *this conveyance* is related to the term invalid by reason of a known relation of each of these terms to a common third term, oral conveyance of real estate. The common term is called the "middle term." *This conveyance,* which appears as the subject of the conclusion is known as the "minor term," and *invalid,* which appears as predicate, is the "major term."

There are three propositions in any syllogism, called, in order, "major premise," "minor premise" and "conclusion." The major premise relates the major term to the middle term, as the minor premise relates the minor to the middle term. The conclusion, as indicated, relates the minor to the middle term as subject to the major term as predicate.

Symbolically, if S, M, and P are taken to represent the minor, middle, and major terms respectively and the letter *a* to indicate that the proposition is universal and affirmative, the above syllogism assumes the following form: MaP
SaM
SaP

Judicial opinions sometimes fall into clear syllogistic form; e.g.,

One has a right to the fruits of his (All M is P)
labor (i.e., Fruits of labor are the
property of their authors)

Private correspondence is a fruit of the (All S is M)
author's labor

Therefore, private correspondence is ($\therefore$ All S is P)
the property of the author.

* * *

Rarely, however, do judicial opinions spell out such syllogistic reasoning explicitly. Attention has been called to this by Mr. Justice Holmes' eloquent phrase "the inarticulate major premise." Frequently a rule of law is such a commonplace that while a court may be conscious of each premise, the style of juristic writing bars a cumbersome elaboration. Often it is argued "a promise given for what the promisor is already bound to do is without consideration and void." All such opinions can be expressed in complete syllogistic form:

[A promise without consideration is void]

A promise given for what the promisor is already bound to do is without consideration.

[Therefore, such a promise] is void

The conclusion of a syllogism is formally correct if it follows necessarily from the premises regardless of their material sense and thus regardless of the factual truth of the conclusion; e.g.

All men are penguins.

Ghandi is a man.

Therefore, Ghandi is a penguin.

or

All men are mortal.

Charley McCarthy is a man.

Therefore, Charley McCarthy is mortal.

Although the major premise or the minor premise be false in fact, the conclusion in each case follows necessarily from the accepted premises and is formally correct.

HOLMES, THE COMMON LAW
pp. 1–2, 35–36 (1909).

The life of the law has not been logic: it has been experience. The felt necessities of the time, the prevalent moral and political theories, intuitions of public policy, avowed or unconscious, even the prejudices which judges share with their fellowmen, have had a good deal more to do than the syllogism in determining the rules by which men should be governed. The law embodies the story of a nation's development through many centuries, and it cannot be dealt with as if it contained only the axioms and corollaries of a book of mathematics. In order to know what it is, we must know what it has been, and what it tends to become. We must alternately consult history and existing theories of legislation. But the most difficult labor will be to understand the combination of the two into a new product at every stage. * * *

* * *

In substance the growth of the law is legislative. And this in a deeper sense than that what the courts declare to have always been the law is in fact new. It is legislative in its grounds. The very considerations which judges most rarely mention, and always with an apology, are the secret root from which the law draws all the juices of life. I mean, of course, considerations of what is expedient for the community concerned. Every important principle which is developed by litigation is in fact and at bottom the result of more or less definitely understood views of public policy; most generally, to be sure, under our practices and traditions, the unconscious result of instinctive preferences and inarticulate convictions, but none the less traceable to views of public policy in the last analysis. And as the law is administered by able and experienced men, who know too much to sacrifice good sense to a syllogism, it will be found that, when ancient rules maintain themselves in the way that has been and will be shown in this book, new reasons more fitted to the time have been found for them, and that they gradually receive a new content, and at last a new form, from the grounds to which they have been transplanted. * * *

The truth is, that the law is always approaching, and never reaching, consistency. It is forever adopting new principles from life at one end, and it always retains old ones from history at the other, which have not yet been absorbed or sloughed off. It will become entirely consistent only when it ceases to grow.

LEONARD G. BOONIN, CONCERNING THE RELATION OF LOGIC TO LAW

17 Journal of Legal Education 155–160, 165–166 (1965) [footnotes omitted].*

Questions concerning the relation of logic to law have been of perplexing concern to legal theorists, jurists, and others seeking to understand and make intelligible the basic structure of the law. The problems which have arisen concerning their relation have been due largely to a failure to clarify conceptually the nature of "legal logic." The purpose of this article is both to explain how some of this confusion concerning the relation of logic to law arose, and to introduce certain distinctions as a way of clarifying their relation.

I

Very broadly speaking, and with some notable exceptions, the general legal theory which prevailed from the time of Blackstone until the Twentieth Century treated the law as a coherent and complete rational system. It was thought to contain legal rules, principles, standards, and maxims, by the application of which one could deductively arrive at the appropriate decision in any given case. The rules and principles were sometimes conceived as eternal and unchanging natural laws, at other times as the historically authentic "living law" embedded in the customs of society, and again as simply the valid enactments of the sovereign. These three representative views as to the source and criteria of the validity of legal rules are, respectively, natural law doctrine, historical jurisprudence, and legal positivism. While proponents of these varying views disagreed as to the criteria of valid law, there seems to have been general agreement in the view of the law as coherent and complete, and of the judicial process as essentially a deductive application of existing rules of law.

While this conception of the law may appear more fitting for a legal system based on a code developed by legal authorities consciously seeking to systematize the law, it was also a widely held view of Anglo–American legal theorists. These theorists were in some way able to reconcile this conception of the law with the fact that in Anglo–American law legal decisions are authoritative sources of legal rules and law grows, to a large extent, out of such legal decisions.

Law was even compared with mathematics and the judge was considered a kind of geometrician, which implied that judges' decisions were as bound by rules and as logically necessary as mathematical proofs. In addition, legal decisions were justified as logically following from the application of those principles and rules. An important corollary of this view of the law was that there is as little justification for holding the judiciary responsible for judicial decisions as for holding mathematicians personally responsible for simply deriving what is implicit within a given mathematical system. The judge's function is simply to apply existing principles of law, whether such principles be conceived in terms of natural law, living law or valid legislative enactments. The judiciary does not make or create law, but rather finds it and applies it. Even cases in which a judge reverses a previous interpretation of the law are not to be characterized as changing the law. What is being done in such cases is simply to restore the "true" rule and remove its previous misinterpretation. That this "traditional theory" did permeate the conception of law until recently can be gathered from the reflections of an American lawyer:

> In days that men of my generation can remember, it was popular for lawyers to assert that judges do not make the law; they merely find it as it already exists in law books and other source material of recognized authority. This notion went unchallenged and exercised a dominant influence over the practical life of the law. . . . That it is a myth is now generally recognized. The breakdown of its effect on the law, not yet complete but far enough advanced to be unmistakable, represents a major change in the climate of professional legal opinion within my generation.

II

It is perhaps fair to identify the beginnings of the systematic attack on the rational deductive model of the law in the United States with the writings and legal opinions of Justice Oliver Wendell Holmes. Holmes can best be understood in the context of the general "revolt against formalism" that occurred in various disciplines at the turn of the century. The influence on Holmes of the doctrines of evolution and pragmatism is unmistakable. Holmes was even a participant in the "Metaphysical Club" of C.S. Pierce. His concern with legal history and the evolution and development of legal principles made it difficult for him to conceive the law as based on eternal and unchanging rational principles. His pragmatic concern with the operative effects and consequences of legal doctrine is clearly expressed in his famous address, "The Path of the Law."

> What constitutes the law? You will find some text writers telling you that it is something different from what is decided by the courts of Massachusetts or England, that it is a system of reason, that it is a deduction from principles of ethics or admitted axioms or what not, which may or may not coincide with the decisions. But if we take the view of our friend the bad man we shall find that he does not care two straws for the axioms or deductions, but that he does want to know what the Massachusetts or English courts are likely to do in fact. I am much of his mind. The prophecies of what the courts will do in fact, and nothing more pretentious, are what I mean by the law.

It is this concern with the actual consequences and operative effects of legal doctrine, as opposed to the mere formal normative content, that becomes the central concern of the movement called "legal realism."

* * * *

* * *

III

While the traditional view of the judicial process was apparently widely expressed, one can perhaps raise questions as to how literally it was meant. In a way, it seems implausible that anyone with the least familiarity with the judicial process could have conceived it in such a simple manner. While the traditional theory may appear more plausible in a period characterized by relatively stable conditions, as opposed to one in which great changes and developments are clearly evident, it is still difficult to see how one could literally believe the law to be a coherent and complete system, and the judicial process to be only a logical application of existing rules of law. Professor Cooperrider has made the plausible suggestion that the traditional theory was not intended as an accurate descriptive account of the judicial process:

> . . . I am also inclined to doubt that it is sound to think of it as a conscious attempt at scientific description. It did, however, represent a view which at one time was generally held as to the *attitude* which the judge should bring to his task: that it should be his *objective* to deal with the case before him in that way which was indicated by an interpretation of existing authorities, rather than in that way which seemed to him on the facts to be the fairest or most desirable from a social point of view. It called for the subordination of his judgment to that of the collectivity of his predecessors, for a primary reliance on a reasoned extrapolation of accumulated experience.

According to this interpretation, the traditional theory represents more a practical regulative *ideal* of how the judicial process *ought* to be conceived by the judiciary than a theoretical analysis of its actual structure and functioning. If this analysis adequately explains why the traditional theory was, and perhaps to some extent still is, deeply embedded in the legal consciousness, it of course does not constitute a justification for it. Part of the message of contemporary jurisprudence is that the judge does, to some extent, unavoidably exercise a creative "legislative" choice, and that he has the responsibility to exercise it in an intelligent manner. To conceal the inevitable elements of discretion involved in the judicial process behind a theory which denies their existence cannot contribute to a responsible use of that discretion. The attack on the traditional theory has been valuable and important in making us sensitive to the variety and complexity of values involved in the judicial process. It has also led, unfortunately, to some confusion concerning the relation of logic to law.

IV

The attack on the conception of law as a coherent and complete system has often shifted into an attack on logic itself. One can find numerous instances in legal literature and legal opinions in which logic is deprecated and its value questioned. One of Justice Holmes' most famous remarks has often been employed by those objecting to logic in the law:

> The life of the law has not been logic: it has been experience. The felt necessities of the time, the prevalent moral and political theories, intuitions of public policy, avowed or unconscious, even the prejudices which judges share with their fellow men, have had a good deal more to do than the syllogism in determining the rules by which men should be governed.

While this statement is perhaps susceptible to more than one interpretation, Holmes can be construed as making two points which are essentially sound and true. First, that the changes and development of legal rules and principles cannot be fully explained and made intelligible in terms of purely logical analysis of legal concepts. Second, that such logical analysis is not a sufficient tool for rationally deciding legal controversies.

Whether Holmes intended it or not, his remark has been repeated in many contexts that import a sharp antithesis between "logic" and "experience." Holmes himself appears to adopt this interpretation elsewhere when he says:

> . . . the whole outline of the law is the resultant of a conflict at every point between logic and good sense—the one striving to work fiction out to consistent results, the other restraining and at last overcoming that effort when the results become too manifestly unjust.

* * *

Logic is concerned with the general and formal principles of valid reasoning. Legal logic is correspondingly concerned with the particular principles of legally sound and valid reasoning and decision-making. The whole body of authoritative legal material constitutes a complex network in terms of which legal inferences can be made and evaluated. It is this material sense of legal logic that underlies most of the remarks of legal theorists concerning the relation of logic to law.

When legal theorists say that the law is not logical, one of the main things they mean is that the law is not a wholly consistent and complete system. A legal system is open-textured in the sense that new rules and principles can be created and old ones changed. In addition, it is often the case that competing rules have applicability to the same set of facts. To say that the law is not wholly logical is a way of saying that judges are not merely tools for deriving legal conclusions. Judges exercise a creative function in various ways. The basic problem is one of setting up rational standards to guide judges in exercising their creative functions. This is a fundamental problem for normative jurisprudence.

NOTE BY THE EDITORS: TYPES OF LEGAL REASONING

Deductive Reasoning. Treusch describes a type of reasoning generally referred to as "deductive reasoning." This category of reasoning is appropriate when a rule of law clearly covers the facts of a litigated case and is therefore applied by the judge through the use of syllogistic logic.

Inductive Reasoning. In some cases, no ready-made rule is available to the judge to guide him in his decision, but he may be able to distill a pertinent rule or principle from a string of earlier decisions. The earlier cases may have been decided on extremely narrow grounds, but the judge may find implicit in them a general principle fit to serve as a rule of decision in the case at bar. In that event, the judge is said to derive a general rule from particular instances by the method of inductive reasoning. Thus, a sequence of cases might show that the courts, without spelling out a comprehensive general principle, had granted injunctions or damages to homeowners who had been seriously inconvenienced by noisy blasting operations, or noxious smells, or the barking of dogs in a nearby kennel. From these decisions, a judge could derive a rule to the effect that a homeowner is entitled to protection against nuisances interfering with the enjoyment of his property rights.

Reasoning by Analogy. This form of reasoning involves the extension of a legal rule to a fact situation not covered by its express words, but deemed to be within the purview of a policy principle underlying the rule. If there is a rule, for example, that the executor of a will is precluded from bringing an action outside of the state of his appointment, this rule might be extended by analogy to an administrator of an estate. This extension would be predicated on the rationale, held to be implicit in the rule in question, that the authority of court-appointed functionaries to act in a representative capacity should be confined to the jurisdictional limits of the state in which they are performing official acts. Reasoning by analogy is widely used in relation to judicial precedent.

Dialectical Reasoning. This type of reasoning is used by judges and lawyers in the following groups of cases: (1) novel problems in which no suitable rule or principle is provided by the law; (2) situations where two or more competing rules or major premises are available for the determination of an issue, among which a genuine choice must be made; and (3) instances in which a rule or precedent covering the case at hand exists, but where the court rejects its application as unsound, either generally or at least in the context of the litigated facts. In these three types of cases, it is impossible for the court to dispose of the controversy by means of an analytic form of argumentation, that is, by deduction, induction, or analogy.

In these situations, judges or lawyers will rely on arguments that they deem to be plausible, reasonable, and convincing. A careful evaluation of points speaking for and against the contemplated solution is frequently an important part of the process. In other words, a balance sheet of opposing considerations is drawn up, and a comparison of their relative weight and utility in the light of the problem to be solved is undertaken. The result finally reached will usually gain in persuasiveness if it rests not only on a single ground, but is strengthened by the cumulative force of a number of reasons.

In some cases, the courts use complex or mixed modes of reasoning. For example, when the words of a statute are ambiguous, a simple deductive application of the statute is not possible. If the legislative history of the statute throws a clear light on the meaning of an ambiguous term, a two-step form of deduction becomes necessary, i.e., a deduction from the text of the statute combined with a deduction from the legislative history clarifying the ambiguous term. If the legislative history is also unclear or ambiguous, dialectical reasoning becomes necessary in order to determine which of two or more interpretations is the most persuasive one.

Problems

(1) A loans a valuable painting to B for an indefinite period of time. B sells the painting to C. A causes B to be indicted for larceny. B is sentenced to a term in prison. The conviction is based on a state statute reading as follows: "Whoever unlawfully appropriates a chattel belonging to another is guilty of larceny and shall be punished by imprisonment not exceeding five years or by a fine."

Some time thereafter E took a car belonging to D for the purpose of stealing a ride to a neighboring town. Upon arrival he abandoned the car. It was restored to D a week later. D, having been seriously inconvenienced by the temporary loss of the car, caused E to be indicted for larceny. E was acquitted. The court took the position that the drafters of the larceny statute had in mind a permanent acquisition of a chattel by the thief. A merely temporary use of a car belonging to another, even though unlawful, was not in the court's view within the meaning of the term "appropriate."

Considering the four types of legal reasoning discussed in the preceding Note, which of these was employed by the court in this case?

(2) In Muskopf v. Corning Hospital District, 55 Cal.2d 211, 11 Cal. Rptr. 89, 359 P.2d 457 (1961), the Supreme Court of California overruled earlier decisions recognizing the doctrine of sovereign immunity, a doctrine that denied the responsibility of the state for tortious acts committed by its agents. The court pointed out that the principle of sovereign immunity originated in England as a personal prerogative of the Stuart kings, was thoughtlessly received into American law, became riddled with exceptions in the course of time, and caused many serious and unnecessary injustices. The court referred to the argument made on behalf of the state that the rule has existed for such a long time that only the legislature can abolish it. The court countered this argument by stating that not only the courts, but also the legislature had imposed many restrictions on the doctrine, implying by this statement that ever-increasing dissatisfaction with the doctrine had marked its history in this century. For these reasons the Court concluded that the doctrine should be abandoned because it was obsolete and thoroughly unfair.

What type of legal reasoning was used by the Court in this case?

B. LOGIC AND POLICY IN JUDICIAL OPINIONS

When reading the next two cases, you should know that, at common law, the duty of a landowner to a stranger regarding risks created by a dangerous condition on his property varied, depending upon whether the stranger was located on or off the premises. A landowner was required to exercise reasonable care to see that strangers using an adjacent public highway or waterway passed by safely. By contrast, he owed no duty of care whatsoever to trespassers who came upon his property without an invitation. See generally W. Prosser and P. Keeton, *The Law of Torts* §§ 57–58 (5th ed. 1984.)

HYNES v. NEW YORK CENTRAL R.R. CO.
Supreme Court of New York, Appellate Division, 1919.
188 A.D. 178.

Putnam, J.: The complaint alleged defendant's neglect in improperly erecting, constructing and maintaining its poles and appurtenances and the wires attached thereto, and in failing to secure said wires and repair the poles, appurtenances and wires, with the result that the same fell.

The learned court rightly held that the deceased was a trespasser. The plank was part of defendant's property, and was so annexed as to become part of the realty. Decedent's entry upon defendant's close from the waters of the ship canal was an unlawful intrusion. On this plank, he was still a trespasser—even when he stepped outward across defendant's technical boundary line and stood near the outer end, over the waters of the ship canal.

Appellant's point that defendant did not own the extremity of this plank, because it projected over the waterway, is against ancient doctrines, that such an object supported from the place of annexation carries the title to the whole thing so annexed, even if it protrudes over and across a vertical boundary line. This applies to tree branches which overhang a neighbor's land. (Masters v. Pollie, (1619) 2 Roll's Rep. 141.)[1] In Hoffman v. Armstrong (48 N.Y. 201) such an instance of an overhanging branch led the court to declare that "if an adjoining owner should build his house so as to overhang it, such an encroachment would not give the owner of the land the legal title to the part so overhanging." (p. 203). In support of which is cited Aiken v. Benedict (39 Barb. 400), which held that ejectment would not lie in such a case. While the owner of land so overhung may cut off the branches above his land (Lemon v. Webb, L.R. (1895) A.C. 1), he cannot, in removing the nuisance, appropriate the materials, and convert to his use the severed branches, or fruit thereon. (Mills v. Brooker, L.R. (1919) 1 K.B. 555.)

The plank cannot be held an unlawful interference with navigation, in view of the apparent shallowness of the water and the circumstances that neither the Federal nor the State authorities had taken any steps for its removal. (1 Franham, Waters, § 95.)

The owner of a wharf, pier or like projection, even if run out beyond the proper exterior line, has a good right against all private intruders or trespassers. (Wetmore v. Atlantic White Lead Co., 37 Barb. 70; Wetmore v. Brooklyn Gas Light Co., 42 N.Y. 384.)[2] As Grover, J. said in the case last cited, the State may have a remedy, but this "gives the plaintiff no right of entry upon such land for any purpose" (p. 393). The same was laid down in Crooked Lake Navigation Co. v. Keuka Navigation Co. (26 Wkly.Dig. 145; affd., 115 N.Y. 667).

In another view, an argument that the extremity of such plank was not defendant's property cannot aid the plaintiff, since, for all that here appears, the entire plank was in defendant's possession; and such possession, even without legal title, is good against an intruder committing a trespass. (Jackson v. Harder, 4 Johns. 202; Cutts v. Spring, 15 Mass. 134; Beardslee v. New Berlin, L. & P., 207 N.Y. 34, 41.)

1. Editors' note: In Masters v. Pollie, 2 Rolle 141 (1619), the plaintiff brought an action of trespass, alleging that the defendant had carried away his timber. The defendant replied that the timber came from a tree that was partly on his land. The Court found that the main part of the tree was on the plaintiff's land, and that some roots only extended into the defendant's land. On the basis of these facts the Court found that the tree belonged to the plaintiff, and that defendant was not entitled to any part of the timber which the plaintiff had cut into boards.

2. Editors' note: In Wetmore v. Atlantic White Lead Co., 37 Barb. (N.Y.) 70 (1862), the defendant owned a wharf extending into the public river. The construction and maintenance of the wharf had been authorized by a legislative act of the State of New York. The plaintiff attempted to unload one of his ships at the wharf and was prevented from doing so by the defendant. He sued for damages. The Court held that the wharf was the exclusive property of the defendant, although it extended into the public stream, and that the plaintiff had no easement for its use.

This complaint was for breach of duty whereby the poles and wires broke and "fell to the ground." The suggestion that plaintiff might recover in analogy to a like accident to a boy swimming in the canal, I think cannot apply. The duty toward persons passing in the fairway, whether in vessels or swimming, is widely different from the duty to one intruding against warning signs, and wrongfully occupying defendant's property.

Therefore, the fall of defendant's wires, not being a willful or wanton injury, violated no duty which defendant owed to the deceased.

The order setting aside the verdict for plaintiff and granting a new trial should be affirmed, with costs.

JENKS, P.J., KELLY, J., concurred; JAYCOX, J. read for reversal, with whom BLACKMAR, J. concurred.

JAYCOX, J., dissenting:

The plaintiff's intestate was not a trespasser in the sense which brings him within the operation of the rule that the owner of the premises owes no duty to trespassers. Ordinarily it clearly appears that the accident would not have happened but for the trespass. In this case, however, the falling wires would have been as fatal to this boy swimming in the river at that point as standing upon a plank attached to the defendant's premises. If a wagon of the defendant had been left standing in the highway and the plaintiff's intestate had climbed into that wagon and while there had been killed by the defendant's wires falling into the highway, there would have been no question as to the plaintiff's right to recover. The situation is exactly analogous to the situation involved in this action. The boy's death was not caused by a defect in the premises upon which he trespassed, but by the negligence of the defendant which permitted its wires to fall into navigable waters of the river. If the boy's death had been caused by the breaking of the plank upon which he was standing, the reasoning of the prevailing opinion herein would apply. I dissent.

BLACKMAR, J. concurred.

Order setting aside verdict for plaintiff and granting new trial affirmed, with costs.

HYNES v. NEW YORK CENTRAL R.R. CO.

Court of Appeals of New York, 1921.
231 N.Y. 229, 131 N.E. 898.

CARDOZO, J. On July 8, 1916, Harvey Hynes, a lad of sixteen, swam with two companions from the Manhattan to the Bronx side of the Harlem River or United States Ship Canal, a navigable stream. Along the Bronx side of the river was the right of way of the defendant, the New York Central railroad, which operated its trains at that point by high tension wires, strung on poles and crossarms. Projecting from the defendant's bulkhead above the waters of the river was a plank or springboard from which boys of the neighborhood used to dive. One end of the board had been placed under a rock on the defendant's land, and nails had been driven at its point of contact with the bulkhead. Measured from this point of contact the length behind was five feet; the length in front eleven. The bulkhead itself was about three and a half feet back of the pier line as located by the government. From this it follows that for seven and a half feet the springboard was beyond the line of the defendant's property, and above the public waterway. Its height measured from the stream was three feet at the bulkhead, and five feet at its outermost extremity. For more than five years swimmers had used it as a diving board without protest or obstruction.

On this day Hynes and his companions climbed on top of the bulkhead intending to leap into the water. One of them made the plunge in safety. Hynes followed to the front of the springboard, and stood poised for his dive. At that moment a crossarm with electric wires fell from the defendant's pole. The wires struck the diver, flung him from the shattered board, and plunged him to his death below. His mother, suing as administratrix, brings this action for her damages. Thus far the courts have held that Hynes at the end of the springboard above the public waters was a trespasser on the defendant's land. They have thought it immaterial that the board itself was a trespass, an encroachment on the public ways. They have thought it of no significance that Hynes would have met the same fate if he had been below the board and not above it. The board, they have said, was annexed to the defendant's bulkhead. By force of such annexation, it was to be reckoned as a fixture, and thus constructively, if not actually, an extension of the land. The defendant was under a duty to use reasonable care that bathers swimming or standing in the water should not be electrocuted by wires falling from its right of way. But to bathers diving from the springboard, there was no duty, we are told, unless the injury was the product of mere willfulness or wantonness, no duty of active vigilance to safeguard the impending structure. Without wrong to them crossarms might be left to rot; wires highly charged with electricity might sweep them from their stand, and bury them in the subjacent waters. In climbing on the board, they became trespassers and outlaws. The conclusion is defended with much subtlety of reasoning, with much insistence upon its inevitableness as a merely logical deduction. A majority of the court are unable to accept it as the conclusion of the law.

We assume, without deciding, that the springboard was a fixture, a permanent improvement of the defendant's right of way. Much might be said in favor of another view. We do not press the inquiry, for we are persuaded that the right of bathers does not depend upon these nice distinctions. Liability would not be doubtful, we are told, had the boy been diving from a pole, if the pole had been vertical. The diver in such a situation would have been separated from the defendant's freehold. Liability, it is said, has been escaped because the pole was horizontal. The plank when projected lengthwise was an extension of the soil. We are to concentrate our gaze on the private ownership of the board. We are to ignore the public ownership of the circumambient spaces of water and of air. Jumping from a boat or a barrel, the boy would have been a bather in the river. Jumping from the end of a springboard, he was no longer, it is said, a bather, but a trespasser on a right of way.

Rights and duties in systems of living law are not built upon such quicksands.

Bathers in the Harlem river on the day of this disaster were in the enjoyment of a public highway, entitled to reasonable protection against destruction by the defendant's wires. They did not cease to be bathers entitled to the same protection while they were diving from encroaching objects or engaging in the sports that are common among swimmers. Such acts were not equivalent to an abandonment of the highway, departure from its proper uses, a withdrawal from the waters, and an entry upon land. A plank of private right has been interposed between the river and the air, but the public ownership was unchanged in the space below it and above. The defendant does not deny that it would have owed a duty to this boy if he had been leaning against the springboard with his feet upon the ground. He is said to have forfeited protection as he put his feet upon the plank. Presumably the same result would follow if the plank had been a few inches above the surface of the water instead of a few feet. Duties are thus supposed to arise and to be extinguished in alternate zones or strata. Two boys walking in the country or swimming in a river stop to rest for a moment along the side of the road or the margin of the stream. One of them throws himself beneath the overhanging branches of the tree. The other perches himself on a bough a foot or so above the ground (Hoffman v. Armstrong, 48 N.Y. 201). Both are killed by falling wires. The defendant would have us say that there is a remedy for the representatives of one, and none for the representatives of the other. We may be permitted to distrust the logic that leads to such conclusions.

The truth is that every act of Hynes from his first plunge into the river until the moment of his death, was in the enjoyment of the public waters, and under cover of the protection which his presence in those waters gave him. The use of the springboard was not an abandonment of his rights as a bather. It was a mere by-play, an incident, subordinate and ancillary to the execution of his primary purpose, the enjoyment of the highway. The by-play, the incident, was not the cause of the disaster. Hynes would have gone to his death if he had been below the springboard or beside it (Laidlaw v. Sage, 158 N.Y. 73, 97). The wires were not stayed by the presence of the plank. They followed the boy in his fall, and overwhelmed him in the waters. The defendant assumes that the identification of ownership of a fixture with ownership of land is complete in every incident. But there are important elements of difference. Title to the fixture, unlike title to the land, does not carry with it rights of ownership usque ad coelum. There will hardly be denial that a cause of action would have arisen if the wires had fallen on an aeroplane proceeding above the river, though the location of the impact could be identified as the space above the springboard. The most that the defendant can fairly ask is exemption from liability where the use of the fixture is itself the efficient peril. That would be the situation, for example, if the weight of the boy upon the board had caused it to break and thereby thrown him into the river. There is no such causal connection here between his position and his injuries. We think there was no moment when he was beyond the pale of the defendant's duty—the duty of care and vigilance in the storage of destructive forces.

This case is a striking instance of the dangers of "a jurisprudence of conceptions" (Pound, Mechanical Jurisprudence, 8 Columbia Law Review, 605, 608, 610), the extension of a maxim or a definition with relentless disregard of consequences to "a dryly logical extreme." The approximate and relative become the definite and absolute. Landowners are not bound to regulate their conduct in contemplation of the presence of trespassers intruding upon private structures. Landowners are bound to regulate their conduct in contemplation of the presence of travelers upon the adjacent public ways. There are times when there is little trouble in marking off the field of exemption and immunity from that of liability and duty. Here structures and ways are so united and commingled, superimposed upon each other, that the fields are brought together. In such circumstances, there is little help in pursuing general maxims to ultimate conclusions. They have been framed alio intuitu. They must be reformulated and readapted to meet exceptional conditions. Rules appropriate to spheres which are conceived of as separate and distinct cannot both be enforced when the spheres become concentric. There must then be readjustment or collision. In one sense, and that a highly technical and artificial one, the diver at the end of the springboard is an intruder on the adjoining lands. In another sense, and one that realists will accept more readily, he is still on public waters in the exercise of public rights. The law must say whether it will subject him to the rule of the one field or of the other, of this sphere or of that. We think that considerations of analogy, of convenience, of policy, and of justice, exclude him from the field of the defendant's immunity and exemption, and place him in the field of liability and duty (Beck v. Carter, 68 N.Y. 283; Jewhurst v. City of Syracuse, 108 N.Y. 303; McCloskey v. Buckley, 223 N.Y. 187, 192.)

The judgment of the Appellate Division and that of the Trial Term should be reversed, and a new trial granted, with costs to abide the event.

HOGAN, POUND, and CRANE, JJ., concur; HISCOCK, CH. J., CHASE and MCLAUGHLIN, JJ., dissent.

Judgments reversed, etc.

BORER v. AMERICAN AIRLINES, INC.

Supreme Court of California, 1977.

19 Cal.3d 441, 138 Cal.Rptr. 302, 563 P.2d 858.

TOBRINER, ACTING CHIEF JUSTICE.

In Rodriguez v. Bethlehem Steel Corp. (1974) 12 Cal.3d 382, 115 Cal.Rptr. 765, 525 P.2d 669 we held that a married person whose spouse had been injured by the negligence of a third party may maintain a cause of action for loss of "consortium." We defined loss of "consortium" as the "loss of conjugal fellowship and sexual relations" (12 Cal.3d at p. 385, 115 Cal.Rptr. at p. 766, 525 P.2d at p. 670), but ruled that the term included the loss of love, companionship, society, sexual relations, and household services. Our decision carefully avoided resolution of the question whether anyone other than the spouse of a negligently injured person, such as a child or a parent, could maintain a cause of action analogous to that upheld in Rodriguez. We face that issue today: the present case presents a claim by nine children for the loss of the services, companionship, affection and guidance of their mother; the companion case of Baxter v. Superior Court, Cal., 138 Cal.Rptr. 315, 563 P.2d 871 presents the claim of a mother and father for the loss of the companionship and affection of their 16–year–old son.

* * *

Since this appeal arises following a trial court order sustaining a demurrer to plaintiffs' complaint without leave to amend, we focus first on the specific allegations of plaintiffs' complaint. Plaintiffs, the nine children of Patricia Borer, allege that on March 21, 1972, the cover on a lighting fixture at the American Airlines Terminal at Kennedy Airport fell and struck Patricia. Plaintiffs further assert that as a result of the physical injuries sustained by Patricia, each of them has been "deprived of the services, society, companionship, affection, tutelage, direction, guidance, instruction and aid in personality development, all with its accompanying psychological, educational and emotional detriment, by reason of Patricia Borer being unable to carry on her usual duties of a mother." The complaint sets forth causes of action based upon negligence, breach of warranty, and manufacture of a defective product; it names as defendants American Airlines, two companies which manufactured and assembled the lighting fixture, and various fictitious defendants. Each plaintiff seeks damages of $100,000.

* * *

Rodriguez * * * does not compel the conclusion that foreseeable injury to a legally recognized relationship necessarily postulates a cause of action; instead it clearly warns that social policy must at some point intervene to delimit liability. Patricia Borer, for example, foreseeably has not only a husband (who has a cause of action under Rodriguez) and the children who sue here, but also parents whose right of action depends upon our decision in the companion case of Baxter v. Superior Court; foreseeably, likewise, she has brothers, sisters, cousins, inlaws, friends, colleagues, and other acquaintances who will be deprived of her companionship. No one suggests that all such persons possess a right of action for loss of Patricia's consortium; all agree that somewhere a line must be drawn. As stated by Judge Breitel in Tobin v. Grossman (1969) 24 N.Y.2d 609, 619, 301 N.Y.S.2d 554, 561, 249 N.E. 2d 419, 424; "Every injury has ramifying consequences, like the ripplings of the waters, without end. The problem for the law is to limit the legal consequences of wrongs to a controllable degree."

The decision whether to limit liability for loss of consortium by denying a cause of action in the parent-child context, or to permit that action but deny any claim based upon more remote relationships, is thus a question of policy. * * *

In the first instance, strong policy reasons argue against extension of liability to loss of consortium of the parent-child relationship. Loss of consortium is an intangible, nonpecuniary loss; monetary compensation will not enable plaintiffs to regain the companionship and guidance of a mother; it will simply establish a fund so that upon reaching adulthood, when plaintiffs will be less in need of maternal guidance, they will be unusually wealthy men and women. To say that plaintiffs have been "compensated" for their loss is superficial; in reality they have suffered a loss for which they can never be compensated; they have obtained, instead, a future benefit essentially unrelated to that loss.

* * *

A second reason for rejecting a cause of action for loss of parental consortium is that, because of its intangible character, damages for such a loss are very difficult to measure.

* * *

Plaintiffs point out that similar policy arguments could be, and to some extent were, raised in *Rodriguez* and that our decision to uphold the wife's action for loss of consortium rejected those arguments. We do not, however, read *Rodriguez* as holding that arguments based upon the intangible character of damages and the difficulty of measuring such damages do not merit consideration. Such a holding would imply an indefinite extension of liability for loss of consortium to all foreseeable relationships, a proposition *Rodriguez* plainly repudiates.

Rodriguez, then, holds no more than that in the context of a spousal relationship, the policy arguments against liability do not suffice to justify a holding denying a cause of action. Plaintiffs contend, however, that no adequate ground exists to distinguish a cause of action for loss of spousal consortium from one for loss of parental consortium. We reject the contention for three reasons.

First, as *Rodriguez* pointed out, the spousal action for loss of consortium rests in large part on the "impairment or destruction of the sexual life of the couple." (12 Cal.3d 382, 405, 115 Cal.Rptr. 765, 780, 525 P.2d 669, 684.) No similar element of damage appears in a child's suit for loss of consortium.

Second, actions by children for loss of parental consortium create problems of multiplication of actions and damages not present in the spousal context.

* * *

The instant case illustrates the point. Patricia Borer has nine children, each of whom would possess his own independent right of action for loss of consortium. Even in the context of a consolidated action, the assertion of nine independent causes of action for the children in addition to the father's claim for loss of consortium and the mother's suit for ordinary tort damages, demonstrates the extent to which recognition of plaintiffs' asserted cause of action will multiply the tort liability of the defendant.

Finally, the proposition that a spouse has a cause of action for loss of consortium, but that a child does not, finds overwhelming approval in the decisions of other jurisdictions. Over 30 states, a clear majority of those who have decided the question, now permit a *spousal* suit for loss of consortium. *No* state permits a child to sue for loss of parental consortium. That claim has been presented, at latest count, to 18 jurisdictions, and rejected by all of them.

* * *

In summary, we do not doubt the reality or the magnitude of the injury suffered by plaintiffs. We are keenly aware of the need of children for the love, affection, society and guidance of their parents; any injury which diminishes the ability of a parent to meet these needs is plainly a family tragedy, harming all members of that community. We conclude, however, that taking into account all considerations which bear on this question, including the inadequacy of monetary compensation to alleviate that tragedy, the difficulty of measuring damages, and the danger of imposing extended and disproportionate liability, we should not recognize a nonstatutory cause of action for the loss of parental consortium.

The judgment is affirmed.

NIX v. PREFORMED LINE PRODUCTS CO.

California Court of Appeal, 1985.
170 Cal.App.3d 975, 216 Cal.Rptr. 581.

PAULINE DAVIS HANSON, ACTING PRESIDING JUSTICE.

I

On September 1, 1982, Ronald Nix (Ronald), father of appellants Shane and Nicholas Nix, was severely injured when a wooden utility pole broke and caused him to fall to the ground. [The pole was manufactured by the respondent. The appellants filed a complaint against the respondent for loss of parental consortium. Respondent filed a demurrer, and it was granted without leave to amend.]

* * *

Discussion

Action for Loss of Parental Consortium.

Appellants urge that because of society's increased recognition of the need to protect the rights of children, the California Supreme Court's reasons for denying a cause of action for loss of parental consortium must be reevaluated. Appellants' challenge is based in part on recent holdings in other jurisdictions recognizing such a cause of action.

The issue of parental consortium was addressed in Borer v. American Airlines, Inc. (1977) 19 Cal.3d 441, 138 Cal.Rptr. 302, 563 P.2d 858, a case directly on point. In *Borer,* the California Supreme Court addressed the issue of extending or limiting liability for loss of consortium as a question of policy. Its major concern was to limit the legal consequences of wrongs to a controllable degree. (Id., at p. 446, 138 Cal. Rptr. 302, 563 P.2d 858.)

Only three years before *Borer,* the Supreme Court recognized the existence of a cause of action for loss of spousal consortium in Rodriguez v. Bethlehem Steel Corp. (1974) 12 Cal.3d 382, 115 Cal.Rptr. 765, 525 P.2d 669. To deny a similar cause of action to the children of an injured parent, the *Borer* court limited the holding of *Rodriguez* and attempted to distinguish its facts. * * *

* * *

The *Borer* court, did not feel compelled by *Rodriguez* to conclude that any foreseeable injury to a legally recognized relationship necessarily created a cause of action. The *Borer* court explained *Rodriguez* merely held that the policy arguments against liability did not justify denying a cause of action in a marital relationship. (Borer v. American Airlines, Inc., supra, 19 Cal.3d at p. 446, 448, 138 Cal.Rptr. 302, 563 P.2d 858.) The court was not persuaded to reach the same conclusion in a parent-child relationship.

* * *

Decisions of the Supreme Court that have never been reversed or modified are binding (County of Butte v. Superior Court (1960) 178 Cal. App.2d 310, 311, 2 Cal.Rptr. 913); we must follow the holding in *Borer.* It is not the function of an intermediate court to reexamine a Supreme Court decision for the purpose of enunciating and enforcing a different rule of law. (Goncalves v. S.F. Unified School Dist. (1958) 166 Cal.App. 2d 87, 89, 332 P.2d 713.)

Borer is directly on point; its reasons for denying a cause of action for loss of parental consortium have not been supplanted. No court in California has ruled that *Borer* should be overruled. In addition, with the exception of one case,[3] the availability of loss of consortium actions

---

3. The case of Butcher v. Superior Court (1983) 139 Cal.App.3d 58, 188 Cal. Rptr. 503, recognized a cause of action for loss of consortium brought by an unmarried cohabitant of the negligently injured victim. The *Butcher* court held that there had to be a showing that the nonmarital relationship is both stable and significant, and that it possesses every characteristic of the spousal relationship except formaliza-

has not been extended beyond the spousal context in California. Under the authority of *Borer,* we can only agree with the sustaining of the demurrer without leave to amend.

However, at the time of the *Borer* decision, as noted by the *Borer* court in support of its holding, no state recognized such a claim. (Borer v. American Airlines, Inc., supra, 19 Cal.3d at p. 449, 138 Cal.Rptr. 302, 563 P.2d 858.) Since the *Borer* decision, a change of some importance has occurred in the development of loss of parental consortium actions in other jurisdictions.

Massachusetts was the first state to recognize a cause of action for loss of parental consortium. In Ferriter v. Daniel O'Connell's Sons, Inc. (1980) 381 Mass. 507, 413 N.E.2d 690, the Massachusetts Supreme Court noted that minors have a strong interest in their parents' society—an interest closely analogous to that of the wife, the former relationship no less intense than the latter. (Id., 413 N.E.2d at p. 692.) The court thought it entirely appropriate to protect the child's reasonable expectations of parental society when the parent suffered negligent injury rather than death, noting that similar damages were available to a child under a wrongful death statute. (Id., 413 N.E.2d at p. 695.)

Refusing to wait for legislative recognition of the cause of action, the Massachusetts court stated:

> " 'In a field long left to the common law, change may well come about by the same medium of development. Sensible reform can here be achieved without the articulation of detail or the creation of administrative mechanisms that customarily comes about the legislative enactments * * *. In the end the Legislature may say that we have mistaken the present public understanding of the nature of the [parent-child] relation, but that we cannot now divine or anticipate.' " (Ferriter v. Daniel O'Connell's Sons, Inc., supra, 413 N.E.2d at p. 695–696.)

Minors in Massachusetts must show they are minors dependent on the parent, and the dependence is rooted not only in economic requirements, but also in "filial needs for closeness, guidance and nurture." (Id., 413 N.E.2d at p. 696.)

[Michigan and Iowa were the next states to recognize the cause of action.]

Wisconsin followed, recognizing a cause of action for loss of parental consortium in Theama By Bichler v. City of Kenosha (1984) 117 Wis. 2d 508, 344 N.W.2d 513. The Wisconsin Supreme Court noted that the genius of the common law is its ability to adapt itself to the changing needs of society, and resolution of whether a cause of action for loss of parental consortium should be recognized is just another step in the evolution of the courts' views of the changing nature of the family unit. (Id., 344 N.W.2d at p. 514.)

tion. This case, along with cases from other districts denying a similar cause of action, was granted a hearing by the Su-preme Court. The appeal was ultimately dismissed, leaving this conflict unresolved.

The *Theama* court discussed three reasons in favor of recognizing this cause of action: the importance of the family unit in society, the increasing recognition of a child as a person deserving of constitutional rights and protection by the courts, and the necessity of a parent's love, care, education and protection in contributing to the wholesome and complete development of the child. A combination of these elements, said the Wisconsin court, indicates it would be contrary to justice to deny the gravity of harm suffered by a child who is deprived of his or her parent's society and companionship because of another's negligence. (344 N.W.2d at p. 518.)

The *Theama* court specifically criticized the *Borer* opinion. In rejecting the *Borer* analysis, the court stated that a monetary award may be a poor substitute for the loss of a parent's society and companionship, but it is the only workable way our legal system has found to ease the injury of a tragic loss. It would be "perpetuation of the error" to deny recovery. (Theama By Bichler v. City of Kenosha, supra, 344 N.W.2d at p. 520.) The court reasoned that by drawing the line at the children, the *Borer* approach ignores the importance of the nuclear family in present day society, not to mention the factor of foreseeability. The *Theama* court noted that the problem of double recovery could be cured by limiting the injured parent's recovery to the child's loss of the parent's ability to support the child, while limiting the child's recovery to the loss of the parent's society and companionship. (Id., 344 N.W.2d at p. 522.)

The court concluded the reasons for allowing the cause of action clearly outweighed the reasons for disallowing it but limited recovery to the child's minority. (344 N.W.2d at p. 522.)

* * *

[Washington also recognized the cause of action.]

Not all courts recently addressing the issue decided to recognize such a cause of action. (Zorzos v. Rosen By and Through Rosen (Fla. 1985) 467 So.2d 305; De Angelis v. Lutheran Medical Center (1983) 58 N.Y.2d 1053, 462 N.Y.S.2d 626, 449 N.E.2d 406; Norwest v. Presbyterian Intercommunity Hosp. (1982) 293 Or. 543, 652 P.2d 318; Morgel v. Winger (N.D.1980) 290 N.W.2d 266; Salin v. Kloempken (Minn.1982) 322 N.W.2d 736.) However, one reason these courts refused to recognize the cause of action was a belief that because debates over social policy were involved, resolution of the issue should be left to the Legislature. (Norwest v. Presbyterian Intercommunity Hosp., supra, 652 P.2d at p. 324; Morgel v. Winger, supra, 290 N.W.2d at p. 267.) Other courts concerned with their responsibility to resolve the issue concluded the line had to be drawn somewhere and, as in the *Borer* case in California, the line was drawn at the children. (Zorzos v. Rosen By and Through Rosen, supra, 467 So.2d 305, at p. 307; Salin v. Kloempken, supra, 322 N.W.2d at pp. 737–738; De Angelis v. Lutheran Medical Center, supra, 462 N.Y.Supp.2d at pp. 627–628.) * * *

* * *

Borer v. American Airlines, Inc., supra, 19 Cal.3d 441, 138 Cal. Rptr. 302, 563 P.2d 858 is a Supreme Court case, and we are bound by its decision (Auto Equity Sales, Inc. v. Superior Court (1962) 57 Cal.2d 450, 455, 20 Cal.Rptr. 321, 369 P.2d 937). However, even though we must affirm the judgment of dismissal, the recent developments in other jurisdictions, plus the many discussions in criticism of the *Borer* result prompt us to point to the inconsistency in the law between husband and wife, and parent and child.   *   *   *

*   *   *

MARTIN, J., concurs.

BEST, JUSTICE, concurring.

I concur in the result but, to the extent that the majority opinion may be read as supporting and encouraging judicial creation of causes of action for loss of consortium in the parent-child relationship, I must voice reservations.

*   *   *

In my view, the courts are ill equipped to decide questions of public policy which are essentially political in nature. Such decisions should be made by the duly elected representatives of the people and, only then, after the opportunity for full legislative investigation and debate. Only through the legislative process can the conflicting public policies and the procedural safeguards appropriate and necessary to protect the interests of *all* of those affected be given due consideration.

Further References

Bodenheimer, E., "A Neglected Theory of Legal Reasoning," 21 Journal of Legal Education 373 (1969).

Joseph, H.W.B., *An Introduction to Logic* (2d ed. 1916), pp. 249–286.

Newman, J.O., "Between Legal Realism and Neutral Principles," 72 California Law Review 200 (1984).

Patterson, E.W., "Logic in the Law," 90 University of Pennsylvania Law Review 875 (1942).

Perelman, Ch., *Justice, Law, and Argument* (1980), pp. 125–135, 163–174.

Chapter VI

FUNDAMENTALS OF
STATUTORY INTERPRETATION

A. OVERVIEW

In the previous three chapters, we examined judicial precedent as a source of law. In this chapter, we will turn our attention to the other major source of law—legislation. You will recall that legislation is more authoritative than judicial precedent. A statute supersedes any prior inconsistent case law, and a judge is not free to disregard or "overrule" a statute except upon a finding of unconstitutionality. Nor can a judge alter the language of a statute in the same way that he or she can modify the rule of a prior case by reformulating its *ratio decidendi*.

The application of statutes to individual fact situations by a process of deductive reasoning is often rendered difficult by the substantial indeterminacy inherent in human language; words in many instances are inexact symbols of communication. For this and other reasons—among them the limited range of human imagination—statutes are rarely capable of identifying in precise terms the results intended by the legislature in all cases that might conceivably arise under them.

As we have already seen, case law cannot be applied mechanistically or formalistically. There will often be some doubt about the more appropriate formulation of the *ratio decidendi,* and considerations of policy, justice, and *stare decisis* may pull judicial decisionmakers in different directions. We now explore the parallel problems of statutory interpretation. While the greater authoritativeness of legislation keeps the judiciary under tighter rein when interpreting statutes than when applying precedent, excessive formalism may be as dangerous in the former situation as in the latter.

H.L.A. HART, THE CONCEPT OF LAW
pp. 123–26.*

Even when verbally formulated general rules are used, uncertainties as to the form of behaviour required by them may break out in particular concrete cases. * * * In all fields of experience, not only that of rules, there is a limit, inherent in the nature of language, to the guidance which general language can provide. * * * Canons of "interpretation" cannot eliminate, though they can diminish, these uncertainties; for these canons are themselves general rules for the use of language, and make use of general terms which themselves require interpretation. They cannot, any more than other rules, provide for their own interpretation. * * *

* * *

Whichever device, precedent or legislation, is chosen for the communication of standards of behaviour, these, however smoothly they work over the great mass of ordinary cases, will, at some point where their application is in question, prove indeterminate; they will have what has been termed an *open texture*. So far we have presented this, in the case of legislation, as a general feature of human language; uncertainty at the borderline is the price to be paid for the use of general classifying terms in any form of communication concerning matters of fact. * * * It is, however, important to appreciate why, apart from this dependence on language as it actually is, with its characteristics of open texture, we should not cherish, even as an ideal, the conception of a rule so detailed that the question of whether it applied or not to a particular case was always settled in advance, and never involved, at the point of actual application, a fresh choice between open alternatives. Put shortly, the reason is that the necessity for such choice is thrust upon us because we are men, not gods. It is a feature of the human predicament (and so of the legislative one) that we labour under two connected handicaps whenever we seek to regulate, unambiguously and in advance, some sphere of conduct by means of general standards to be used without further official direction on particular occasions. The first handicap is our relative ignorance of fact: the second is our relative indeterminacy of aim. * * *

* * * When we are bold enough to frame some general rule of conduct (e.g. a rule that no vehicle may be taken into the park), the language used in this context fixes necessary conditions which anything must satisfy if it is to be within its scope, and certain clear examples of what is certainly within its scope may be present to our minds. They are the paradigm, clear cases (the motor-car, the bus, the motor-cycle); and our aim in legislating is so far determinate because we have made a certain choice. We have initially settled the question that peace and quiet in the park is to be maintained at the cost, at any rate, of the

exclusion of these things. On the other hand, until we have put the general aim of peace in the park into conjunction with those cases which we did not, or perhaps could not, initially envisage (perhaps a toy motor-car electrically propelled) our aim is, in this direction, indeterminate. We have not settled, because we have not anticipated, the question which will be raised by the unenvisaged case when it occurs: whether some degree of peace in the park is to be sacrificed to, or defended against, those children whose pleasure or interest it is to use these things. When the unenvisaged case does arise, we confront the issues at stake and can then settle the question by choosing between the competing interests in the way which best satisfies us. In doing so we shall have rendered more determinate our initial aim, and shall incidentally have settled a question as to the meaning, for the purposes of this rule, of a general word.

Different legal systems, or the same system at different times, may either ignore or acknowledge more or less explicitly such a need for the further exercise of choice in the application of general rules to particular cases. The vice known to legal theory as formalism or conceptualism consists in an attitude to verbally formulated rules which both seeks to disguise and to minimize the need for such choice, once the general rule has been laid down.

NOTE BY THE EDITORS

For an earlier but no less eloquent presentation of Professor Hart's views on the role of judges in construing legislation, see Hart, "Positivism and the Separation of Law and Morals," 71 Harvard Law Review 593, 606–615 (1958). For a complex and engaging counterpoint to Hart's analysis of how judges faced by "the unenvisaged case" are to "settle the question by choosing between the competing interests," see Dworkin, "Hard Cases," 88 Harvard Law Review 1057, 1082–87 (1975). The approaches of Professors Hart and Dworkin are compared in Oakley, "Taking Wright Seriously: Of Judicial Discretion, Jurisprudents, and the Chief Justice," 4 Hastings Constitutional Law Quarterly 789, 801–809 (1977).

Problems

Professor Hart, in the preceding excerpt, refers to an ordinance, apparently enacted by a municipality, which prohibits the taking of vehicles into a public park. In your opinion, would the ordinance apply to the following facts?

(1) A child seeks to take his large, battery-powered toy automobile into the park. The toy is designed for use upon a sidewalk. The sidewalks of the park are used by many pedestrians.

(2) A child has been injured in the park and her father calls for an ambulance. The ambulance seeks to enter the park in order to pick up the child at the place of injury.

B. APPROACHES TO STATUTORY INTERPRETATION

As the preceding materials demonstrate, judges do more than apply statutes—they interpret them. Over the centuries, Anglo–American courts have taken different approaches to the task of statutory interpretation.

HISTORICAL INTRODUCTION

The ancient Roman law, in its period of maturity, took a liberal attitude toward the interpretation of statutes. If the application of a broadly-phrased statute to a particular combination of facts led to a serious injustice, a judge was under no constraint to follow the words but could disregard them. This was in effect an application of Aristotelian equity. Conversely, when the words of a statute did not fit a particular case but the policy rationale behind the statute clearly covered it, the courts applied the statute by analogy. The Roman pattern has been widely followed in the orbit of the modern Civil Law.

Samuel Thorne has shown that, during certain periods of English medieval history, the position of the Common Law toward the construction of statutes was similar to the general attitude of the Roman and Civil Law. Statutes were sometimes extended to situations not expressly covered by them. Conversely, if the application of a broadly phrased statute to a particular complex of facts led to a hardship or injustice, a judge was under no constraint to follow the words of the statute. In the early fourteenth century, the freedom with which statutes were treated by common-law judges was so great that a substantial rewriting of statutory law by the judiciary was not at all uncommon. In the words of Thorne, statutes were viewed as "suggestions of policy to be treated with an easy unconcern as to their precise content." While this freedom of interpretation was gradually curbed and far-reaching extensions of statutory norms came to be looked upon as improper, the emerging doctrine of the equity of the statute still permitted a liberal interpretation of legislation according to its purpose and the use of analogy within moderate limits. The reporter Plowden stated in 1573 that "the intent of statutes is more to be regarded and pursued than the precise letter of them, for oftentimes things which are within the words of statutes, are out of the purview of them, which purview extends no further than the intent of the makers of the Act, and the best way to construe an Act of Parliament is according to the intent rather than according to the words."

In the eighteenth century Blackstone, in his *Commentaries on the Laws of England,* still recognized the doctrine of the equity of the statute. He pointed out that judges are under no obligation to follow the words of a statute if its application to a particular case would lead to an unreasonable result not foreseen by the legislature. But it seems that Blackstone did not favor the method of applying statutes by analogy.

During the nineteenth century, the remaining force of the equity of the statute doctrine was destroyed. It is held today in England, at least as a general proposition, that supplying omitted particulars or writing equitable exceptions into statutes in hardship cases is beyond the powers of a judge. The judge is directed to gather the intent of the legislature from the words used, except perhaps when the consequences of such an interpretation would be shockingly unfair. Until relatively recent times, recourse to the legislative history of a statute was not permitted for any interpretative purpose. At the present time, committee reports and other preparatory materials are inadmissible for the direct purpose of explaining the intention of Parliament, but admissible under the second criterion of *Heydon's Case* (see infra) in order to ascertain the mischief against which the statute was directed.[1]

NOTE ON THREE BASIC APPROACHES

The three fundamental approaches to statutory interpretation under Anglo–American law, as articulated by the English courts, are set forth below:

1. THE LITERAL RULE

If the language of a statute be plain, admitting of only one meaning, the Legislature must be taken to have meant and intended what it has plainly expressed, and whatever it has in clear terms enacted must be enforced though it should lead to absurd or mischievous results. Lord Atkinson in Vacher & Sons, Ltd. v. London Society of Compositors, (1913) A.C. 107, at 121 (House of Lords).

2. THE GOLDEN RULE

But it is to be borne in mind that the office of the Judges is not to legislate, but to declare the expressed intention of the Legislature, even if that intention appears to the Court injudicious; and I believe that it is not disputed that what Lord Wensleydale used to call the golden rule is right, viz., that we are to take the whole statute together, and construe it all together, giving the words their ordinary signification, unless when so applied they produce an inconsistency, or an absurdity or inconvenience so great as to convince the Court that the intention could not have been to use them in their ordinary signification, and to justify the Court in putting on them some other signification which, though less proper, is one which the court thinks the words will bear. Lord Blackburn in River Wear Commissioners v. Adamson, 2 App.Cas. 742, at 764–765 (House of Lords, 1877).

1. G. Williams, *Learning the Law* (11th ed. 1982), p. 102. For a statement of contemporary basic rules of statutory interpretation in England see R. Cross, *Statutory Interpretation* (1976), pp. 42–52.

3. THE SOCIAL PURPOSE APPROACH

HEYDON'S CASE

30 Co. 7a, 76 Eng.Rep. 637, at 638 (Exchequer, 1584).

And it was resolved by them that for the sure and true interpretation of all statutes in general (be they penal or beneficial, restrictive or enlarging of the common law), four things are to be discerned and considered:

1st.　What was the common law before the making of the act?

2nd.　What was the mischief and defect for which the common law did not provide?

3rd.　What remedy the Parliament hath resolved and appointed to cure the disease of the commonwealth?

4th.　The true reason of the remedy; and then the office of all the Judges is always to make sure construction as shall suppress the mischief, and advance the remedy, and to suppress subtle inventions and evasions for continuance of the mischief, and *pro privato commodo*, and to add force and life to the cure and remedy, according to the true intent of the makers of the Act, *pro bono publico*.

NOTE BY THE EDITORS

Which of the three approaches to statutory interpretation was applied in each of the following cases? How would the outcome have differed had one of the other two approaches been invoked?

WHITELEY v. CHAPPELL

L.R. 40.B. 147 (Court of Queen's Bench, 1868).

[This was the appeal of a defendant convicted of voting fraud. The relevant statute prohibited impersonating "any person entitled to vote" with the intent to influence an election. It had been proved at the defendant's trial that a Mr. Marston had been qualified to vote at a certain election, but had died before the election took place. The defendant, purporting to be Marston, voted in Marston's name.]

Lush, J. I do not think we can, without straining them, bring the case within the words of the enactment. The legislature has not used words wide enough to make the personation of a dead person an offense. The words "A person entitled to vote" can only mean, without a forced construction, a person who is entitled to vote at the time at which the personation takes place; in the present case, therefore, I feel bound to say the offense has not been committed.

Hannen, J. I regret we are obliged to come to the conclusion that the offense charged was not proved; but it would be wrong to strain words to meet the justice of the present case, because it might make a precedent, and lead to dangerous consequences in other cases.

UNITED STATES v. KIRBY

74 U.S. (7 Wall.) 482, 19 L.Ed. 278 (1868).

Golden Rule

[This case arose under the Act of Congress of March 3, 1825, providing for the conviction of any person who "shall knowingly and willfully obstruct or retard the passage of the mail, or of any driver * * * carrying the same." The Court held that the statute had no application to a sheriff who arrested a mailman upon a warrant issued by a state court, thereby retarding delivery of the mail.]

social purpose approach

All laws should receive a sensible construction. General terms should be so limited in their application as not to lead to injustice, oppression, or an absurd consequence. It will always, therefore, be presumed that the legislature intended exceptions to its language which would avoid results of this character. The reason of the law in such cases should prevail over its letter.

[74 U.S. (7 Wall.) 486–487, 19 L.Ed. 280.]

HOLY TRINITY CHURCH v. UNITED STATES

Supreme Court of the United States (1892).
143 U.S. 457, 12 S.Ct. 511, 36 L.Ed. 226.

social purpose approach

[This case involved an 1885 statute making it "unlawful for any person, company, partnership, or corporation, in any manner whatsoever, to * * * in any way assist or encourage the * * * migration of any alien * * * into the United States * * * under contract or agreement * * * made previous to the * * * migration of such alien * * * to perform labor or service of any kind in the United States." The defendant church was a corporation which had entered into a contract with an Englishman to come to the United States to act as its pastor. The Supreme Court reversed a judgment against the church for a penalty payable to the United States for violation of the 1885 act.]

It must be conceded that the act of the corporation is within the letter of this section, for the relation of rector to his church is one of service, and implies labor on the one side with compensation on the other. Not only are the general words labor and service both used, but also, as it were to guard against any narrow interpretation, and emphasize a breadth of meaning, to them is added "of any kind;" and, further, as noticed by the Circuit Judge in his opinion, the fifth section, which makes specific exceptions, among them professional actors, artists, lecturers, singers and domestic servants, strengthens the idea that every other kind of labor and service was intended to be reached by the first section. While there is great force to this reasoning, we cannot think Congress intended to denounce with penalties a transaction like that in the present case. It is a familiar rule, that a thing may be within the letter of the statute and yet not within the statute, because not within its spirit, nor within the intention of its makers. This has been often asserted, and the reports are full of cases illustrating its

application. This is not the substitution of the will of the judge for that of the legislator, for frequently words of general meaning are used in a statute, words broad enough to include an act in question, and yet a consideration of the whole legislation, or of the circumstances surrounding its enactment, or of the absurd results which follow from giving such broad meaning to the words, makes it unreasonable to believe that the legislator intended to include the particular act.
* * *

Again, another guide to the meaning of a statute is found in the evil which it is designed to remedy; and for this the court properly looks at contemporaneous events, the situation as it existed, and as it was pressed upon the attention of the legislative body. United States v. Union Pacific Railroad, 91 U.S. 72, 79, 23 L.Ed. 224. The situation which called for this statute was briefly but fully stated by Mr. Justice Brown when, as District Judge, he decided the case of United States v. Craig, 28 F. 795, 798: "The motives and history of the act are matters of common knowledge. It has become the practice for large capitalists in this country to contract with their agents abroad for the shipment of great numbers of an ignorant and servile class of foreign laborers, under contracts, by which the employer agreed, upon the one hand, to prepay their passage, while, upon the other hand, the laborers agreed to work after their arrival for a certain time at a low rate of wages. The effect of this was to break down the labor market, and to reduce other laborers engaged in like occupations to the level of the assisted immigrant. The evil finally became so flagrant that an appeal was made to Congress for relief by the passage of the act in question, the design of which was to raise the standard of foreign immigrants, and to discountenance the migration of those who had not sufficient means in their own hands or those of their friends, to pay their passage."

It appears, also, from the petitions, and in the testimony presented before the committees of Congress, that it was this cheap unskilled labor which was making the trouble, and the influx of which Congress sought to prevent. It was never suggested that we had in this country a surplus of brain toilers, and, least of all, that the market for the services of Christian ministers was depressed by foreign competition. Those were matters to which the attention of Congress, or of the people, was not directed. So far, then, as the evil which was sought to be remedied interprets the statute, it also guides to an exclusion of this contract from the penalties of the act.

[143 U.S. at 458–459, 463–464, 12 S.Ct. at 511–512, 513–514.]

CHUNG FOOK v. WHITE

264 U.S. 443, 44 S.Ct. 361, 68 L.Ed. 781 (1924).

[Chung Fook was a native born citizen of the United States. Lee Shee, his wife, was an alien Chinese woman who was ineligible for naturalization. In 1922, she was refused admission to the United States and was detained at the immigration station on the ground that she was an alien who was afflicted with a dangerous contagious disease, clonorchiasis. Section 22 of the Immigration Act of February 5, 1917, provided that the "wife of a naturalized alien shall be admitted without detention for treatment in hospital. * * *" Chung Fook filed a petition for writ of habeas corpus to release his wife from detention, arguing that Congress could not have intended "to accord to a naturalized citizen a right and preference beyond that enjoyed by a native born citizen." The Supreme Court refused to grant relief.]

The words of the statute being clear, if it unjustly discriminates against the native born citizen, or is cruel and inhuman in its results, as forcefully contended, the remedy lies with Congress and not with the courts. Their duty is simply to enforce the law as it is written, unless clearly unconstitutional.

[264 U.S. at 446, 44 S.Ct. at 352.]

NOTE BY THE EDITORS

The three previously quoted Supreme Court cases were all decided without dissent.

CAMINETTI v. UNITED STATES

Supreme Court of the United States (1917).
242 U.S. 470, 37 S.Ct. 192, 61 L.Ed. 442.

[In this case the Supreme Court of the United States sundered over the construction of the "White Slave Traffic Act" of 1910. Caminetti had been convicted under that Act of transporting a woman from Sacramento to Reno for immoral purposes. The proof at trial established only that Caminetti had induced the woman to travel to Reno to have an affair with him, and that the couple had indeed engaged in sexual relations. For this Caminetti was fined $1,500 and sentenced to imprisonment for 18 months. His appeal was premised on the argument that Congress had intended only to outlaw the use of channels of interstate commerce for purposes of prostitution. The literal words of the statute, however, made it a crime to transport or assist the transportation of, in interstate commerce, "any woman or girl for the purpose of prostitution or debauchery, or for any other immoral purpose." With one justice not participating, five members of the Court affirmed Caminetti's conviction. The three dissenters invoked *Holy Trinity Church,* and relied heavily on the legislative history of the Act, which showed concern exclusively with the interstate transportation of women for purposes of commercial prostitution, as reflected in the name "White Slave Traffic Act" under which the statute was enacted. The majority did not mention *Holy Trinity Church* and rejected the dissenters' arguments as follows:]

It is elementary that the meaning of a statute must, in the first instance, be sought in the language in which the act is framed, and if that is plain, and if the law is within the constitutional authority of the law-making body which passed it, the sole function of the courts is to enforce it according to its terms. * * *

Where the language is plain and admits of no more than one meaning the duty of interpretation does not arise and the rules which are to aid doubtful meanings need no discussion. * * * There is no ambiguity in the terms of this act. It is specifically made an offense to knowingly transport or cause to be transported, etc., in interstate commerce, any woman or girl for the purpose of prostitution or debauchery, or for "any other immoral purpose," or with the intent and purpose to induce any such woman or girl to become a prostitute or to give herself up to debauchery, or to engage in any other immoral practice.

Statutory words are uniformly presumed, unless the contrary appears, to be used in their ordinary and usual sense, and with the meaning commonly attributed to them. To cause a woman or girl to be transported for the purposes of debauchery, and for an immoral purpose, to-wit, becoming a concubine or mistress, for which Caminetti [was] convicted * * * would seem by the very statement of the facts to embrace transportation for purposes denounced by the act, and therefore fairly within its meaning.

While such immoral purpose would be more culpable in morals and attributed to baser motives if accompanied with the expectation of pecuniary gain, such considerations do not prevent the lesser offense against morals of furnishing transportation in order that a woman may be debauched, or become a mistress or a concubine from being the execution of purposes within the meaning of this law. To say the contrary would shock the common understanding of what constitutes an immoral purpose when those terms are applied, as here, to sexual relations. * * *

* * *

It is true that § 8 of the act provides that it shall be known and referred to as the "White-slave traffic Act," and the report accompanying the introduction of the same into the House of Representatives set forth the fact that a material portion of the legislation suggested was to meet conditions which had arisen in the past few years, and that the legislation was needed to put a stop to a villainous interstate and international traffic in women and girls. Still, the name given to an act by way of designation or description, or the report which accompanies it, cannot change the plain import of its words. If the words are plain, they give meaning to the act, and it is neither the duty nor the privilege of the courts to enter speculative fields in search of a different meaning.

Reports to Congress accompanying the introduction of proposed laws may aid the courts in reaching the true meaning of the legislature in cases of doubtful interpretation [citing cases]. But, as we have already said, and it has been so often affirmed as to become a recognized rule, when words are free from doubt they must be taken as the final expression of the legislative intent, and are not to be added to or subtracted from by considerations drawn from titles or designating names or reports accompanying their introduction, or from any extraneous source. In other words, the language being plain, and not leading to absurd or wholly impracticable consequences, it is the sole evidence of the ultimate legislative intent.

[242 U.S. at 485–486, 489–490, 37 S.Ct. at 194–195, 196.]

UNITED STATES v. AMERICAN TRUCKING ASS'NS

310 U.S. 534, 60 S.Ct. 1059, 84 L.Ed. 1345 (1940)
[footnotes omitted].

There is, of course, no more persuasive evidence of the purpose of a statute than the words by which the legislature undertook to give expression to its wishes. Often these words are sufficient in and of themselves to determine the purpose of the legislation. In such cases we have followed their plain meaning. When that meaning has led to absurd or futile results, however, this Court has looked beyond the words to the purpose of the act. Frequently, however, even when the plain meaning did not produce absurd results but merely an unreasonable one "plainly at variance with the policy of the legislation as a whole" this Court has followed that purpose, rather than the literal words. When aid to construction of the meaning of words, as used in the statute, is available, there certainly can be no "rule of law" which forbids its use, however clear the words may appear on "superficial examination." The interpretation of the meaning of statutes, as applied to justiciable controversies, is exclusively a judicial function. This duty requires one body of public servants, the judges, to construe the meaning of what another body, the legislators, has said. Obviously there is danger that the courts' conclusion as to legislative purpose will be unconsciously influenced by the judges' own views or by factors not considered by the enacting body. A lively appreciation of the danger is the best assurance of escape from its threat but hardly justifies an acceptance of a literal interpretation dogma which withholds from the courts available information for reaching a correct conclusion. Emphasis should be laid, too, upon the necessity for appraisal of the purposes as a whole of Congress in analyzing the meaning of clauses or sections of general acts. A few words of general connotation appearing in the text of statutes should not be given a wide meaning, contrary to a settled policy, "excepting as a different purpose is plainly shown."

[310 U.S. at 543–544, 60 S.Ct. at 1063–1064.]

NOTE BY THE EDITORS

The approach of the *American Trucking* case was reiterated in Cass v. United States, 417 U.S. 72, at 77–78, 94 S.Ct. 2167, at 2170–2171, 40 L.Ed.2d 668 (1974) and Train v. Colorado Public Interest Research Group, Inc., 426 U.S. 1, at 9, 96 S.Ct. 1938, at 1942, 48 L.Ed.2d 434 (1976). Plain meaning language has reappeared in some of the more recent decisions of the United States Supreme Court without, however, affecting the continued validity of the *American Trucking* rule. As Judge Patricia Wald has observed in commenting on the 1981–82 Term of the Court, "Not once last Term was the Supreme Court sufficiently confident of the clarity of statutory language *not* to double check its meaning with the legislative history. The language of 'plain meaning' lingers on in Court opinions, but its spirit is gone. In its application of the plain meaning rule, the Court now shifts onto the legislative history the burden of proving that the words do not mean what they appear to say." [2]

C. GUIDES TO LEGISLATIVE INTENT

NOTE BY THE EDITORS

To the extent that legislative purpose or intent is deemed relevant to statutory construction, there arise numerous questions about how that intent is best determined. We now survey some of the common sources of legislative intent, and the problems which these sources pose.

1. CANONS OF STATUTORY CONSTRUCTION

In attempting to ascertain the intent of the legislature, American courts have developed various "canons" of statutory construction. These canons of construction are simply a specialized body of precedent derived from cases in which courts have, in interpreting legislation, articulated *rationes decidendi* which address the problem of statutory construction in general terms. Unfortunately, the grand generalities of these canons ignore the particular facts of the decisions in which they were articulated. The most frequently invoked canons are described below.

(a) The Construction of Penal Statutes

"The rule that penal laws are to be construed strictly is perhaps not much less old than construction itself. It is founded on the tenderness of the law for the rights of individuals; and on the plain principle that the power of punishment is vested in the legislative, not in the judicial department. It is the legislature, not the Court, which is to define a crime, and ordain its punishment.

"It is said that notwithstanding this rule, the intention of the lawmaker must govern in the construction of penal, as well as other statutes. This is true. But this is not a new independent rule which subverts the old. It is a modification of the ancient maxim, and amounts to this, that though penal laws are to be construed strictly, they are not to be construed so strictly as to defeat the obvious intention of the legislature. The maxim is not to be so applied as to narrow the words of the statute to the exclusion of cases which those words, in their ordinary acceptation, or in that sense in which the

2. P. Wald, "Some Observations on the Use of Legislative History in the 1981 Supreme Court Term," 68 Iowa Law Review 195, at 197–198 (1983).

legislature has obviously used them, would comprehend." Chief Justice Marshall in United States v. Wiltberger, 18 U.S. (5 Wheat.) 76, 95, 5 L.Ed. 37 (1820).

"Although it is not likely that a criminal will carefully consider the text of the law before he murders or steals, it is reasonable that a fair warning should be given to the world in language that the common world will understand, of what the law intends to do if a certain line is passed." Justice Holmes in McBoyle v. United States, 283 U.S. 25, 27, 51 S.Ct. 340, 75 L.Ed. 816 (1931).

(b) The Ejusdem Generis Rule

Under the *ejusdem generis* rule, "when particular words of description are used, followed by general words, the latter are to be limited in their meaning so as to embrace only a class of the things indicated by the particular words." State ex rel. School Dist. of Sedalia v. Harter, 188 Mo. 516, 520, 87 S.W. 941, 944 (1905).

In McBoyle v. United States, 283 U.S. 25, 51 S.Ct. 340, 75 L.Ed. 816 (1931), the United States Supreme Court held that the National Motor Vehicle Theft Act did not apply to airplanes. Section 2 of the Act provided: "The term 'motor vehicle' shall include an automobile, automobile truck, automobile wagon, motor cycle, or any other self-propelled vehicle not designed for running on rails." The Court declared that this definition covered vehicles running on land only.

In United States v. Alpers, 338 U.S. 680, 70 S.Ct. 352, 94 L.Ed. 457 (1950), the question was whether the shipment of obscene phonograph records in interstate commerce was prohibited by a provision in the Federal Criminal Code which made illegal the interstate shipment of any "obscene * * * book, pamphlet, picture, motion-picture film, paper, letter, writing, print, or other matter of indecent character." The Court of Appeals for the 9th Circuit had invoked the rule of *ejusdem generis*. Since the specific words "book, pamphlet, etc." appearing in the statute refer to objects comprehensible by sight only, the Court of Appeals construed the general words "other matter of indecent character" to be limited to matter of the same genus. The 9th Circuit held phonograph records to be excluded from the scope of the statute, since phonograph records are comprehended by the sense of hearing.

The United States Supreme Court disagreed. The Court stated that the rule of *ejusdem generis,* when properly applied, was a useful canon of construction. But, in the opinion of the Court, "it is to be resorted to not to obscure and defeat the intent and purpose of Congress, but to elucidate its words and effectuate its intent. It cannot be employed to render general words meaningless." (338 U.S. at 682, 70 S.Ct. at 354). The Court deemed controlling in the present case the obvious purpose of Congress to prohibit the interstate shipment of obscene material.

The *ejusdem generis* rule often dovetailed in the past with another ancient maxim of statutory construction, namely, the rule that statutes in derogation of the common law were to be strictly construed. This maxim is rarely used by the courts today. Remedial statutes designed to correct certain shortcomings of the common law are interpreted liberally by the federal courts and most state courts. See, for example, Caspar v. Lewin, 82 Kan. 604, 83 Kan. 799, 109 P. 657 (1910), one of the early cases abandoning the derogation canon in the field of social legislation. Many states have statutes expressly abrogating the rule of strict construction of statutes in derogation of the common law.

Problems

(1) The English Sunday Observance Act, dating from the 17th century, provides that "no tradesman, workman, labourer, or any other person whatsoever shall do or exercise any worldly labour, business, or work of their ordinary callings upon the Lord's day or any part thereof" (excepting only works of necessity or charity).

The question arose in 1953 whether real estate agents were forbidden to work on Sundays under the terms of the Act. Assuming that the *ejusdem generis* rule was in full force and effect in England in 1953, how should an English court decide this question?

(2) Do you think that, in light of the *Alpers* decision, the case of *McBoyle v. United States,* supra, would be decided differently today?

(3) In *Caminetti v. United States,* would the defendant have been acquitted if the Supreme Court had used the *ejusdem generis* rule for the purpose of interpreting the phrase "any other immoral purpose"? Would it have been proper for the Court to use the rule in that case?

(c) Express Mention, Implied Exclusion Rule

A rule of statutory construction often relied upon by courts is the maxim *Expressio unius est exclusio alterius* [Expression of one thing means exclusion of another thing]. In Townsley v. County of Ozaukee, 60 Wis. 251, 18 N.W. 840 (1884), the plaintiff, a county surveyor of the defendant county, presented to the board of supervisors a claim against the county for fuel and stationery used in his office. A Wisconsin statute enumerated a number of county officers, not including the county surveyor, who were entitled to be supplied with fuel and stationery by the county. The Supreme Court of Wisconsin disallowed the plaintiff's claim on the ground that the statute, by not mentioning county surveyors, meant to exclude them from the benefit provided.

In Tennessee Valley Authority v. Hill, 437 U.S. 153, 98 S.Ct. 2279, 57 L.Ed.2d 117 (1978), the United States Supreme Court upheld an injunction against the completion of the Tellico Dam in order to prevent the extinction of the snail darter, a fish of three-inch size without food value and existing only in relatively small numbers. The Court deemed the injunction required by the Endangered Species Act of 1973, which provided in Section 7 that federal departments and agencies should utilize their authority in furtherance of the Act by carrying out programs for the conservation of endangered species and "by taking such action necessary to insure that actions authorized, funded, or carried out by them do not jeopardize the continued existence of such endangered species. * * * " The Act was passed seven years after construction of the dam had commenced, and Congress had continued appropriations for Tellico, with full awareness of the snail darter problem.

After citing some examples of on-going projects which Congress realized would in some way be altered by passage of the Act, the Court, in an opinion by Chief Justice Burger, continued:

> One might dispute the applicability of these examples to the Tellico Dam by saying that in this case the burden on the public through the loss of millions of unrecoverable dollars would greatly outweigh the loss of the snail darter. But neither the Endangered Species Act nor Art. III of the Constitution provides federal courts with authority to make such fine utilitarian calculations. On the contrary, the plain language of the Act, buttressed by its legislative history, shows clearly that Congress viewed the value of endangered species as "incalculable." Quite obviously, it would be difficult for a court to balance the loss of a sum certain—even $100 million—against a congressionally declared "incalculable" value, even assuming we had the power to engage in such a weighing process, which we emphatically do not.

> In passing the Endangered Species Act of 1973, Congress was also aware of certain instances in which exceptions to the statute's broad sweep would be necessary. Thus, § 10, 16 U.S.C.A. § 1539, creates a number of limited "hardship exemptions," none of which would even remotely apply to the Tellico Project. In fact, there are no exemptions in the Endangered Species Act for federal agencies, meaning that under the maxim *expressio unius est exclusio alterius,* we must presume that these were the only "hardship cases" Congress intended to exempt.

[437 U.S. at 187–88, 98 S.Ct. at 2298.]

Reliance by the defendant on the *Holy Trinity* case, supra p. 138 was held unjustified by the Chief Justice on the ground that the principle of that case was to apply only in "rare and exceptional circumstances," and when there was "something to make plain the intent of Congress that the letter of the statute is not to prevail." 437 U.S. at 187 n. 33, 98 S.Ct. at 2298 n. 33.

Justices Powell, Blackmun, and Rehnquist dissented. Justice Powell argued that nothing in the language of the Act called for its retrospective application to projects nearing completion, and that this interpretation of Congressional intent was corroborated by the continuation of appropriations for Tellico subsequent to the passage of the Act. He also rejected Chief Justice Burger's narrow construction of the holding in *Holy Trinity* and accused the majority of ignoring canons of statutory construction firmly recognized in United States v. American Trucking Assns. and Supreme Court decisions following it. 437 U.S. at 195–207, 98 S.Ct. at 2302–2308 (see especially Justice Powell's footnote 14).

After the decision was handed down, Congress overturned it and ordered the completion of the dam.

(d) Special Statutes Take Precedence Over General Statutes

Another generally recognized canon of statutory construction is that special statutes take precedence over general statutes. This maxim was set forth more fully in People v. Ruster, 16 Cal.3d 690, 694, 129 Cal.Rptr. 153, 155, 548 P.2d 353, 355 (1976):

> Prosecution under a general statute is precluded by a special statute when the general statute covers the same matter as, and thus conflicts with, the special statute. * * * However, a special statute does not supplant a general statute unless *all* of the elements of the general statute are included in the special statute.

In People v. Ruster, the defendant had obtained unemployment insurance benefits by making false representations regarding his identity. The defendant had been convicted of committing the felony of grand theft, in violation of § 484 of the California Penal Code, which provides in pertinent part: "Every person who shall * * * knowingly and designedly, by any false or fraudulent representation or pretense, defraud any other person of money * * * is guilty of theft." The court reversed the conviction on the ground that he should have been prosecuted for violating § 2101 of the Unemployment Insurance Code, which provides: "It is a misdemeanor to willfully make a false statement or representation or knowingly fail to disclose a material fact to obtain * * * any benefit or payment."

2. LEGISLATIVE HISTORY AND OTHER EXTRINSIC AIDS

In addition to the canons of statutory construction, which serve as intrinsic guides to ascertaining legislative intent, the courts often rely on extrinsic aids, such as legislative history. The first three excerpts in this section demonstrate that there is a difference of opinion regarding the appropriateness of relying on extrinsic aids to ascertain legislative intent. The subsequent case illustrates the use of such extrinsic aids and the limitations on their utility.

RADIN, "STATUTORY INTERPRETATION"
43 Harvard Law Review 863, 870–871 (1930).*

That the intention of the legislature is undiscoverable in any real sense is almost an immediate inference from a statement of the proposition. The chances that of several hundred men each will have exactly the same determinate situations in mind as possible reductions of a given determinable, are infinitesimally small. The chance is still smaller that a given determinate, the litigated issue, will not only be within the minds of all these men but will be certain to be selected by all of them as the present limit to which the determinable should be narrowed. In an extreme case, it might be that we could learn all that was in the mind of the draftsman, or of a committee of half a dozen men who completely approved of every word. But when this draft is submitted to the legislature and at once accepted without a dissentient voice and without debate, what have we then learned of the intentions of the four or five hundred approvers? Even if the contents of the minds of the legislature were uniform, we have no means of knowing that content except by the external utterances or behavior of these hundreds of men, and in almost every case the only external act is the extremely ambiguous one of acquiescence, which may be motivated in literally hundreds of ways, and which by itself indicates little or nothing of the pictures which the statutory descriptions imply. It is not impossible that this knowledge could be obtained. But how probable it is, even venturesome mathematicians will scarcely undertake to compute.

And if it were discoverable, it would be powerless to bind us. What gives the intention of the legislature obligating force? In theology or in literature, that question answers itself; but in law, the specific individuals who make up the legislature are men to whom a specialized function has been temporarily assigned. That function is not to impose their will even within limits on their fellow-citizens, but to "pass statutes," which is a fairly precise operation. That is, they make statements in general terms of undesirable and desirable situations, from which flow certain results. * * * When the legislature has uttered the words of a statute, it is *functus officio*,[1] not because of the Montesquieuan separation of powers, but because that is what legislating means. The legislature might also be a court and an executive, but it can never be all three things simultaneously.

LANDIS, "A NOTE ON STATUTORY INTERPRETATION"

43 Harvard Law Review 886, 888–892 (1930) [footnotes omitted].*

The assumption that the meaning of a representative assembly attached to the words used in a particular statute is rarely discoverable, has little foundation in fact. The records of legislative assemblies once opened and read with a knowledge of legislative procedure often reveal the richest kind of evidence. To insist that each individual legislator besides his aye vote must also have expressed the meaning he attaches to the bill as a condition precedent to predicating an intent on the part of the legislature, is to disregard the realities of legislative procedure. Through the committee report, the explanation of the committee chairman, and otherwise, a mere expression of assent becomes in reality a concurrence in the expressed views of another. A particular determi-

---

1. Editors' note: *functus officio* means "through."

nate thus becomes the common possession of the majority of the legislature, and as such a real discoverable intent.

Legislative history similarly affords in many instances accurate and compelling guides to legislative meaning. Successive drafts of the same act do not simply succeed each other as isolated phenomena, but the substitution of one for another necessarily involves an element of choice often leaving little doubt as to the reasons governing such a choice. The voting down of an amendment or its acceptance upon the statement of its proponent again may disclose real evidence of intent. Changes made in the light of earlier statutes and their enforcement, acquiescence in a known administrative interpretation, the use of interpreted language borrowed from other sources, all give evidence of a real and not a fictitious intent, and should be deemed to govern questions of construction. The real difficulty is twofold: that strong judges prefer to override the intent of the legislature in order to make law according to their own views, and that barbaric rules of interpretation too often exclude the opportunity to get at legislative meaning in a realistic fashion. The latter, originating at a time when records of legislative assemblies were not in existence, deserve no adherence in these days of carefully kept journals, debates, and reports. Unfortunately they persist with that tenaciousness characteristic of outworn legal rules. Strong judges are always with us; no science of interpretation can ever hope to curb their propensities. But the effort should be to restrain their tendencies, not to give them free rein in the name of scientific jurisprudence. * * * To ignore legislative processes and legislative history in the processes of interpretation, is to turn one's back on whatever history may reveal as to the direction of the political and economic forces of our time.

SCHWEGMANN BROS. v. CALVERT DISTILLER'S CORP.

Supreme Court of the United States (1951).
341 U.S. 384, 71 S.Ct. 745, 95 L.Ed. 1035.

MR. JUSTICE JACKSON, whom MR. JUSTICE MINTON joins, concurring.

Resort to legislative history is only justified where the face of the Act is inescapably ambiguous, and then I think we should not go beyond Committee reports, which presumably are well considered and carefully prepared. I cannot deny that I have sometimes offended against that rule. But to select casual statements from floor debates, not always distinguished for candor or accuracy, as a basis for making up our minds what law Congress intended to enact is to substitute ourselves for the Congress in one of its important functions. The Rules of the House and Senate, with the sanction of the Constitution, require three readings of an Act in each House before final enactment. That is intended, I take it, to make sure that each House knows what it is passing and passes what it wants, and that what is enacted was formally reduced to writing. It is the business of Congress to sum up its own debates in its legislation. Moreover, it is only the words of the bill that have presidential approval, where that approval is given. It is not to be supposed that, in signing a bill the President endorses the whole Congressional Record. For us to undertake to reconstruct an enactment from legislative history is merely to involve the Court in political controversies which are quite proper in the enactment of a bill but should have no place in its interpretation.

Moreover, there are practical reasons why we should accept whenever possible the meaning which an enactment reveals on its face. Laws are intended for all of our people to live by; and the people go to law offices to learn what their rights under those laws are. * * * Aside from a few offices in the larger cities, the materials of legislative history are not available to the lawyer who can afford neither the cost of acquisition, the cost of housing, or the cost of repeatedly examining the whole congressional history. Moreover, if he could, he would not know any way of anticipating what would impress enough members of the Court to be controlling. To accept legislative debates to modify statutory provisions is to make the law inaccessible to a large part of the country.

By and large, I think our function was well stated by Mr. Justice Holmes: "We do not inquire what the legislature meant; we ask only what the statute means." Holmes, Collected Legal Papers, 207.

[341 U.S. at 395–396, 71 S.Ct. at 751.]

SECURITIES & EXCHANGE COMMISSION v. ROBERT COLLIER & CO.

Court of Appeals, Second Circuit (1935).
76 F.2d 939, 941.

HAND, L., CIRCUIT JUDGE.

* * *

* * * The amendments of a bill in committee are fertile sources of interpretation. [Citation omitted.] It is of course true that members who vote upon a bill do not all know, probably very few of them know, what has taken place in committee. On the most rigid theory possible we ought to assume that they accept the words just as the words read, without any background of amendment or other evidence as to their meaning. But courts have come to treat the facts more really; they recognize that while members deliberately express their personal position upon the general purposes of the legislation, as to the details of its articulation they accept the work of the committees; so much they delegate because legislation could not go on in any other way.

SILVERMAN v. ROGERS

Court of Appeals, First Circuit (1970).
437 F.2d 102 [footnotes omitted except as indicated].

McENTEE, CIRCUIT JUDGE.

The principal issue raised by this appeal is one of statutory construction. The relevant facts are not in dispute and may be stated briefly as follows. In July 1964 Ulku Gurkan, an unmarried Turkish citizen, came to the United States as an exchange visitor under the auspices of the Agency for International Development (AID) [2]. Her purpose in coming here was to study psychiatric nursing in order to qualify as an instructor at the Florence Nightingale School of Nursing in Istanbul. She obtained several extensions of her original visa which enabled her to complete her studies and obtain a master's degree in psychiatric nursing from Boston University. The last extension expired on January 30, 1969. On March 9, 1969, she married Charles A. Silverman, an American citizen, and on April 24th of the same year applied to the Immigration and Naturalization Service (INS) for a waiver of the statutory two-year foreign residence requirement which normally she would have to meet before being allowed to return to the United States. 8 U.S.C.A. § 1182(e). In her application for the waiver she stated that to require her to leave this country would impose exceptional hardship on her husband because of his ill health. The relevant statutory waiver provision upon which she relies reads as follows:

> "*Provided further*, That upon the favorable recommendation of the Secretary of State, pursuant to the request of an interested United States Government agency, or of the Commissioner of Immigration and Naturalization after he has determined that departure from the United States would impose exceptional hardship upon the alien's spouse or child (if such spouse or child is a citizen of the United States or a lawfully resident alien), the Attorney General may waive the requirement of such two-year foreign residence abroad in the case of any alien whose admission to the United States is found by the Attorney General to be in the public interest; * * *" 8 U.S.C.A. § 1182(e).

Despite strenuous objection from AID, the INS found that the applicant's compliance with the two-year foreign residency requirement would impose exceptional medical hardship on her new husband and requested that the Secretary of State recommend whether the waiver should be granted. The Secretary recommended that the waiver not be granted.[4] On December 11, 1969, INS notified Mrs. Silverman, *inter*

---

2. AID is an agency in the United States Department of State. See 22 C.F.R. ch. II (1970).

4. In reply to INS, the Secretary stated, "we have had extended discussions with the Agency for International Development and the Turkish Government concerning the training given to Mrs. Silverman. The

Turkish Government believes her services are indispensable, and a position is being held open for her at the Florence Nightingale Nursing Home in Istanbul. In addition, she has signed a bond which obligates her to serve for a period of ten years in Turkey after finishing her training here. If she does not return, those who signed as

alia, that both the State Department and INS had carefully reviewed the facts in her case; that the State Department had recommended against granting her waiver; that accordingly her application had been denied and that she must arrange to leave the United States on or before a specified date.

On January 30, 1970, the Silvermans brought the instant suit to enjoin the commencement of deportation proceedings against Mrs. Silverman and for a judgment instructing the defendants to issue the waiver. They argued that under the statute only the INS was authorized to make the decision in hardship waiver applications and that the Secretary of State's recommendation was a mere matter of form. Alternatively, they contended that to deny Mrs. Silverman residency in the United States would deprive both plaintiffs of their right to liberty under the Fifth Amendment. The defendants moved for dismissal of the complaint or in the alternative for summary judgment. The district court took jurisdiction of the case and decided for the plaintiffs, granting a preliminary injunction on February 25, 1970, 309 F.Supp. 570, and a final injunction on March 9, 1970. The Government appealed.

The district court construed the statutory waiver proviso set out above "to provide that decision by the Attorney General whether to waive the foreign residence requirement may be based either upon the favorable recommendation of the Secretary of State or upon that of the [INS] Commissioner after determination of exceptional hardship." The court then went on to say,

> "This construction seems to be required by the plain language of [the proviso], especially the punctuation and the word 'of' as underlined in the following excerpt, 'That upon the favorable recommendation of the Secretary of State, pursuant to the request of an interested United States Government Agency, or of the Commissioner of Immigration and Naturalization after he has * * *.'" Silverman v. Rogers, 309 F.Supp. 570, 574 (D.Mass.1970).

The court noted that its decision was "at odds" with regulations implementing the exchange-visitor program [6] but felt that its interpretation guarded "the interest obviously underlying the particular proviso, to wit, protection of a United States citizen against exceptional hardship, which interest ordinarily conflicts with considerations of foreign policy of prime concern to the Secretary of State."

guarantors for the bond will be required by the Turkish Government to pay approximately $40,000 as compensation."

6. The court saw a conflict between its opinion and 22 C.F.R. §§ 63.6 and 63.7 (1970), but not with 8 C.F.R. § 212.7(c) (1970). Others commenting on the waiver proviso in the instant case also appear to disagree with the district court. See Mendez v. Major, 340 F.2d 128, 130 (8th Cir. 1965) (dictum), affirming 226 F.Supp. 364, 366 (E.D.Mo.1963) (dictum); Gras v. Becchie, 221 F.Supp. 422, 423 (S.D.Tex. 1963) (dictum); Matter of Tran, 11 I. & N.Dec. 395 (Dist.Dir., 1965); contra, Samala v. Immigration and Naturalization Service, 336 F.2d 7, 9 n. 4 (5th Cir.1965) (dictum); see also 1 Gordon & Rosenfield, Immigration Law and Procedure § 6.8h(3) (1970) (ambiguity noted).

We start with the thought that in spite of some awkwardness in its structure, the statute lends itself to a construction unfavorable to appellees. It also lends itself to a construction favorable, but we cannot agree with the district court's view that this latter is "required by the plain language." 309 F.Supp. at 574. The question is, which clause modifies which. The ultimate provision for the waiver of the two-year foreign residence requirement may be read to be conditioned upon, (a) the favorable recommendation of the Secretary of State pursuant to the request of an interested United States Government agency, or (b) the request of the Commissioner of Immigration and Naturalization after he has determined hardship. However, it is equally possible to read the statute as authorizing waiver conditioned upon the recommendation of the Secretary of State when he (a) has received a request of a government agency, or (b) has received a request of the Commissioner after he had determined hardship.

In the light of this ambiguity it becomes important to examine the legislative history. The proviso in question was added by the 1961 revision of the statute. It was derived from a then-existing provision which read,

> "upon request of an interested Government agency and the recommendation of the Secretary of State, the Attorney General may waive such two-year period of residence abroad in the case of any alien whose admission to the United States is found by the Attorney General to be in the public interest." Act of June 4, 1956, ch. 356, 70 Stat. 241.

Although the 1956 statute did not make any provision for hardship cases, the State Department's regulations took them into account. 22 Fed.Reg. 10840 (1957).[8] Between June 1956 and the end of 1960, the State Department approved 2104 waiver applications out of 2674 such applications received, and 1812 of those approved were hardship cases.[9] This liberal policy [10] was strongly disapproved by Subcommittee No. 1 of the House Committee on the Judiciary. The subcommittee stated:

> "It is believed to be detrimental to the purposes of the program and to the national interests of the countries concerned to apply a lenient policy in the adjudication of waivers *including cases where marriage occurring in the United States, or the birth of a child or children, is used to support the contention that the exchange alien's departure from this country would cause personal hardship.*" H.R.Rep. No. 721, 87th Cong., 1st Sess. 121 (1961) (emphasis in original).

8. The hardship dealt with in the regulations was that of the exchange visitor and not that of his spouse or child as is the case under the instant statute.

9. H.R.Rep. No. 721, 87th Cong., 1st Sess. 81 (1961). Only 499 applications had been refused during that period and 71 were still pending at the end of the period.

10. The State Department referred to its policy as a "liberal attitude." H.R.Rep. No. 721, supra at 33. But the rare refusal of waiver was made "when the foreign government strongly desires the individual's return abroad." Id.

In light of this, the subcommittee proposed language in place of the then-existing proviso, which is substantially similar to that finally adopted, to wit:

> "*Provided further,* That upon the favorable recommendation of the Secretary of State, pursuant to the request of a Government agency desiring to obtain the alien's services for the prospective benefit to the national defense, economy, welfare or cultural interest, or of the Commissioner of Immigration and Naturalization after he has determined that departure from the United States would impose exceptional hardship upon the alien's spouse or child (if such spouse or child is a citizen of the United States or a lawfully resident alien), the Attorney General may waive the requirement of such two-year foreign residence abroad in the case of any alien whose admission to the United States is found by the Attorney General to be in the public interest." Id. at 122.

The House Committee on Foreign Affairs specifically adopted this suggestion for the 1961 bill. 1961 U.S.Code Cong. & Admin.News, p. 2773. In particular, it noted that it was reenacting and amplifying the earlier proviso—and it also noted that it made only one "important change" in the existing law, namely, to allow the Secretary of State to approve variances in the place where the two-year foreign residence requirement could be fulfilled. Id. at 2774. The House approved the committee language as reported. 107 Cong.Rec. 18281 (1961).

The Senate version would have kept the language of the then-existing proviso, Act of June 4, 1956, ch. 356, 70 Stat. 241. It should be noted that the Senate report on the bill stated that "The waiver is subject to a request by an interested agency of the Federal Government *and recommendation by the Secretary of State to the Attorney General.*" S.Rep. No. 372, 87th Cong., 1st Sess. 19 (1961) (emphasis added). When the Senate received the House version, it voted to substitute the language of its own bill for the House bill and send the bill to conference. 107 Cong.Rec. 18515 (1961). The language of the then-existing proviso (as readopted by the Senate) and the new version drafted by Subcommittee No. 1 of the House Committee on the Judiciary were combined to make the final version. In its conference report, the House managers said:

> "[The House bill] reenacted and amplified [Act of June 4, 1956, ch. 356, 70 Stat. 241] but contained one modification, namely, the requirement of the finding by the Secretary of State that the 2 years' residence abroad of an exchange alien, if not occurring in the country from which he came to the United States, is in accord with the basic purpose of the exchange program. *The Senate amendment contained language similar in intent but different in wording.* The Senate conferees accepted the House language with amendments." 1961 U.S. Code Cong. & Admin.News, pp. 2779–2780 (emphasis added).

We conclude, therefore, that the intent of both the House and Senate versions of the 1961 proviso now in 8 U.S.C.A. § 1182(e), supra, was the same, namely, to include the Secretary of State in the hardship waiver process. Indeed, it would have been illogical to *reduce* the number of agencies wielding a veto, given the expressed purpose of Subcommittee No. 1 to grant fewer hardship waivers.

Weight must also be given to the regulations, which have consistently given the Secretary a decisive voice in all waivers. See note 3, supra; 35 Fed.Reg. 5958 (1970), 1970 U.S.Code Cong. & Admin.News, p. 1132. "In case of ambiguity it is appropriate to give weight to the view of the body entrusted to administer the act." Massachusetts Trustees of Eastern Gas and Fuel Associates v. United States, 312 F.2d 214, 222 (1st Cir.1963), aff'd, 377 U.S. 235, 84 S.Ct. 1236, 12 L.Ed.2d 268 (1964); accord, American Power & Light Co. v. SEC, 141 F.2d 606, 621 (1st Cir. 1944), aff'd, 329 U.S. 90, 67 S.Ct. 133, 91 L.Ed. 103 (1946). Finally, we note that Congress has not seen fit to question the administrative practice. See, 8 U.S.C.A. § 1182(e), amending 8 U.S.C.A. § 1182(e); 1970 U.S.Code Cong. & Admin.News, p. 874. We therefore resolve the statutory ambiguity in favor of giving the Secretary a veto over hardship waiver applications.

R. POSNER, "ECONOMICS, POLITICS, AND THE READING OF STATUTES AND THE CONSTITUTION"

49 University of Chicago Law Review 263, 274–75 (1982) (footnotes omitted).*

* * *

[There are] two recurrent issues in the use of legislative history to interpret statutes. The first is whether it is proper to use legislative history at all, and if so, which parts of that history to use. Because legislators vote on the statutory language rather than on the legislative history, they cannot be presumed to have assented to all that has been said, either in the committee reports or on the floor, about a bill that becomes law.

This matters, however, only if one holds the unrealistic view that each enacted bill reflects the convictions of a majority of legislators voting for it. If instead it is assumed that some unknown fraction of all bills are passed at the behest of politically powerful interest groups, it is not so clear that each member of the legislative majority behind a particular bill has studied the details of the bill he voted for. It may be more realistic to assume that he assented to the deal struck by the sponsors of the bill. The terms of the deal presumably are stated accurately in the committee reports and in the floor comments of the sponsors (otherwise the sponsors will have difficulty striking deals in the future), though not necessarily by opponents of the bill, who may take the floor or write minority opinions in committees to create a specious legislative history that they hope will influence judicial interpretation of the statute.

This picture is especially persuasive if we assume a considerable amount of "log rolling"—that is, vote trading—in the legislative process. Log rolling implies that legislators often vote without regard to their personal convictions. This process makes it unrealistic to demand that each legislator assent only to those aspects of statutory meaning that are fixed in the language of the bill, divorced from the intentions of its sponsors as reflected in their statements in the committee reports and on the floor.

My analysis is also germane to the question what weight to give post-enactment expressions of legislative intent. The answer it suggests, which is also the traditional answer, is that such expressions should be given little or no weight. The deal is struck when the statute is enacted. If courts paid attention to subsequent expressions of legislative intent not embodied in any statute, they would be unraveling the deal that had been made; they would be breaking rather than enforcing the legislative contract. Nor, if one takes seriously the interest group theory of politics, can subsequent expressions of legislative understanding be treated simply as impartial interpretations of the law; they are as likely to be a gambit in the practice of interest group politics.

P. WALD, "SOME OBSERVATIONS ON THE USE OF LEGISLATIVE HISTORY IN THE 1981 SUPREME COURT TERM"

68 Iowa Law Review 195, 195 (1983) (footnotes omitted except as indicated).*

The Supreme Court increasingly is using legislative history in construing and applying federal statutes. An article in a recent issue of *Jurimetrics* surveyed the Court's use of legislative history in the four decades from 1938 to 1979.[1] In 1938 there were nineteen citations to items of legislative history; in the late 1970's there were 300 to 400 per Term. * * *

[T]he Court has greatly expanded the types of materials and events that it will recognize in the search for congressional intent. Floor debates and hearings, for example, are now routinely cited, as is evidence that the legislature did not act to override or alter administrative or judicial interpretation at either the time of passage or later.

3. UNFORESEEN CIRCUMSTANCES

In the preceding cases, it was reasonable to assume that the legislature had thought about the problem before the court. But suppose, for example, a statute of State X passed in the 1870's provides that "a person qualified to vote for representatives and senators of the state legislature shall be liable to serve as a Juror." At the time of

---

1. Carro & Brann, *The U.S. Supreme Court and the Use of Legislative Histories: A Statistical Analysis*, 22 JURIMETRICS J. 294 (1982). [See also Carro & Brann, *Use of Legislative Histories by the United States Supreme Court: A Statistical Analysis*, 9 J.LEGIS. 282 (1982) (analyzing the use of legislative histories by year; by subject matter; and by the name of the judge authoring the opinion).]

enactment of this statute women did not possess the franchise under the constitution of that state. In 1920, the Nineteenth Amendment to the United States Constitution went into effect, providing that "the right of citizens of the United States to vote shall not be denied or abridged by the United States or by any State on account of sex." Thereupon State X passed a statute conferring upon women the right to vote. Did that bring women into the category of persons liable to serve as jurors?

State courts have taken conflicting views on that question. In Commonwealth v. Welosky, 276 Mass. 398, 177 N.E. 656 (1931), the Supreme Judicial Court of Massachusetts held that inclusion of women among those subject to jury duty was wholly outside the contemplation of those who passed the early statute defining the qualifications of jurors. "Manifestly, * * * the intent of the Legislature must have been, in using the word 'person' in statutes concerning jurors and jury lists, to confine its meaning to men. That was the only intent constitutionally permissible."

The same result was reached by the Supreme Court of Illinois in People ex rel. Fyfe v. Barnett, 319 Ill. 403, 150 N.E. 290 (1925). The Court stated its reasons as follows:

> It is a primary rule in the interpretation and construction to be placed upon a statute that the intention of the legislature should be ascertained and given effect. * * * If in a statute there is neither ambiguity nor room for construction the intention of the legislature must be held free from doubt. What the framers of the statute would have done had it been in their minds that a case like the one here under consideration would arise is not the point in dispute. The inquiry is what, in fact, they did enact, possibly without anticipating the existence of such facts. * * * The true rule is that statutes are to be construed as they were intended to be understood when they were passed. Statutes are to be read in the light of attendant conditions and that state of the law existent at the time of their enactment. The words of a statute must be taken in the sense in which they were understood at the time the statute was enacted. * * *

> At the time of the passage by the legislature of the act above mentioned, providing for the appointment of a jury commission and the making of jury lists, the words "voters" and "electors" were not ambiguous terms. * * * At that time the legislature did not intend that the name of any woman should be placed on the jury list, and must be held to have intended that the list should be composed of the names of male persons, only. * * * The word "electors" in the statute here in question, meant male persons, only, to the legislatures who used it * * *: Petitioner was not entitled to have her name replaced upon the jury list of Cook County.

But in Commonwealth v. Maxwell, 271 Pa. 378, 114 A. 825 (1921), the Supreme Court of Pennsylvania came to the opposite conclusion on the basis of the following considerations:

We then have the act of 1867, constitutionally providing that the jury commissioners are required to select "from the whole qualified electors of the respective county * * * persons, to serve as jurors in the several courts of such county," and the Nineteenth Amendment to the federal Constitution, putting women in the body of electors.

"The term 'elector' is a technical, generic term, descriptive of a citizen having constitutional and statutory qualifications that enable him to vote, and including not only those who vote, but also those who are qualified, yet fail to exercise the right of franchise." 20 Corpus Juris, 58.

If the act of 1867 is prospective in operation, and takes in new classes of electors as they come to the voting privilege from time to time, then, necessarily, women, being electors, are eligible to jury service. That the act of 1867 does cover those who at any time shall come within the designation of electors there can be no question.

"Statutes framed in general terms apply to new cases that arise, and to new subjects that are created from time to time, and which come within their general scope and policy. It is a rule of statutory construction that legislative enactments in general and comprehensive terms, prospective in operation, apply alike to all persons, subjects, and business within their general purview and scope coming into existence subsequent to their passage." 25 Ruling Case Law, 778.

D. REASONING FROM STATUTES BY ANALOGY

In Chapter V, we observed that courts sometimes resolve a controversy by referring to an analogous judicial precedent. The following excerpt suggests that statutes could be used in precisely the same manner.

POUND, "COMMON LAW AND LEGISLATION"

21 Harvard Law Review 383, 385–386 (1908). *

Four ways may be conceived of in which courts in such a legal system as ours might deal with a legislative innovation. (1) They might receive it fully into the body of the law as affording not only a rule to be applied but a principle from which to reason, and hold it, as a later and more direct expression of the general will, of superior authority to judge-made rules on the same general subject; and so reason from it by analogy in preference to them. (2) They might receive it fully into the body of the law to be reasoned from by analogy the same as any other rule of law, regarding it, however, as of equal or co-ordinate authority in this respect with judge-made rules upon the same general subject. (3) They might refuse to receive it fully into the body of the law and give effect to it directly only; refusing to reason from it by analogy but giving it, nevertheless, a liberal interpretation to cover the whole field it was intended to cover. (4) They might not only refuse to reason from it by analogy and apply it directly only, but also give to it a strict and narrow interpretation, holding it down rigidly to those cases which it covers expressly. The fourth hypothesis represents the orthodox common law attitude toward legislative innovations. Probably the third hypothesis, however, represents more nearly the attitude toward which we are tending. The second and first hypotheses doubtless appeal to the common law lawyer as absurd. He can hardly conceive that a rule of statutory origin may be treated as a permanent part of the general body of the law. But it is submitted that the course of legal development upon which we have entered already must lead us to adopt the method of the second and eventually the method of the first hypothesis.

NOTE BY THE EDITORS

Despite the possibility of using statutes as analogous precedents, most courts "have rejected the civil law notion that the general principles drawn from statutes may be made use of as bases for analogy in the decision of cases which do not fall within the broadest possible meaning of statutory language." Jones, "Statutory Doubts and Legislative Intention," 40 Columbia Law Review 957, 974 (1940).[1] A rare case based on analogous reasoning in the application of a federal statute is International Stevedoring Co. v. Haverty, 272 U.S. 50, 47 S.Ct. 19, 71 L.Ed. 157 (1926), where a special type of action for damages accorded to "seamen" was extended to longshoremen, although the Court acknowledged that in common usage such workers were not considered seamen. Another statute that has been applied by analogy is the Uniform Commercial Code, which you will study extensively in your contracts class. See Williams, R.F., "Statutes as Sources of Law Beyond Their Terms," 50 George Washington Law Review 554 (1982); Note, "The Uniform Commercial Code as a Premise of Judicial Reasoning," 65 Columbia Law Review 880 (1965).

Problem

We have encountered a number of United States Supreme Court decisions, such as the *Holy Trinity* case, in which the Court gave a broadly worded statute an extremely narrow construction. On the other hand, the Court has been very reluctant to expand the scope of statutes by applying them analogically. Can you see convincing reasons why courts, in civil litigation, should be hospitable to the restriction of statutory language but hostile to an expansion of such language?

E. A CONCLUDING QUERY

In an article entitled "Remarks on the Theory of Appellate Decision and the Rules or Canons About How Statutes Are to be Con-

---

1. It should be noted that the civil law approach is not used in the area of criminal law.

strued," 3 Vanderbilt Law Review 395 (1950), Karl Llewellyn said: "There are two opposing canons [of statutory construction] on almost every point. * * * Every lawyer must be familiar with them all: they are still needed tools of argument."

Among the examples of opposing canons listed by Llewellyn are the following. Some courts have said that "a statute cannot go beyond its text." Other courts have stated "To effect its purpose a statute may be implemented beyond its text." Some courts have declared that "statutes in derogation of the common law will not be extended by construction." Others have taken the position that "such acts will be liberally construed if their nature is remedial." Some courts have held that "when design has been distinctively stated no place is left for construction." Others have insisted that "courts have the power to inquire into real—as distinct from ostensible—purpose." Some courts have stated categorically that "if language is plain and unambiguous it must be given effect." Others have rejected this rule "when literal interpretation would lead to absurd or mischievous consequences or thwart manifest purpose." Some courts have applied the *ejusdem generis* rule. Others have declared that "*ejusdem generis* is only an aid in getting the meaning and does not warrant confining the operations of a statute within narrower limits than were intended."

Do you think that Llewellyn's viewpoint is borne out by the court decisions included in this chapter? Do the canons which he juxtaposes actually contradict one another, or can some of them be considered as embodying general principles subject to exceptions?

Further References

Eskridge, W.N., Jr., "Dynamic Statutory Interpretation," 135 University of Pennsylvania Law Review 1479 (1987).

Frank, J.N., "Words and Music: Some Remarks on Statutory Interpretation," 47 Columbia Law Review 365 (1947).

Kernochan, J.M., "Statutory Interpretation: An Outline of Method," 3 Dalhousie Law Journal 333 (1965).

Murphy, A.W., "Old Maxims Never Die: The 'Plain–Meaning Rule' and Statutory Interpretation in the 'Modern' Federal Courts," 75 Columbia Law Review 1299 (1975).

Posner, R., "Statutory Interpretation—in the Classroom and in the Courtroom," 50 University of Chicago Law Review 800 (1983).

Thorne, S., *A Discourse upon the Exposition & Understandings of Statutes* (1942), pp. 1–99 (discussing the early English history).

Index of Subjects

References are to Pages

TRIAL, MODES OF
Battle, 28.
Jury trial, 28, 36, 37, 38, 51–52.
Ordeal, 28.
Wager of law, 28, 36, 38.

TROVER
Characteristics of action, 37.
History of action, 37.

TRUSTS
See Uses and Trusts.

UNITED NATIONS
Law developed by, 7.
Power to enforce decisions, 7.

UNJUST ENRICHMENT
See Quasi Contract.

USES AND TRUSTS
Jurisdiction in Chancery, 44.

WAGER OF LAW
See Trial, Modes of.

WAR POWERS RESOLUTION
Purpose and chief provisions, 21–22.

WESTMINSTER II, STATUTE OF
Provisions regarding writs, 31–32.

WRIT SYSTEM
See Common Law; Forms of Action.

†